The UK Parliament

Moyra Grant

Edinburgh University Press

© Moyra Grant, 2009

Edinburgh University Press Ltd
22 George Square, Edinburgh
www.euppublishing.com

Typeset in 11/13pt Monotype Baskerville by
Servis Filmsetting Ltd, Stockport, Cheshire, and
printed and bound in Great Britain by
CPI Antony Rowe, Chippenham and Eastbourne

A CIP record for this book is available from the British Library

ISBN 978 0 7486 2261 0 (paperback)

The right of Moyra Grant to be identified as author of this
work has been asserted in accordance with the Copyright,
Designs and Patents Act 1988.

Published with the support of the Edinburgh University
Scholarly Publishing Initiatives Fund.

Books in the Politics Study Guides series

Contents

Boxes

Tables

Figures

CHAPTER 1

A Brief History of Parliament

Overview

This introductory chapter offers an outline – sometimes light-hearted – of the origins and history of the United Kingdom's Westminster Parliament from Saxon times through to the present day: its buildings; evolution; functions; key officials; procedures; pomp; and language. It ends with an outline and analysis of the limited legislative role of the United Kingdom's constitutional monarchy.

Key issues to be covered in this chapter

- The origins and history of Parliament
- The functions of Parliament
- The buildings of Parliament
- Parliamentary procedures
- Pomp and ceremony
- Parliamentary officials
- Parliament and the monarch today

The origins and history of Parliament

The Westminster Parliament is the national law-making institution of the United Kingdom. It is widely seen as the historical heart of the United Kingdom political system, the main creator and guardian of its constitution and the 'mother of democracies'. How far these attributes ever were, or remain, true is the subject of this book.

The history of Parliament can be divided into four main periods. The first, covering the Middle Ages, is concerned with the early growth of Parliament, when only (a version of) the House of Lords existed. The word 'Parliament' derives from the French word *parler* – to speak – because Parliament dates from the days when monarchs summoned advisers to discuss the affairs of state. The origins of Parliament lie in Saxon times when monarchs consulted with their 'wise men' – the Witenagemot, which included the archbishops, bishops and abbots, earls, thegns and knights, and was later known as the Great Council. This was the foundation of the House of Lords. The barons' grievances against the monarch, including the excessive levying of taxes, formed the basis for the Magna Carta of 1215.

The Commons was created in the thirteenth century because the expense of wars weighed so heavily upon successive monarchs that they extended taxation from the lords to the freemen of the country. This necessitated a form of representation. In 1227, four knights from each county, elected in the shire courts, were sent to Westminster. The feudal Council now represented the three great classes of the kingdom: the clergy; the barons; and the commoners: that is, the prayers, the fighters and the workers.

The gradual separation of the Lords and Commons began in the fourteenth century, when the inferiors of Parliament – the common-ers – were sent away to an antechamber once the monarch had expressed his or her wishes. Westminster, therefore, became **bicameral**: that is, it has two 'chambers' or Houses: the House of Commons and the House of Lords. From 1376, the Commons began regularly to choose one of their members to speak for them – a **Speaker** – to convey their views to the monarch and lords. Whenever the monarch needed money for war, the Commons were in a strong position to make such provision dependent upon the granting of their petitions. The presentation of such petitions eventually developed into the process of legislation. In 1414 King Henry V agreed that henceforth 'nothing be enacted to the petitions of the Commons that be contrary to their asking, whereby they should be bound without their consent'. By the middle of the fifteenth century the formula was adopted whereby statutes were made 'by the advice and consent of the Lords Spiritual and Temporal and Commons, and by the authority of the same'. This established the authority of the whole Parliament for the first time. The Lords and Commons were then of equal status. Still today, every new parliamentary **Bill** (draft law) has to go through all three parts of Parliament – Commons, Lords and Crown – before it can become a **statute law**, that is, an Act of Parliament.

The second period of Parliament's development, from 1485 to the seventeenth century, covers the period when it was engaged in a definitive struggle with British monarchs over the exercise of ultimate sovereignty. During this period Parliament won the right to punish royal officials who broke the rules in the collection of taxes. This was the origin of parliamentary scrutiny of the **executive**: that is, the government. The Commonwealth period was a brief departure from the organic development of England's constitution, when the Protector, Oliver Cromwell, and Parliament, without an Upper House, governed the country. The restoration of the monarchy in 1660 marked a return to government by the monarch through a bicameral Parliament. The Civil War had settled once and for all the legal sovereignty of Parliament. This was also the period (in 1678) when the Commons asserted its sole right against the Lords, by powerful convention, to approve matters of government taxation and finance as it was the commoners who were paying the taxes.

The third period, dating from 1688 to 1832, witnessed the beginning of the party system in Parliament, the establishment of the doctrines of ministerial responsibility and the foundations of the Cabinet system. The Bill of Rights 1689 and the Act of Settlement 1701 limited many **royal prerogative** powers by statute and entrenched the right of Parliament to approve all new laws and taxes. The life of each Parliament was increased from three to seven years by the Septennial Act 1716. New institutions appeared within Parliament: parties; the Prime Minister and the Cabinet; and, with them, the gradual decline of the powers and political functions of the monarch. In 1771, largely through the efforts of radical English

Member of Parliament (MP), John Wilkes, the Commons permitted the public reporting of parliamentary debates, a key step toward more open and democratic government.

The final period was from 1832 until the present day, when the relationships between Parliament and government, and Commons and Lords, were established to ensure the legal sovereignty of Parliament in conformity with the wishes of the people as expressed at the ballot box. The Reform Act 1832 was seminal because it established the political sovereignty of the electorate – albeit a then very limited electorate – which was extended from the Second Reform Act 1867 onwards. The period from 1832 to 1867 is described by historians as the 'golden age' of the Commons when neither the monarch nor the electorate had the power to choose the government, and the Commons truly held sway, with real powers to remove ministers, introduce and reject legislation at will and overrule government policies.

As the electorate was extended, governments were increasingly made and unmade by votes at general elections rather than by MPs' votes in the Commons. As party organisation and discipline strengthened in order to win voters' loyalty, MPs' voting patterns in the Commons became increasingly controlled and predictable. By the late nineteenth century, most legislation came from the government rather than from individual MPs, virtually all divisions were on party lines and the government changed the rules of procedure so that it effectively controlled the Commons timetable (a development flagged by Bagehot as early as 1867). **Parliamentary government** had become party government.

For example, a number of Irish MPs persistently disrupted the business of the Commons as part of their battle to win Home Rule, by using a tactic known as **filibustering** – talking-out a bill for hours, sometimes days, on end. In response, in 1881 the government introduced a process known as the **guillotine** – a drastic time limit on debates of Bills. Early clauses could therefore be debated at length, while later clauses were not considered at all. Ministers blamed opposition MPs for time-wasting; opposition MPs argued that the guillotine negated the parliamentary processes of debate and scrutiny. Since 2002, guillotine motions have largely been superseded by the timetabling of Bills in advance.

This trend towards executive dominance of the **legislature** – the law-making assembly – continued throughout the twentieth century and into the twenty-first and has long been the main feature, and point of controversy, of the United Kingdom system of parliamentary government.

Members of Parliament, meanwhile, have evolved from being part-time amateurs into career politicians who tend to put their own political survival and advancement first. Their resources, salaries and allowances have all increased (though not on a par with some other legislatures, notably the United States Congress), and their jobs have grown in complexity with ever more weighty and intricate legislation, the creation of special scrutiny committees, growing pressures from outside lobbies and interest groups and the expanding burden of European legislation. The twentieth century also saw a decisive shift in the balance of power from the Lords to the Commons, as the Lords lost their legal right to amend money bills and their power to delay legislation was reduced.

The functions of Parliament

Parliament has three main functions within the United Kingdom political system:

- making the law;
- scrutinising and controlling the executive;
- representing the people.

These are outlined and assessed in detail throughout this book. They, in turn, give rise to certain subsidiary functions, including:

- debate and deliberation;
- controlling government finance;
- channel of communication between government and electorate.

Parliamentary sovereignty

Parliament is said to be the sovereign law-making body in the political system of the United Kingdom: that is, it has legal supremacy. In theory – *de jure* – it can make, amend or repeal any law, and no other domestic institution can challenge, veto or override its laws.

Parliament's law-making power is supposed to be based on authority – from elections for the House of Commons and tradition for the

House of Lords. The legitimacy of these sources of authority is debatable and is discussed in later chapters.

Parliamentary government

It is not the function of Parliament to govern the country. That responsibility rests with the executive: that is, the Prime Minister; Cabinet; and junior ministers. In 'presidential' systems, the executive and the legislature are separate bodies. However, in the UK system of parliamentary government, they are overlapping bodies: the members of the executive are drawn from within Parliament – both Commons and Lords – and remain within it. Each individual, therefore, wears 'two hats' as both lawmaker and government minister, and thus, there is a fusion of the legislature and the executive. 'Cabinet is a combining committee – a hyphen which joins, a buckle which fastens the legislative part of the state to the executive part of the state. In its origin it belongs to the one, in its function it belongs to the other.'[1]

Also, according to the theory of parliamentary government, Parliament should have the power to scrutinise and hold to account the executive, through debates, votes, Question Time, **Her Majesty's Opposition** (the second largest party in the Commons – a nineteenth-century development), Select Committees, the Ombudsman, etc. This holds particularly true when the executive does not have a majority in the Commons – for example, John Major's Conservative Government before the 1997 General Election. Much more frequently, however, the government has a majority of party-affiliated and supportive MPs in the Commons and can get its legislation through the House of Commons with little genuine difficulty. There has, therefore, long been criticism that Parliament is too executive-dominated. Again, this central feature of the UK political system is explained and analysed more fully in later chapters.

Representation through Parliament

Parliament is also given the authority and power to represent the people through the first-past-the-post system of election for the Commons. Though the Lords are not elected and, therefore, have limited legislative powers compared with the Commons, they derive authority from factors such as tradition and expertise – at least in the eyes of traditional conservatives.

Theory and practice

In theory, *de jure*, therefore, Parliament is the linchpin of the United Kingdom's constitution – the powerful, democratic heart of the political system.

However, the actual *de facto* powers of Parliament are limited, above all by majority governments appointed from, and residing within, Parliament. The executive can usually effectively dominate Parliament due to party loyalty and discipline, control of the Commons timetable, the exercise of official secrecy, the weaknesses of the mechanisms of parliamentary scrutiny and the limited powers of House of Lords.

The European Union (EU) can, since the United Kingdom's entry in 1973, override Westminster legislation in a growing range of policy areas. This also means that both the European and UK courts can override Parliament's law where it conflicts with EU law. Because the EU has this formal, legal predominance, it is known as a **supranational** institution. No other external body of which the United Kingdom is a member has such power; although other international bodies such as the International Monetary Fund (IMF), UN and NATO do have some influence upon Westminster legislation.

Other, informal constraints on the actual power of Parliament include the City and other powerful economic and business interests, pressure groups and the media. However, against the 'legal sovereignty' of Parliament it is widely said that UK voters exercise ultimate 'political sovereignty' because they hire and fire the MPs in the Commons and may, occasionally, simply refuse to obey the law of Parliament. One prime example of this was the community charge or 'poll tax' – a flat-rate charge paid for local council services by every adult, unconnected with property, income or wealth. This measure – introduced by the Local Government Finance Act 1988 – was controversial because it was unrelated to voters' ability to pay. It sparked a widespread campaign of civil disobedience (illegal non-payment), culminating in a violent anti-poll tax demonstration in London in 1990. It was one of the issues that helped to bring down Margaret Thatcher as Prime Minister in 1990 and her successor, John Major, was quick to replace the poll tax with a banded property tax per household – the current council tax.

The buildings of Parliament

The palace of Westminster

The parliamentary buildings are, in fact, a royal palace. Before the Norman Conquest, King Edward the Confessor built his palace upon the site by the River Thames, and it was the monarch's main residence until the reign of Henry VIII. Thereafter, the buildings were gradually set aside for the two chambers of Parliament and the Law Lords, although significant royal occasions, such as George IV's coronation in 1821, were held there throughout the nineteenth century.

The buildings, collectively known as the Palace of Westminster, cover eight acres and contain over 1,100 rooms – including the chambers, the offices of MPs, peers and officials, libraries, bars and restaurants, medical surgeries, hairdressers, shops and florists. Some buildings are of special architectural significance, such as St Stephen's Chapel and Westminster Hall. The great fire of 1834 – started by the over-stoking of the House of Lords' furnaces – allowed the opportunity for skilled restructuring of the palace by architect, Sir Charles Barry, and interior designer, Augustus Welby Pugin.

Several people actually live in the palace, most notably the Commons Speaker and former Lord Chancellors. One recent Lord Chancellor, Labour's Lord Irvine, was famously criticised because, in 1998, he spent £650,000 of taxpayers' money redecorating the Lord Chancellor's apartment in the House of Lords, including £59,000 on Pugin wallpaper at £350 a roll. The refurbishment also included £32,000 worth of mirrors and £24,430 worth of hand-woven fabrics. Irvine defended his actions without remorse. Future generations, he said, would be thankful for his 'noble' effort. The hand-made flock wallpaper 'was not the sort of thing you'd pick up at B&Q which would fall down after a couple of years', he said. On the one hand, Lord Irvine was simply protecting the prestige and status of the Lords building; on the other hand, according to his critics, he was an arrogant profligate.

The most famous feature of the sumptuous Lords chamber is the Woolsack, upon which successive Lord Chancellors sat for centuries as presiding officers of the chamber. The Woolsack is a seat stuffed with wool, deriving from the time of Edward III, who decreed that this would be a useful reminder to the country of its debt to the sheep farmers of the kingdom for the economic well-being and stability of England.

While the Lords chamber is quite breathtaking in its magnificence, the Commons chamber is quite plain and austere. It is rectangular in shape, with government and opposition MPs' benches facing each other on opposite sides of the chamber. Lines are drawn in front of the benches on each side, over which members may not step when speaking from the front benches. Famously, these lines are two sword-lengths apart. This structure encourages a more adversarial atmosphere than in those legislatures structured, for example, in a semi-circle, such as the devolved Scottish Parliament at Holyrood, the United States Congress and most European legislatures.

Although there are currently 646 MPs in the Commons, the chamber was built to seat under 430. This was a deliberate decision, made when the chamber was rebuilt after German bombing in 1941. As Winston Churchill then argued, 'If the House is big enough to contain all its members, nine-tenths of the debates will be conducted in the depressing atmosphere of an almost empty or half-empty chamber . . . There should be, on great occasions, a sense of crowd and urgency.'

A new office block for MPs opposite Big Ben, called Portcullis House, was built in 2000. It cost £234 million, £28 million more than estimated. Perhaps the most famous extravagance was the cost of leasing fig trees for the courtyard from Belgium at £150,000 for five years. A further £1 million was spent on works of art and £30 million on bronze cladding.

Parliament is also an environmentally wasteful institution according to a report by Liberal Democrat MP Norman Baker in 2005. The amount of energy used by Parliament has risen by 45 per cent since 1997 and the amount of water by 50 per cent. Lights and TV monitors are left on all night, escalators meant to be motion sensitive are set to run constantly, and bottled water for MPs' use costs over £11,000, whereas tap water would cost just £25.

Westminster authorities are currently considering plans to move out of the Gothic palace for an extended period for a £250 million project to replace the disintegrating roofing and wiring and, perhaps, to turn the shooting gallery into a swimming pool: 'A splendid building is not necessarily a practical building, nor does it necessarily house a splendid institution.'[2]

Security at the Palace of Westminster

Parliament has always jealously guarded its right to control its own proceedings and protect itself from attack. It has its own officials to oversee security and deal with intruders. They are the Serjeant at Arms and his or her forty staff, who also preside at ceremonial occasions. Under the headline 'It cost the taxpayer £19,000 last year to dress the "men in tights"',[3] it was revealed that the £9,000 wardrobe of the Serjeant at Arms includes a gilt fine blade sword, black cutaway jacket with a wig bag, waistcoat, lace ruffles at throat and cuffs, knee breeches, black silk stockings and black patent shoes with steel buckles. The 'men in tights' were increasingly disparaged as ineffectual guardians of the security of Parliament and, following the storming of the Commons chamber by pro-hunt protesters in 2004, a plan was forced through to create a new post of parliamentary security coordinator and an MI5 counter-terrorism officer was swiftly appointed over the parliamentary officials, despite opposition to the move from within Parliament.

In 2005 a waist-high steel barrier was erected around the Palace of Westminster to protect it from terrorist attack by vehicle bombs. This barrier replaced the concrete blocks put in place after the 11 September 2001 attacks on the Twin Towers in New York. A high transparent security screen, costing over £1 million, was also erected in front of the public gallery in the Commons to protect MPs from a biological or chemical attack. This followed the throwing of purple flour down on to the Prime Minister during Question Time in 2004 by Fathers4Justice protesters. (Previous protests since the 1970s involved the throwing of leaflets, manure and CS gas canisters into the Commons chamber from the public gallery, and the abseiling of three lesbian demonstrators into the Lords chamber in protest against section 28, a 1988 law which banned the 'promotion' of homosexuality in schools.)

The new security measures did not prevent the theft of cash and valuables worth £160,000 in 2005, according to information released by the police in response to a freedom of information request. Inspector Paul Barden told the *Evening Standard* newspaper, 'This is an establishment which is centuries old. It is hardly surprising that most of the things in it are worth a few bob.' The police also revealed that 119 weapons had been confiscated from people trying to enter Parliament in that year, including 79 gas sprays, 37 knives and three batons. Nor did the security measures prevent six protesters against the expansion of Heathrow airport from gaining access to the roof of Westminster Palace in 2008, to unfurl banners and throw paper planes.

Parliamentary procedures

Westminster is renowned for its arcane and quaint procedures. In the Commons chamber, for example, MPs are not allowed to refer to each other by name. Instead, they use phrases such as 'the honourable member' and 'my honourable friend'. This is intended to encourage courteous and considered debate and to deter personal insults. In 2004, MPs finally voted to stop referring to members of the public as 'strangers', a tradition dating back to 1575. This custom has also generated the Strangers' Bar and Strangers' Gallery (public viewing area) in the Palace of Westminster. In 2004 Commons Leader, Peter Hain, called the use of the term 'an ancient, mediaeval practice . . . we should get rid of.' However, his Conservative counterpart, Oliver Weald, warned against 'stripping away the charm and magic' of Parliament.

The conduct of parliamentary business is based partly upon customs and conventions, and partly upon **Standing Orders**: that is, written rules of procedure enforced by the Speaker and his or her deputies. These rulings are then included in newer editions of **Erskine May**, *Practical Treatise on the Law, Privileges, Proceedings and Usage of Parliament.* This book has been revised regularly by successive Clerks of the House and is commonly known as *Parliamentary Practice* or simply Erskine May. Sir Thomas Erskine May was Clerk of the House of Commons between 1871 and 1886.

Erskine May includes a long, growing and entertaining list of insults which MPs are not allowed to hurl at each other across the chamber, ranging from 'cad', 'knave' and 'bounder' in the nineteenth century to more earthy epithets today. Labour's Tam Dalyell was suspended from the House for describing Margaret Thatcher as 'a bounder, a liar, a deceiver, a cheat and a crook'. Surprisingly, however, former Labour MP, Tony Banks, escaped rebuke for accusing Margaret Thatcher of acting 'with the sensitivity of a sex-starved boa-constrictor', and for describing former Conservative MP, Terry Dicks, as 'living proof that a pig's bladder on the end of a stick can be elected to Parliament'. Labour's Michael Foot was not censured for describing Conservative Norman Tebbit as a 'semi-house-trained polecat'. In proud response, Tebbit included a polecat in his coat-of-arms when he entered the House of Lords. In 2004, SNP MP, Annabelle Ewing, was ejected from the Commons when she refused to apologise for calling Defence Secretary, Geoff Hoon, a 'back-stabbing coward' over his plans to merge historic Scottish regiments. In 2005, Labour MP, Dennis Skinner, was banned from the Commons for a day for his comments about Shadow Chancellor George Osborne and cocaine. Referring to the economy of the 1980s, Mr Skinner said, 'The only thing that was growing then was the lines of coke in front of Boy George and the rest of the Tories.' (Skinner, nicknamed 'the Beast of Bolsover' after his constituency and for his confrontational style, has been required to leave the Commons ten times since 1979, including a five-day ban in 1981.) In 2006, a Conservative Party anti-debt video urged young people to 'ignore the tosser in you'. They claimed that they were using the dubious expression in the old sense of someone who tossed their money away without thought; but most commentators reckoned that they were coyly trying to boost their street cred. Labour's Deputy Prime Minister, John Prescott, then employed the word in the Commons against the serried ranks of Conservative MPs, and the Speaker merely smiled.

Accusations of lying usually mean expulsion from the chamber; although Prime Minister, Gordon Brown, escaped with a warning from the Speaker when he accused Opposition leader, David Cameron, of 'misleading people' during Prime Minister's Question Time (PMQT) in 2007, because Brown had not accused Cameron of misleading the House itself. And Winston Churchill, famously, got away with describing a lie as a 'terminological inexactitude'.

Hansard

Hansard is the official report of the proceedings of Parliament. It is published daily when Parliament is sitting and records everything that is officially said and done in both the House of Commons and House

Sharia Law

4. Mr Hugo Swire (East Devon) (Con): What recent assessment her Department has made of the implications of sharia law practices for community cohesion. [226339]

The Parliamentary Under-Secretary of State for Communities and Local Government (Mr Sadiq Khan): Community cohesion is about building better relationships between people from different backgrounds, including those from new and settled communities. The use of religious courts, such as sharia councils, to resolve private family and contractual disputes is well established, and in itself does not have an impact on community cohesion. It is, however, important that all practices are compliant with our framework of equality legislation, as equality is essential in the underpinning of cohesion.

14 October 2008: Column 660

Mr Swire: I congratulate the Minister on his debut on the Front Bench in his new role. He said over the weekend that he would be: "very concerned about sharia courts applying in the UK." Presumably no one had told him that last year the Government licensed a whole lot of what they call Muslim arbitration tribunals. I appreciate that their powers are limited, but they are presided over by sharia judges and are therefore, in effect, state-licensed sharia courts. Is the Minister satisfied that individual women in particular who come before such courts will do so voluntarily in every case?

Mr Khan: I thank the hon. Gentleman for his question, but I wish that he had read the entire quotation. For the avoidance of any doubt, I tell the House that sharia law has no jurisdiction in England and Wales, and there is no intention to change that. His point about women is one that I referred to in the answer that I gave a minute and a half ago. We are conscious of the fact that all sharia councils should abide by equality legislation. That is at the core of cohesion.

Mrs Ann Cryer (Keighley) (Lab): Is my hon. Friend aware that only two of the eight mosques in my constituency are registered for marriage? Therefore, there can be problems, as couples are married in sharia law, but not in the law of this country. Sometimes there are problems – if the marriage breaks down and a settlement needs to be arrived at about the division of assets, for instance, where the woman can be let down by a sharia judge. Can my hon. Friend's Department do anything to encourage mosques to register for marriage, so that those marriages take place within the law of the land?

http://www.publications.parliament.uk/pa/cm200708/cmhansrd/cm081014/
debtext/81014-0002.htm#08101459000017

Figure 1.1 Extract from *Hansard*, Tuesday, 14 October 2008

of Lords, for which separate reports are issued. *Hansard* also publishes written answers by government ministers in response to questions formally posed by MPs. Since 1909 – and for important votes before then – *Hansard* has listed how MPs have voted in divisions. The proceedings and debates in parliamentary committees are also published in separate volumes.

The name *Hansard* was officially adopted in 1943 after Luke Hansard (1752–1828) who was the printer of the *House of Commons Journal* from 1774. The first detailed official reports were published in 1803 by the journalist William Cobbett in his *Political Register*. For many years *Hansard* did not formally acknowledge the existence of parties in the House, though in 2003 this changed and so MPs' party affiliations are now identified.

Pomp and ceremony

The Queen's Speech
The Queen's Speech is written by the government of the day and delivered by the reigning monarch at the annual state opening of Parliament. It sets out the government's legislative agenda for the year ahead. The Queen is simply a mouthpiece and, famously, would have to announce her own abolition if government, parliamentary and public opinion so willed it. The ceremonial trappings surrounding the occasion make the event one of the high points in the parliamentary calendar, redolent of tradition, ceremony and spectacle. Some of the more arcane practices have been abolished in recent years: for example, the tradition that the Lord Chancellor must walk backward down the steps of the grand throne in the House of Lords after handing the speech to the Queen. The symbolic point of this was that no one must turn their back on the Queen; but some recent Lord Chancellors, such as Lord Hailsham in the 1980s, were deemed too frail to risk the manoeuvre.

Parliamentary officials

The Speaker
'Order, order!' is one of the most famous of parliamentary expressions, summoning the image of the Speaker imposing discipline upon

Box 1.1 The current duties of the Speaker

- To chair meetings of the House of Commons with independence and impartiality.
- To decide the allocation of time to parties and MPs.
- To call MPs to speak.
- To regulate MPs' speeches, questions and parliamentary motions while also protecting them from an overweening executive. 'Catching the Speaker's eye' requires his or her attention to a balance of party time and opportunities for critical backbenchers, or it may sometimes be achieved by a word with him or her beforehand.
- To order individual MPs to apologise or withdraw if they make unacceptable remarks.
- To 'name' and exclude MPs who refuse to obey the authority of the Chair.
- To adjourn or suspend the whole House if order is unduly disrupted (as when pro-hunt protesters stormed into the Commons chamber in 2004).
- To exercise a casting vote on a Bill where votes are tied; by convention, the Speaker votes for the *status quo* and arranges for the vote to be taken again.
- To accept or reject points of order, urgency motions, closures and so on.
- To select chairpersons for, and allocate Bills to, standing committees.
- To decide whether a Bill is a 'money Bill' – a tax law – under the Parliament Act 1911.
- To decide on *prima facie* breaches of parliamentary privilege.
- To bear messages between the House and the monarch.
- To issue warrants for holding by-elections to fill vacancies.

a House of unruly MPs. Since the televising of the Commons began this has become internationally well known and often copied.

When the Commons first assembled separately, a spokesman was necessary to report the commoners' views to the monarch and the Lords. The first record of such a Speaker was Sir Thomas Hungerford in 1377. However, for three centuries, the loyalties of Commons' Speakers were divided between Parliament and executive. It was not until 1642, when Charles I attempted to arrest five Members of Parliament, that Speaker Lenthall famously declared: 'Sire, I have neither eyes to see nor tongue to speak in this place, but as the House is pleased to direct me, whose servant I am here.' Since then, the Speaker has traditionally been committed to serving and protecting the interests of the whole House of Commons, especially against executive pressure, regardless of party affiliation or interests.

Traditionally, Speakers are backbench MPs with long experience of the House. They need to be popular, trusted, authoritative and, at best, charismatic. They are elected by all members of the Commons who (a rare event) seek to rise above party affiliations and to resist frontbench pressures. Since, at one time, the office involved conveying unpopular messages to angry monarchs who could punish the Speaker with imprisonment or death, there developed the quaint tradition that a new Speaker feigns resistance and is gently and reluctantly 'dragged to the Chair' by two fellow MPs, one on each arm. (Nine Speakers have died violent deaths: one was murdered; another was killed in battle; and seven were beheaded – including two on the same day in 1510.)

The Speaker holds office until he or she retires (after which they are given a life peerage) but, meanwhile, remains a sitting MP, on the ground that this gives electoral authority to his or her office. However, it also denies his or her constituents a functioning MP, since the Speaker is required to be non-party political. The Speaker, therefore, nominates a neighbouring MP to do his or her constituency work. This effectively disenfranchises the Speaker's voters – especially since, by convention, usually no one stands against the incumbent in the Speaker's constituency. However, most voters do not seem to mind. They appear to enjoy having an MP of the Speaker's status and renown, and always re-elect him or her, even when the election is contested. The Speaker is paid a salary similar to that of cabinet ministers – £137,000 in 2008.

One of the most famous and respected of recent speakers (1992–2000) was Betty Boothroyd – the only woman ever to have held the office. On taking up her position she instructed bemused MPs, accustomed only to men holding the position, to 'call me Madam':

> The first time she presided over Prime Minister's Questions, she astonished MPs by bringing it to a close with the now immortal words: 'Right, time's up.' It was like Bet Lynch calling time in the Rovers Return – an impression helped by her gravelly voice, the result of a

20-a-day cigarette habit – and it stunned MPs into silence. Over eight years she made it as much a Commons tradition as slamming the door in Black Rod's face during the state opening of Parliament.[4]

The current, and 156th, Speaker, Labour MP Michael Martin, was elected in 2000. He is the first Roman Catholic Speaker since the Reformation and, as a working-class Glaswegian, nicknamed 'Gorbals Mick', he has encountered some prejudice and snobbery and has generated some controversy. For example, in 2001, he welcomed Home Secretary David Blunkett's announcement of the end of the voucher support system for asylum seekers. He apologised the next day for appearing to depart from the strict tradition of the Speaker's impartiality. He was also criticised in 2007 for spending over £20,000 of taxpayers' money on legal fees to challenge negative press stories about his rulings, the exemption of his wife from Westminster security checks and his attempts to block the publication of MPs' expenses under the Freedom of Information Act. Whatever the controversy, no one has the power to remove the Speaker after election – including MPs themselves – in order to safeguard his or her independence.

The Speaker has an opulent official residence at the Westminster Bridge end of the Palace of Westminster. From here begins a formal Speaker's procession before every sitting of the House, via the Library Corridor, the Lower Waiting Hall, Central and Members' Lobbies to the Chamber. The Speaker is preceded in the procession by a Bar Doorkeeper and the Serjeant at Arms with the Mace (a staff of office symbolising the authority of the House), and followed by the Chaplain, Secretary and Trainbearer. This daily procession is a favourite with tourists. On normal sitting days, the Speaker wears a black cloth court suit with linen bands, over which is worn a black silk robe with train. Betty Boothroyd decided against wearing the full-bottomed wig used by her predecessors, and Michael Martin has followed suit. On state occasions, such as the opening of Parliament, he or she wears a robe of black satin damask trimmed with gold, with a lace jabot at the neck and lace frills at the sleeves.

The Serjeant at Arms
We have already touched upon the role of the Serjeant at Arms in the context of parliamentary security. He also plays a role in the disciplining

of MPs: if the Speaker decides to suspend or remove an MP from the chamber and the MP refuses to leave, the Serjeant at Arms comes to eject him or her. He and his staff also preside at ceremonial occasions within Westminster. The Serjeant at Arms is best known as the bearer of the Mace during the daily procession of the Speaker into the Commons chamber. His office dates back to 1415.

Former Serjeant at Arms, Peter Grant Peterkin, was embroiled in a row in 2007 for sending out an email ordering Westminster staff 'to give way to MPs when queuing for retail and catering services, the post office, travel office or when using other facilities such as lifts, photocopiers, telephone cubicles etc.' Westminster researchers, secretaries and other staff were incensed at this 'feudal' ruling – 'What will they want us to do next? Doff our caps?' asked a TGWU representative – and Liberal Democrat MP, Lembit Opik, said, 'I suspect it's a cross-party initiative of the "don't you know who I am" brigade.'

In 2008 the first ever female Serjeant at Arms was appointed.

Black Rod

The Gentleman Usher of the Black Rod is more usually known simply as Black Rod. He is responsible for accommodation, security and services in the House of Lords. He has a chair in the House of Lords and wears a distinctive black costume. He is best known to the public for the prominent role he plays in the ceremony of the State Opening of Parliament, when he is sent to the House of Commons to summon MPs to the House of Lords to hear the Queen's Speech. In a symbol of the Commons' independence, the door to their chamber is slammed in his face and not opened until he has knocked on the door three times with his staff of office. Black Rod's role in the Lords is similar to that of the Serjeant at Arms in the Commons, but less powerful.

The Lord Chancellor

The Lord Chancellor was the monarch's chief legal adviser from the thirteenth century onwards. His office predates that of the Prime Minister or any members of the Cabinet, with the legal authority of the Lord Chancellor dating back to a statute of Henry VIII of 1540.

He (there has never been a she) traditionally performed three key functions. First, he was a member of the Cabinet and was responsible for the development and implementation of government policy on the legal system. Secondly, he was also the head of the judiciary and was in charge of the appointment of senior judges, the administration of the courts and the legal system. Thirdly, he sat in the House of Lords and presided over its proceedings from his position on the Woolsack. His office was, therefore, unique in spanning the executive, judiciary and legislature – a major breach of the principle of the separation of powers which is supposed to underpin a liberal democracy.

His legislative function was not exactly equivalent to that of the Speaker of the Commons. He shared his duties equally with his deputies and was not responsible for maintaining order during debates as this is the responsibility of the Lords as a whole. Also, he did not call upon peers to speak during debates as the order of speaking is prearranged. Rather than being impartial, he spoke during debates for the government, was entitled to vote like any other peer and he did not hold a casting vote.

In 2003, the Labour Government announced plans to abolish the office of Lord Chancellor and to separate out the three roles – executive, judicial and legislative. In the 2003 Queen's Speech, the government announced that it would legislate on the following changes:

- abolishing the office of Lord Chancellor;
- creating a 'supreme court' of senior judges separate from the House of Lords;
- creating an independent judicial appointments commission;
- abolishing the remaining 92 hereditary peers;
- retrospectively barring convicted criminals from sitting in the House of Lords (apparently targeted at former Conservative Lord Jeffrey Archer).

The Conservatives were outraged at the proposal to abolish the office of Lord Chancellor and 'destroy 1,200 years of history'. Conservative peer, Lord Howe, described the post as 'the cornerstone of the constitution' and said that its abolition 'could be almost compared with the events of September 11'.[5] They forced a government U-turn on the abolition of the actual title of Lord Chancellor but, since then, the office has simply disappeared. In 2006, the role of head of the judiciary passed to the (second in command) Lord Chief Justice, and an independent appointments commission was created to choose senior judges. The Lord Chancellor was also replaced in 2006 as the presiding officer of the Upper House by the first Speaker of the Lords ever to be elected by fellow peers, former Labour minister, Baroness Hayman.

Since the formation of PM Gordon Brown's first Cabinet in 2007, the Lord Chancellor was no longer even a lord. Instead, Labour MP, Jack Straw, combined the offices of Secretary of State for Justice and Lord Chancellor, with the latter title largely disappearing from government websites. Surprisingly, this caused barely a ripple in the Lords.

Parliament and monarch today

Every Bill that goes through Parliament must receive royal assent to become law. However, since the eighteenth century this has been a formality. There has long been a very strong convention that no modern monarch will refuse royal assent to a Bill, because it would be undemocratic for a non-elected monarch to challenge the will of the elected House of Commons. The last time a monarch successfully refused royal assent for a Bill was in 1707, when Queen Anne vetoed the Scotch Militia Bill.

The monarch's legislative functions today are purely ceremonial – notably, the Queen's Speech at the beginning of each parliamentary session. Even today, this invokes echoes of Parliament's earliest beginnings, with the Queen pronouncing, 'We being desirous and resolved, as soon as may be, to meet Our people and have their advice in Parliament, do hereby make known to all Our loving subjects Our Royal Will and Pleasure to call a new Parliament.'

The royal prerogative

The conventional view of the royal prerogative, that is, the legal powers of the Crown, is that, following the Glorious Revolution of 1688, it was made subject to parliamentary control; and the United Kingdom constitution, based on parliamentary government under the rule of law, dates from that time.

The fact is that the royal prerogative is alive and well and living, for the most part, in 10 Downing Street. A former Lord Chief Justice,

Lord Hewart, has defined the royal prerogative as 'such powers as are exercisable by the executive government without express authority from Parliament'.[6] Prime ministerial (and ministerial) use of the royal prerogative, by convention, allows the executive to bypass parliamentary, and often judicial, control – especially where 'national security' is invoked. Examples include: ministers withholding information in the court case about 'arms to Iraq' in 1995; MI5 officers being allowed to 'bug and burgle' in the United Kingdom without fear of prosecution; the government forbidding some civil servants to be members of trades unions; and the Home Office supplying the police with plastic bullets and CS gas against the wishes of elected local authorities.

Many parliamentarians fear that the conventional use of prerogative powers gives ministers – particularly the Prime Minister – excessive policy-making power beyond democratic scrutiny and control. They would like to see these powers redefined and limited within statute law, and subject to parliamentary approval. One prime example, since the invasion of Iraq in 2003, is the declaration of war and deployment of troops by British Prime Ministers – a topic on which former Labour minister, Clare Short, introduced an unsuccessful Private Member's Bill in 2005. Almost as soon as he took office in 2007, PM Gordon Brown proposed a raft of constitutional reforms, including giving MPs the final say on declaring war.

· ·

✔ What you should have learnt from reading this chapter

- This chapter has provided a brief historical outline of the development of the Westminster Parliament in four stages, from the earliest days when the House of Commons did not even exist, through to the dominance of Parliament – especially the Commons – by party and executive in the twenty-first century.

- It has outlined Parliament's main functions and explained the key concepts of 'parliamentary sovereignty' and 'parliamentary government'.

- It has introduced some of the key controversies surrounding the role of Parliament today, particularly whether its legal sovereignty is, in practice, manipulated by government from within and bypassed by the EU from without.

- This chapter has also taken the reader on a short tour of the buildings of Parliament, introduced its key officials and acquainted you with some of the whimsies of its procedures and ceremonies.

- Finally, it has outlined the role of the monarch and Crown in relation to Parliament, and has highlighted the difference between the very limited powers of the modern monarch and the potentially huge powers which the use of the royal prerogative confers upon the modern executive.

Glossary of key terms

Bicameral legislature A Parliament with two chambers/Houses.
Bill A draft law going through Parliament.
Erskine May The book of rules on parliamentary procedures.
Executive The government.
Filibustering Talking out a Bill.
Guillotine A time limit on parliamentary debate of a Bill in the committee stage, imposed by the government.
Hansard The official written report of the proceedings in Parliament.
Her Majesty's Opposition The second largest party in the House of Commons.
Legislature The law-making institution of the state.
Parliamentary government A system based on overlap rather than separation of powers, that is, the executive is chosen from the legislature and is, in theory, subordinate and accountable to the legislature – the opposite of a presidential system.
Parliamentary sovereignty Parliament has supreme law-making power, and can make, amend or repeal any law without challenge from any domestic body. Thus, it cannot be ruled illegal or unconstitutional, it can legalise illegality and no Parliament can bind its successors. However, since 1973, it is formally overridden by the EU.
Royal prerogative The legal powers of the Crown.
Speaker The person who chairs proceedings of the House of Commons.
Standing orders Written rules of parliamentary procedure.
Statute law An Act of Parliament.
Supranational An international institution with sovereign power over member states.

Likely examination questions

Short questions:

- Describe the UK's 'bicameral legislature'.
- Define 'parliamentary government'.

- Describe the role and functions of the Speaker of the House of Commons.
- Outline the contemporary monarch's legislative functions.

Essay questions:

- Outline and explain the changing balance of power between the executive and the legislature.
- Distinguish between the legal and the actual powers of Parliament.
- How and why did Parliament become 'legally sovereign'?
- Describe and assess the utility of current parliamentary practices and procedures.

 Helpful websites

http://news.bbc.co.uk

http://www.parliament.uk

http://www.explore.parliament.uk

 Suggestions for further reading

Rush, M., *Parliament Today*, Manchester: Manchester University Press, 2005.

Thomas, G. P., *Parliament in an Age of Reform*, Sheffield: Sheffield Hallam University Press, 2000.

Walters, R. and Rogers, R., *How Parliament Works*, London: Longman, 2006.

CHAPTER 2

The United Kingdom Parliamentary System

Overview

This chapter provides an outline of the United Kingdom's parliamentary system of **government**, including an analysis of the changing reality of 'parliamentary **sovereignty**', the theory and practice of 'parliamentary government', contrasts with other contemporary democratic assemblies around the world and an analysis of the current issues and controversies surrounding the roles of Parliament today.

Key issues to be covered in this chapter

- Parliamentary sovereignty
- Parliamentary government
- Other current issues and controversies: political representation and responsibility
- Contrasts with other contemporary legislative assemblies

Parliamentary sovereignty

Sovereignty is unrestricted power and authority. It applies to any body which can act or take decisions without hindrance from any institution above, below or within it. A body has internal sovereignty if it has the power to make decisions binding on all its own citizens. A body has external sovereignty if it can control its own affairs without being blocked by outside bodies and states. Further, to complicate matters, there are different kinds of sovereignty, for example, legal, political and economic.

The political system of the United Kingdom is unitary: that is, it has one sovereign legislature – namely, the Parliament at Westminster, which has ultimate law-making authority over all other bodies within the country. Although there are local government councils and now also local Parliaments throughout the United Kingdom, these bodies are subordinate to the central, sovereign, Westminster Parliament; and their existence and powers are wholly determined by Westminster, which can limit the powers of such local bodies or, indeed, abolish them altogether at any time. The frequent suspension by Westminster of Stormont – the Northern Irish Assembly (because of political conflicts during the peace process) – is one example of Westminster's legal supremacy. This does not mean that the law must be exactly the same throughout the whole of the United Kingdom; but differences, for example, between Scottish law and English law, are only those allowed, or ordered, by Westminster.

This unitary system is in contrast to a **federal constitution** such as that of the United States or Australia, where the local executive and/or legislative bodies have much stronger and more autonomous powers within their own defined areas of responsibility. In a federal system, the centre has decision-making powers over matters such as national security, defence and foreign affairs, but it cannot impede or impose upon the local powers of the local bodies – and the same is true in reverse. The central and local power bodies are, in theory, equal and autonomous and there are mutual checks and balances between them. Internal sovereignty is divided between national and local powers; they are, therefore, based upon the paradoxical idea of shared sovereignty. A federal system is, in summary, much more decentralised than is a unitary system.

In the unitary state of the United Kingdom, the main theoretical pillar of the constitution is the legal sovereignty or supremacy of Parliament. This suggests that the Westminster Parliament is the supreme law-making body in the United Kingdom, and that no other institution in the country can override its laws. As the eminent constitutional writer, A. V. Dicey, stated in 1885, 'Parliament has, under the English constitution, the right to make or unmake any law whatsoever; and, further, no person or body is recognised by the law of England as having a right to override or set aside the legislation of Parliament.'[1]

Box 2.1 The doctrine of parliamentary sovereignty

The doctrine of parliamentary sovereignty implies the following principles:

- The Westminster Parliament is the supreme – ultimate – law-making body within the United Kingdom.
- It can pass, amend or repeal any law without challenge from any other UK institution.
- There is no higher legal authority; whereas, with codified constitutions, the constitution itself is sovereign and sets limits to the powers of the legislature. In the United Kingdom, all rules of the constitution other than Acts of Parliament (e.g. conventions) can be overridden by Parliament, which can also take back, by law, any power given away to any other bodies, for example, the European Union or devolved assemblies.
- Parliament cannot be ruled illegal, nor can it be bound by any laws of any previous Parliament.
- Thus, no Parliament can bind its successors.
- Also, Parliament is not always bound by its own laws (statutes), but instead by a special body of law known as **parliamentary privilege**. This exempts MPs from some ordinary law, the most important example being that they cannot be sued for slander for words spoken in Parliament. For example, Labour MP, Stuart Bell, used parliamentary privilege to expose the Conservative 'cash for questions' scandal in the 1990s, prompting the resignations of three government ministers.
- The Westminster Parliament is subject only to the 'political sovereignty' of the voters at a general election – as long as Parliament chooses not to ban elections.

In theory, no person or body – including the UK courts – can override Westminster legislation. Judges can interpret and enforce the law only as it is written by Parliament. If Parliament is not happy with the courts' interpretation of the law, it can rewrite that law. With a codified constitution, by contrast, some kind of constitutional or supreme court can check or override the law. In the United States, for example, federal courts and the Supreme Court can veto laws of both the national (federal) Congress and the local state legislatures.

In 2005, with reference to clashes between Parliament and the courts over a series of draconian anti-terror laws passed in the United Kingdom since the attacks on America on 11 September 2001, the then Opposition Leader, Michael Howard, restated the principle of parliamentary sovereignty against the judges:

> Given that judicial activism seems to have reached unprecedented levels in thwarting the wishes of Parliament, it is time, I believe, to go back to first principles. The UK constitution, largely unwritten, is based on the **separation of powers**. Ever since the Glorious Revolution established its supremacy, Parliament has made the law and the judiciary has interpreted it. As Lord Reid, a Law Lord from 1948 to 1974, explained in 1969: 'It is often said that it would be unconstitutional for Parliament to do certain things, meaning that the moral, political and other reasons against doing them are so strong that most people would regard it as highly improper. But that does not mean that it is beyond the power to Parliament to do such things. If Parliament chose to do any of them, the courts would not hold the Act of Parliament invalid.'

In conclusion, Howard warned the judges not to 'thwart the will of Parliament'.[2]

The sovereign Westminster Parliament can even pass **retrospective law**, that is, backdated law, which may have effect for days, months or years before it was actually passed. At its most extreme, this means that Parliament could, in unlikely theory, pass a law which says 'As from now, it was illegal for you to have been walking down that particular road last week. Which you did. You are therefore nicked.' Retrospective law breaches the principle (in an important theory called the 'rule of law') that the law should be 'knowable' at the time that it is being broken.

Box 2.2 Four examples of retrospective law in the United Kingdom

- In 1998, retrospective legislation stopped tax exemption for overseas earners (which prompted the Rolling Stones to cancel their UK tour).
- After 11 September 2001, the government – through Parliament – hastily imposed a retrospective increase in the penalty for terrorist hoaxes from six months to seven years.
- In 2003, the government – again, through Parliament – retrospectively abolished the double jeopardy rule, which had prevented people from being tried more than once for the same crime.
- In 2007, Chancellor Alistair Darling announced a change in inheritance tax law, to be applied retrospectively.

Most written constitutions prohibit such retrospective laws.

The theory and practice of parliamentary sovereignty

In theory, Westminster's legislative sovereignty is absolute. However, in practice, Parliament's external sovereignty is now limited by the European Union, whose laws have formal sovereignty over all twenty-seven member states – for example, on the imposition of fishing quotas and the world-wide ban on the sale of UK beef during the BSE ('mad cow') crisis. Even on entry to the EU in 1973, the UK Parliament had to accept forty-three volumes of existing EU legislation. More than 50 per cent of UK legislation now originates from the EU. This is the only formal override upon Westminster's legal supremacy. In theory, however, Parliament could legislate to withdraw from the EU at any time; therefore it remains, technically, sovereign, although, in practice, withdrawal from the EU seems unlikely.

There are also many other, informal, constraints upon parliamentary sovereignty, both external and internal.

Box 2.3 Informal constraints upon parliamentary sovereignty

- Other international courts and laws, such as the European Court of Human Rights (ECHR), which, for example, in 2004 ruled against the United Kingdom's blanket ban on votes for prisoners as a breach of free elections, free expression and non-discrimination. (Note that that the ECHR has no connection with the EU.)
- Big business, the City and other economic power bodies such as the international currency dealers, who, in 1992, forced the UK to pull out of the European exchange rate mechanism (ERM) which was paving the way for the euro.
- Pressure groups, for example, the National Farmers' Union influenced the huge extra subsidies given by the government to UK beef farmers in the 1990s to compensate them for lost sales due to the BSE scandal; and also the Countryside Alliance, which persuaded the Labour Government for years not to fulfil its **manifesto** promise to abolish fox hunting, and which also rendered the eventual hunting ban effectively unenforceable.
- The media, for example, on clamping down on asylum seekers.
- Referenda: although, in theory, these are merely advisory in the United Kingdom, in practice their results could never be ignored by Parliament.
- Ultimately, Parliament's 'legal sovereignty' is constrained by the 'political sovereignty' of the electorate, who may occasionally simply refuse to obey the law of Parliament – for example, the mass refusal to pay the poll tax in 1989–90 – and who choose the MPs in the Commons and can, therefore, in effect, sack Parliament.
- Most importantly, Parliament tends to be dominated, from within itself, by a 'majority' government (that is, an executive whose party holds over 50 per cent of the seats in the Commons) which, with strong party discipline and backbench support, can usually ensure that its legislative proposals are passed by Parliament.

Parliamentary government

Any state has three branches:

- a legislature, which makes the laws;
- an executive, which implements the laws and policies;
- a judiciary, which interprets and enforces the laws.

The UK executive, or government, decides and carries out the policies by which the country is run – whether that means raising or cutting taxes, imposing university tuition fees or going to war. However, all of these policies must be lawful. Therefore, every year, the government must submit its new policy proposals to the legislature to be legalised. If the legislature, that is, Parliament, defeats a government Bill, the government cannot implement that policy because it would not be lawful.

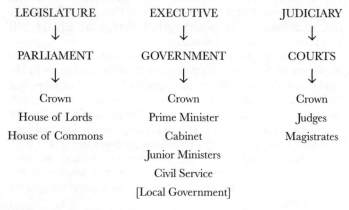

Figure 2.1 The UK system of government

If the three branches of state – legislature, executive and judiciary – are completely united, the system may be a tyranny. Liberal democratic theory advocates the 'separation of powers', that is, non-overlapping personnel and powers of the legislature, executive and judiciary, to ensure checks and balances between the different parts of the system and hence more freedom for the citizen. The United States has a substantial degree of separation between the legislature, that is, Congress; the executive, that is, President and Cabinet; and the American judiciary. The United Kingdom, however, does not.

The main overlap in the UK system is between the legislature and the executive. The term 'parliamentary government' (see Chapter 1) refers to this overlap between Parliament and government: that is, the executive (government – PM and ministers) is chosen from within the legislature (Westminster MPs and peers) and the executive is, in theory, subordinate and accountable to the legislature.

Box 2.4 The formation of parliamentary government in the United Kingdom

Step 1 At each general election, the voters elect 646 MPs into the House of Commons, usually on the basis of a party label. Assuming that one party wins over 50 per cent of the seats . . .

Step 2 The Queen appoints, as Prime Minister, the leader of the majority party in the Commons.

Step 3 The PM then appoints his/her senior Cabinet ministers, and wider team of junior ministers, from within both the Commons and the Lords.

The main example of the government's constitutional subordination to Parliament is an important convention (tradition) of the constitution that, if a government is defeated in a 'vote of no confidence' by the House of Commons, it should resign. This is a motion simply stating 'That this House has no confidence in Her Majesty's government'. It is usually tabled by the Leader of the Opposition. The last time that such a motion forced a government to resign was in 1979, when James Callaghan's Labour government was defeated by just one vote in the Commons. However, it is important to note that this defeat was inflicted upon a **minority government** which had under 50 per cent of the seats in the Commons. No majority government has been so defeated since the 1880s and, therefore, such motions are rarely timetabled even against governments with a small majority, because their own MPs will invariably rally round and just make the Opposition look ineffectual. For this reason, beleaguered governments sometimes turn votes on key issues into 'confidence' votes to be sure of winning them. Conservative Prime Minister John Major did this with the parliamentary vote on the controversial EU Maastricht Treaty in 1993.

Parliament is also supposed to examine, debate, criticise and check the activities of the government, to publicise executive actions, to convey public opinion to government, and to authorise the raising and spending of money by government through, for example, debates, votes on government Bills, Question Time, parliamentary committees and financial scrutiny. Thus, through its link with Parliament – and especially with the elected House of Commons – the UK government is said to be both representative, that is, reflective of the voters' views and interests, and responsible, that is, accountable and answerable for its actions, to Parliament and thus, indirectly, to the voters.

The United States and many other countries, by contrast, have a **presidential system**. This does not (confusingly) refer to the fact that they have a President and the United Kingdom does not. It means that the executive (headed by the President) is directly elected by the voters, quite separately from Congress (the American legislature). The President is not allowed to be a member of Congress, and he is, in theory, equal (rather than subordinate) to the legislature with mutual checks and balances between them. The American President can, for example, veto Congressional Bills, as President George W. Bush did in 2007 on the threatened freezing of funding for troops in Iraq, and in 2008 on a Bill which sought to ban torture by the CIA. He is also directly accountable to the voters through the ballot box, rather than indirectly through the legislature.

The theory and practice of parliamentary government
In theory, the UK Parliament controls government. However, in practice, government usually controls Parliament. This is because the first-past-the-post electoral system almost always produces a 'majority' government with over 50 per cent of the seats in the Commons which, with strong party discipline and backbench support, can usually ensure that its legislative proposals are passed by Parliament.

In his 1976 Dimbleby Lecture, Lord Hailsham, therefore, famously coined the term **'elective dictatorship'** to suggest that a majority government – in control of a sovereign Parliament, with a **flexible constitution** which can be changed by a one-vote majority in the House of Commons – can effectively push through almost any piece of legislation, and even change the constitution, at will. He noted that:

> The sovereignty of Parliament has increasingly become, in practice, the sovereignty of the Commons, and the sovereignty of the Commons has increasingly become the sovereignty of the government, which, in addition to its influence in Parliament, controls the party whips, the party machine and the civil service.[3]

The thesis that modern governments in the United Kingdom constitute elective dictatorships gained renewed strength after the 1997 general election when Labour won a massive 179-seat majority over all of the other parties combined in the House of Commons (although this was on a minority of the votes cast – see Chapter 5) and seemed virtually unassailable. Thus, for example, within its first year in office Labour had pushed through many unpopular policies which were not in its manifesto, such as cuts in the benefits payable to lone parents and disabled people, the introduction of tuition fees for university students, increasing taxation of pension funds and completing the Millennium Dome. Although the Labour Governments since 1997 have suffered many significant backbench revolts, they have very rarely been defeated in the House of Commons.

The dominance of the Commons by the government is enhanced by the so-called 'payroll vote': that is, the total number of MPs with government posts (from Cabinet ministers down to lowly parliamentary private secretaries) who are, therefore, covered by the doctrine of **collective responsibility** and must vote for every government measure or risk losing their jobs. After the 2005 general election, the payroll vote totalled 115 of Labour's 356 MPs.

The rare exceptions to this balance of power and predominance of the executive within Parliament are:

- A minority government: for example, the Conservatives by April 1997.
- A successful backbench revolt: for example, in 2005 the government was defeated in the Commons for the first time since 1997, on the 90-day detention clause in the Terrorism Bill, by thirty-one votes – the largest post-war defeat on such a significant issue.
- Defeat by the House of Lords: for example, repeated rejection of government plans to restrict trial by jury, in complex fraud cases for instance. The government has often been obstructed by the House of Lords (where they do not have an absolute majority) but, usually, only temporarily because the elected House of Commons has the ultimate legal power to overturn the unelected Lords' decisions.

Labour's large majorities in the Commons since 1997 have usually ensured their dominance of Parliament as a whole. However, in the

2005 general election, Labour's majority in the Commons fell to just sixty-six, making their power and strength rather less secure.

Other current issues and controversies

Two key controversies have so far been outlined: the loss of Parliament's sovereignty to the EU, from without; and to the executive, from within.

Representation

A further concern centres upon Parliament's representative role. The House of Commons is the only nationally elected institution in the United Kingdom, and voters look to it – and to their individual MPs – to represent their views and interests. However, the first-past-the-post electoral system creates a number of problems.

MPs require only a **simple majority** of votes to win their seats, that is, more votes than any other single candidate in their constituency, not necessarily 50 per cent. No MP in the 2005 Parliament won over 50 per cent of the votes cast in their constituencies and this begs the question as to how representative MPs are of voters' views and wishes.

Across the country as a whole, this electoral system means that a party can win a majority of seats in the Commons on a minority of votes in the country. In 2005, for example, Labour won 55 per cent of the seats with just 35 per cent of the votes cast. On an almost historically low turnout of 61 per cent, this means that the Labour Government elected in 2005 won just 22 per cent of the votes of the total eligible electorate – which raises serious questions about the strength of their **mandate**, or authority to govern.

MPs are not even very representative of the voters in terms of their social background, with (in 2005) just 19 per cent of Westminster MPs being women and only 2 per cent (15 out of 646) being black or Asian.

The unelected House of Lords, of course, faces even greater problems of legitimacy and perceptions of unrepresentativeness. This issue will be covered in more detail in Chapters 3 and 5.

Responsibility

Voters' doubts about the legitimacy of Parliament are compounded by their general mistrust of politicians and their common perception that most MPs and ministers are self-serving, dishonest and potentially corrupt. 'Sleaze' became the media's shorthand term for political dishonesty and corruption from the 1990s onwards.

A 2004 report by the Committee for Standards in Public Life (established in 1994 after a series of scandals about political 'sleaze') found a 'widespread lack of trust in politicians'. Only estate agents and tabloid newspaper journalists were held in lower esteem than government ministers, who were trusted by just 24 per cent of people to tell the truth. The report found that: 'There is a widespread perception of a culture in which politicians try to cover up the mistakes that they make, which sits uncomfortably alongside a strongly expressed desire among the public for them to come clean.' The report also said that many people feel 'party politics is somehow at odds with the needs of the country', and that the public believe that MPs should vote in Parliament according to the public interest, rather than party loyalties or political self-interest.

The public mistrust of government ministers is compounded by the growing perception that they are not held sufficiently accountable for mistakes and misbehaviour and that the doctrine of **individual ministerial responsibility** is becoming dangerously weak. In other words, ministers often do not resign when they should over departmental or personal errors, or, if they do resign, it is usually belatedly and reluctantly, and they are often brought back into government with unseemly haste. Peter Mandelson and David Blunkett – both brought back into government by former Prime Minister Tony Blair after being forced to resign ministerial office over personal scandals, and then both forced to resign again over new scandals – are cited as examples which highlight Parliament's shortcomings in holding ministers to account. However, they did resign. Other ministers perhaps should have, but did not: for example, former Deputy Prime Minister, John Prescott, over punching a voter who threw an egg at him, or over an affair with a secretary, or over a stay at the Colorado ranch of a would-be super-casino owner. This issue of ministerial accountability is further examined in Chapter 6.

Contrasts with other contemporary legislative assemblies

Flexible versus rigid constitutions

The UK constitution is flexible, that is, it requires no special procedures for amendment, but can be changed by an ordinary Act of Parliament. This means that even a major change to the UK political system, such as the abolition of the monarchy, could be implemented by a one-vote majority in the House of Commons (in the same way as any minor change, such as a law on littering). Thus, there is no distinct body of constitutional law. A **rigid constitution**, by contrast, requires a special process for change: for example, the American constitution requires two-thirds of Congressional votes, plus a majority in three-quarters of all of the state legislatures; and the Irish constitution requires a **referendum** (a direct vote on an issue by the electorate) for major change.

In theory, therefore, the UK Parliament is potentially more powerful than legislatures in states with rigid constitutions. In practice, however, the UK's flexible constitution means that whoever can control even a one-vote majority in the Commons – and that usually means the government of the day – can push through almost any change at will. The flexibility of the UK constitution, therefore, actually undermines the power of Parliament in relation to the executive.

Parliamentary versus presidential systems

Legislatures often serve as forums for the recruitment and training of politicians who enter the executive. This is obviously much more the case in parliamentary systems such as the United Kingdom. However, even in presidential systems such as the United States, several former Presidents have begun, or served some of, their political careers in Congress.

Parliamentary scrutiny

In America, it took Congress just twenty-four hours to launch six inquiries into the fraudulent collapse of the giant energy trading company Enron in 2001. In the United Kingdom, which also had an interest in the affair, Parliament launched not one. In America,

Congress sued the government over contacts between Enron and the President's office, whereas in the United Kingdom such a suit is inconceivable. In America, any citizen can be subpoenaed, that is, summoned to attend, by Congress: in the United Kingdom, even public officials and prime ministerial advisers can simply refuse to appear or to answer questions before Parliament or its committees.

In sum, the UK Parliament which, in theory, is the 'sovereign' and most powerful political institution in the country, is widely seen as a weak and ineffectual scrutinising body, certainly by comparison with the US Congress.

Other Western European Parliaments, however, have also been accused by critics of being largely 'talking shops'. There is even more criticism of the EU Parliament for its lack of power to legislate or effectively to control the EU Commission. This issue is further examined in Chapters 6 and 7.

Bicameralism
In the United Kingdom, the legislature has two houses or 'chambers' – the Commons and the Lords – thus, it is a bicameral legislature. Bicameralism is seen as a key principle of liberal constitutional theory because it helps to ensure checks and balances in the system of state power. In the United States, for example, the legislature is called 'Congress' and it also has two chambers, the House of Representatives and the Senate. However, these are both elected, unlike the UK's House of Lords. In Russia, similarly, the legislature has two chambers, the State Duma and the Federation Council – again, both elected.

Upper chambers commonly house 'elder statesmen' who are perceived to have more experience, expertise and higher status – but often less democratic legitimacy – than members of the lower, but usually more democratic and powerful, chamber. The upper house serves as a check upon the lower house, with powers to amend and delay legislation, to defend the rights of citizens and to reduce the workload of the lower house.

The upper house may also have the power to resolve differences between the centre and the regions or between the regions themselves, especially in unitary states such as France and the Netherlands. In most federal states, the upper chamber represents the states or provinces. For example, in the United States, the Senate comprises two Senators from each state, regardless of geographical or population size, whereas in the lower House of Representatives, states are represented on the basis of population size. This arrangement allows smaller states in the US Senate to exert influence out of proportion to their size – an arrangement designed to ensure that the smaller states are not permanently outvoted in Congress.

The second chamber is usually subordinate to the first, either constitutionally (in theory) or politically (in practice) or both. This is especially true in parliamentary systems where the government is largely drawn from, and accountable to, the more powerful first chamber.

Upper chambers often have less democratic legitimacy than lower chambers. Some are indirectly elected from the various states, for example, in Germany, Austria and India. Some have a combination of election and appointment. In the United Kingdom the House of Lords were, until recently, almost unique in being largely hereditary. Only the Senate of the tiny, landlocked southern African kingdom of Lesotho shared this distinction.

The United Kingdom and Canadian upper houses are rare in being wholly non-elected and are often seen as dumping grounds for cast-off politicians. Canada is the only major country which has an entirely appointed second chamber. The Senate has 105 members and new members are selected as others retire. The members are, in theory, appointed by the Governor General, although in practice the Prime Minister of the day actually selects them and usually appoints from within his or her own party. Although it has some powers, the Canadian Senate rarely challenges legislation, because, first, governments tend to have a majority within it, and secondly, there would be an outcry if the appointed Senate was to act against the elected House of Commons. However, a general election was forced in the 1980s when the Conservatives inherited a Liberal Senate.

Italy is unusual in that the upper house is essentially identical to the lower house: the Senate and the Chamber of Deputies are elected under a proportional representation system on the same day and the houses have equal powers. The system came about because, after the experience of fascism, the country wanted a diffusion of power. However, difficulties often arise with Bills shuttling backwards and forwards between the two houses for some considerable time.

Ireland is unique in that a large proportion of Senate members are elected nominally on the basis of professional groups rather than parties – so-called 'functional representation'. Five-sixths of members are indirectly elected from the universities, by graduates, and from candidates put forward by vocational panels. Other members are nominated by the Prime Minister. It is a weak upper house within a weak Parliament and has little impact on the legislative process, but it has useful scrutiny and committee functions.

The Australian Senate, by contrast, is quite powerful, forcing general elections fairly often because the government, which is elected under direct preferential majority vote, rarely has a majority in the proportionally elected upper house.

States such as Denmark and Sri Lanka, by contrast, are unicameral, that is, their Parliaments have only one (elected) chamber. However, they invariably have other safeguards against an over-centralised system, such as written and rigid constitutions and proportional systems of election, which the United Kingdom lacks.

Representation

Following the 2005 general election, just 19 per cent of Westminster MPs were women. That said, world-wide, the average in 2006 was only 17 per cent. Italy was the worst performer in the EU with only 12 per cent of parliamentary seats filled by women. Finland was something of a trailblazer with 38 per cent female MPs. This trend goes back over one hundred years, when Finnish women became the first in the world to have equal rights both to vote and to stand for Parliament: the 'Eduskunta'. Having substantial female representation in the legislature has, in turn, encouraged unusually progressive social policies in Finland.

Recent political upheavals elsewhere in the world have, however, often boosted women's political rights more vigorously. For example, Rwanda, where quota measures are now in place, currently tops the global table for female MPs with 49 per cent.

The House of Commons is more representative than most other democracies in the sense that each MP represents, on average, 90,000 voters, whereas elsewhere constituencies commonly exceed 100,000 voters. However, the Conservatives, Liberal Democrats and UKIP have all recently advocated cutting the number of Westminster MPs

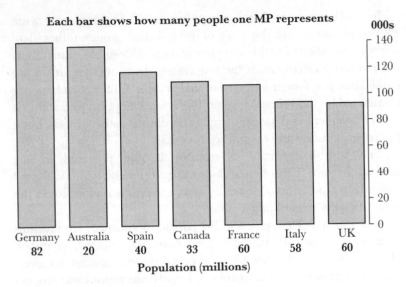

Each bar shows how many people one MP represents

Population (millions)

	Germany	Australia	Spain	Canada	France	Italy	UK
	82	20	40	33	60	58	60

Source: *The Times*, 13 December 2004

Figure 2.2 Graph showing how many people each MP represents

by up to 20 per cent in accordance with their 'smaller state' philoso-phies, arguing that this would save up to £15 million in salary and allowances each year and £10 million in the cost of Commons administration.

Party funding

There has been growing controversy in the United Kingdom about political party funding since the 'cash for honours' scandal of 2006–7 (see Chapter 3), with cross-party talks on reform breaking down as both main parties tried to protect their own financial interests (see Chapter 5).

In America there are statutory controls over funding for federal election campaigns. Individuals cannot donate more than $1,000 to a candidate per election campaign or more than $25,000 for election campaigns in a year. Candidates have to name all individuals who have given them more than $200 in a year and must list all party and political actions committees which have given them financial support. These committees must submit regular reports about money received and spent.

In France, contributions from businesses have been banned since 1995. Donations by individuals – which are tax deductible – are capped at €7,500.

In Germany, individuals can make donations – also tax deductible – of up to £336, and all donations above £6,700 must be disclosed.

In Australia, all candidates and parties must report all donations received to the Australian Electoral Commission. The names and addresses of individuals and organisations who donate over £77 to a candidate or £577 to a party must be declared together with the date and value of each donation made.

Parliamentary procedures

Other legislative assemblies – especially in Commonwealth countries which have inherited UK practices due to the legacy of empire – have often copied the methods and procedures of Westminster. A 'speech from the throne' – announcing the government's legislative plans for the year – is held in other Commonwealth countries and is usually read in the Queen's absence by the relevant Governor General. However, if the Queen is in the country at the time she may give the address in person – as, for example, in Canada in 1957 and 1977.

Hansard (see Chapter 1) is the traditional name for the printed transcripts of parliamentary debates in the Westminster political system. In addition to the Parliament of the United Kingdom, a *Hansard* is maintained for the Parliament of Canada and the Canadian provincial legislatures, the Parliament of Australia and the Australian state Parliaments, the Parliament of South Africa and South Africa's provincial legislatures, the Parliament of New Zealand, the Legislative Council of Hong Kong, the Parliament of Malaysia and the Parliament of Singapore.

Hansard reporters are highly skilled but, occasionally, selectively deaf. One famous example of the influence of *Hansard* in Canada concerned former Canadian Prime Minister Pierre Trudeau, who caused a minor scandal when opposition MPs claimed that he had mouthed the words 'fuck off' to them in the Canadian House of Commons in 1971. Pressed by journalists, Trudeau later said, unconvincingly, that he may have said 'fuddle duddle or something like that'. Trudeau likely got the phrase 'fuddle duddle' from the official *Hansard* transcript of his words for that parliamentary session. The

Hansard reporter could not make out (or, more likely, chose not to record verbatim) what Trudeau had mouthed, and chose to write down the now infamous phrase instead. The phrase has since taken on a humorous connotation for Canadians, with many calling the Canadian dollar (the value of which declined sharply during Trudeau's administration) the 'fuddlebuck'.

Erskine May, the 'bible' of parliamentary rules and procedures (see Chapter 1), is also a very influential document in many Commonwealth states and often has strong impact upon the conventions of their constitutions.

. . . .

☑ **What you should have learnt from reading this chapter**

- This chapter has explained and analysed the theory and practice of both parliamentary sovereignty and parliamentary government, and has concluded that Parliament is less powerful than theory suggests that it should be.

- It has argued that Lord Hailsham's thesis of 'elective dictatorship' has been more valid since 1997 than it was when he first advanced it in 1976.

- It has introduced questions and concerns about Parliament's representative role (covered in detail in Chapter 5), and Parliament's capacity to hold ministers to account (covered in detail in Chapter 6).

- Finally, it has drawn some comparisons and contrasts with other democratic legislatures around the world, which often have stronger representative claims.

🔎 **Glossary of key terms**

Collective responsibility Based on the assumption of collective Cabinet policy making, therefore, all ministers are collectively accountable for government policies, and should publicly and unanimously support those policies or resign.
Elective dictatorship Lord Hailsham's thesis of excessive executive power, between elections, over Parliament and public.
Federal constitution Division of power between central and local executive and legislative bodies, with both, in theory, supreme in their particular fields, that is, there is shared sovereignty and the centre cannot override the local bodies. Contrasts with a unitary system where there can be devolution but no genuine regional autonomy.

Flexible constitution One that needs no special legal process for change, that is, not rigid/entrenched.

Government The executive, policy-making branch of state.

Individual ministerial responsibility Based on the assumption that ministerial heads of department are the chosen representatives of the people (while the non-elected civil servants are anonymous administrators), therefore, ministers should be publicly accountable for the actions of their department and themselves and should resign in the event of serious departmental or personal error.

Mandate Authority to govern granted by the electorate; strictly, the authority or obligation of the government to implement its manifesto proposals.

Manifesto A booklet of policy proposals issued by each party before a general election.

Minority government Executive with fewer than 50 per cent of seats in House of Commons.

Parliamentary privilege The exemption of MPs and peers from some ordinary laws, notably slander and libel within the Houses of Parliament.

Presidential system A system where the executive is separately elected from the legislature and the two bodies are in theory equal, possessing checks and balances against each other.

Referendum A vote by the electorate directly on a specific issue; may be advisory or binding.

Representative government A form of indirect democracy reflecting the views, interests and/or typical social background of the electorate.

Responsible government Executive accountable to Parliament and public (through party system, manifesto and mandate); or wise and sensible government in the best interests of the people.

Retrospective law Backdated law.

Rigid constitution One which requires a special legal process for change.

Separation of powers An arrangement (favoured by liberal democratic thinker Montesquieu) whereby the personnel and structures of the legislature, executive and judiciary do not overlap with each other.

Simple majority More votes or seats than any other single candidate or party, not necessarily 50 per cent.

Sovereignty Ultimate legal and political power and authority.

Unicameral legislature A Parliament with only one chamber/house.

Unitary constitution A political system based upon a single, sovereign, national legislature.

? Likely examination questions

Short questions:

* How does parliamentary government differ from presidential government?

- Define the concept of the electoral mandate.

- Distinguish between a flexible and a rigid constitution.

- How does government acquire its legitimacy?

Essay questions:

- How, and to what extent, does the United Kingdom's parliamentary system produce representative and responsible government?

- Is the United Kingdom an 'elective dictatorship'?

- 'Parliamentary sovereignty is the linchpin of the UK political system.' Discuss.

- Compare and contrast the composition and powers of the UK Parliament with those of other legislatures.

 Helpful websites

http://news.bbc.co.uk

http://www.parliament.uk

http://www.explore.parliament.uk

http://news.bbc.co.uk/1/hi/programmes/bbc_parliament

http://news.bbc.co.uk/1/hi/education/5393394.stm

 Suggestions for further reading

Norton, P., *Parliament in British Politics*, Basingstoke: Palgrave Macmillan, 2005.

Norton, P. (ed.), *Parliaments and Governments in Western Europe*, London: Frank Cass, 1998.

Rush, M., *Parliament Today*, Manchester: Manchester University Press, 2005.

Watts, D., *British Government and Politics: A Comparative Guide*, Edinburgh: Edinburgh University Press, 2006.

CHAPTER 3

The House of Lords

Overview

This chapter examines the composition, functions, power and influence of the House of Lords; how – and how well – the Lords does its work. It assesses the arguments for and against the present upper chamber, analyses recent reforms and considers the possibilities for the future nature and role of the second chamber.

Key issues to be covered in this chapter

- The history of the House of Lords
- The composition of the House of Lords
- The powers and functions of the House of Lords
- Arguments for and against the House of Lords
- Reform of the House of Lords
- The future of the House of Lords

The history of the House of Lords

The House of Lords has existed, in some form, since Saxon times, when monarchs summoned their 'wise men' – the noblemen and churchmen – for consultation. Commoners began to be summoned in the thirteenth century and the two bodies gradually separated in the fourteenth century. The two chambers remained of equal status until the nineteenth century, when the extension of the franchise gave the Commons growing democratic authority and the balance of power gradually shifted away from the Lords.

In the early part of the twentieth century, the Conservative-dominated Lords often rejected Liberal government Bills – in particular, the Home Rule Bill for Ireland was repeatedly rejected. 'The end result, the partition of Ireland . . . led to decades of bloodshed and hatred, providing a grim epitaph on claims by the Conservative peers to be the watchdog of the national interest.'[1]

The Parliament Acts 1911 and 1949

There was a decisive shift in the balance of power between Lords and Commons in the twentieth century, as the Lords lost their legal right to amend **money bills**, and their power to delay legislation was reduced.

The Parliament Act 1911 arose from a clash between the then Liberal Government and the Conservative-dominated House of Lords. When the Lords threw out the government's reforming 'people's Budget', the government introduced the Parliament Act to remove the Lords' right to block legislation and instead to give peers a maximum two-year delaying power (three sessions of Parliament). Peers could impose only a nominal one-month delay on money bills, that is, financial and tax laws (as certified by the Speaker of the Commons). To offset the reduction in the checking power of the Lords against the Commons, this statute also increased the checking power of the electorate against the Commons by reducing the maximum length of time between general elections from seven years to five. The Lords retained a veto only over bills seeking to extend this five-year term, and over **private bills** and **delegated (secondary) legislation**. The Act also paved the way for MPs to be paid a salary for the first time. The Lords, naturally, tried to block the Bill, but King George

V was obliged by the government to threaten to create enough new Liberal peers to swamp the chamber, and the Lords backed down.

The Parliament Act 1949 was brought in by the first ever majority Labour Government when the Lords tried to block the nationalisation of the steel industry. This Bill reduced the Lords' delaying power to just one year (across two parliamentary sessions). After this period the Commons can 'invoke the Parliament Act' and simply override the Lords to push Bills through. Again, the Lords (still with a permanent Conservative majority) tried to block the Bill, and the 1911 Act was used to force the 1949 Act on to the statute book. In other words, the House of Lords was simply bypassed in the passing of the 1949 Act. Ever since, constitutional lawyers have debated whether the 1949 Act is valid, and, therefore, whether any law passed through its use, is valid. This was tested in the courts as recently as 2005, when the law was ruled to be valid. The 1949 Act was also retrospective: it allowed for the reduced delaying power of the Lords to be backdated by two years, to allow the nationalisation of the iron and steel industry. In the event, the government compromised on the timetable for nationalisation and the use of the retrospective powers of the Act proved to be unnecessary.

Since 1911, the Parliament Acts have been used just seven times – three of them, tellingly, by post-1997 Labour Governments.

Box 3.1 Use of the Parliament Acts

- Welsh Church Disestablishment Act 1914, by which the Welsh section of the Church of England was disestablished in 1920.
- Government of Ireland Act 1914, which established Home Rule for Ireland.
- Parliament Act 1949, amending the Parliament Act 1911.
- War Crimes Act 1991, which allowed retrospective prosecution of suspected Nazi war criminals (the only Conservative use of the Parliament Acts).
- European Parliamentary Elections Act 1999, introducing a closed party list system of election for UK members of the EU Parliament.
- Sexual Offences (Amendment) Act 2000, lowering the gay age of consent to sixteen.
- Hunting Act 2004, banning hunting with hounds.

After the Second World War and the passing of the Parliament Act 1949, the Lords – then an almost wholly hereditary chamber – went into near-terminal decline, with diminishing power, authority and attendance as even the peers themselves saw their chamber as increasingly irrelevant. The House usually sat for only three days a week and for about three hours per day. Harold Macmillan's Conservative Government, therefore, introduced the Life Peerages Act 1958, which allowed for the appointment of non-hereditary peers almost for the first time. ('Almost' because life peerages were actually first introduced in 1875 to allow judges to perform the judicial work of the Lords.) This post-war reform gave the chamber a new lease of life, with the appointment of 'working peers' on various forms of merit who would be committed to attending regularly and doing a more conscientious job.

Until the 1960s, **hereditary peers** were not able to give up their titles. This frustrated a few such as Viscount Stansgate – Lord Anthony Wedgwood Benn, a democratic socialist who wanted to stand for election to the Commons but, as a hereditary peer, was not permitted to do so. However, in 1963 the Conservatives wanted Lord Alec Douglas-Home to be their party leader and Prime Minister. Since convention, by then, dictated that the Prime Minister should come from the elected House of Commons, the Conservative Government passed the Peerages Act 1963, allowing peers to renounce their titles. Douglas-Home was found a safe seat in the Commons and was duly appointed Prime Minister; and a few others, such as Tony Benn, also took advantage of the new law to move from the Lords to the Commons. Douglas-Home's premiership only lasted one year; ten years later, he was given a new life peerage and gently elevated once again to the Lords. Labour MP Tony Benn remained in the Commons until 2001.

The House of Lords remained dominated by hereditary peers with a permanent Conservative majority and was persistently obstructive of Labour Governments. In 1969, therefore, the Labour Government proposed further reform of the second chamber to remove the voting rights of the hereditary peers and reduce the House's delaying power to six months. Both front benches favoured the proposals, but they were defeated by an 'unholy alliance' of radical left-wing Labour MPs, for whom the reforms did not go far enough, and right-wing Conservatives, for whom they went too far.

For much of the 1970s, Labour were in power with little or no majority, and the Lords – still Conservative-dominated – defeated the government over 350 times. While Labour were in opposition in the early 1980s, the radical left wing within the Labour Party grew in strength, and the outright abolition of the House of Lords was accepted as party policy and proposed in the 1983 Labour manifesto. However, this radical left-wing document – which also advocated unilateral nuclear disarmament and withdrawal from the EC – was famously described by right-wing Labour MP, Gerald Kaufman, as 'the longest suicide note in history', and Labour went down at that general election to its most ignominious post-war defeat.

The Thatcher Governments of the 1980s were more troubled by the House of Lords than any previous Conservative Government had been. This was largely because the Thatcher Governments were ideological adherents of the 'New Right', whereas the majority in the Lords were traditional Conservatives with a very different philosophical approach to the economy, law and society. However, there was a difference between the 'working' and the 'voting' peers. Although the working peers – mainly **life peers** – challenged the Conservative Government during debates, for crucial votes the whips could call in the 'backwoodsmen', that is, Conservative peers (largely hereditary) who very rarely turned up except to give the government an assured majority on major issues.

The Conservatives were, however, happy to introduce procedural reforms which had no impact on the Lords' composition or powers. In 1985, the proceedings of the Lords began to be televised for the first time, four years ahead of the Commons.

The composition of the House of Lords

The House of Lords is a wholly unelected chamber. Until the 1950s, it was made up entirely of hereditary peers whose right to sit and vote in the chamber derived purely from a title inherited within the family. By that decade the chamber was moribund, with a huge and permanent Conservative majority, plummeting attendance rates and negligible legitimacy. Therefore, in 1958, life peers were established: members appointed by the Prime Minister of the day, for their lifetime only, whose titles were not hereditary. Nevertheless, for most of the twentieth century, hereditary peers still made up two-thirds of the Lords – almost 800 of a potentially huge chamber of 1,200 peers, although many of them rarely attended.

Also entitled to sit and vote in the Lords are the twenty-four senior bishops of the Church of England (including the Archbishops): the **Lords Spiritual**. When a bishop retires, his place is taken by the next in line. The Lords Spiritual, therefore, are the only members of the House of Lords who do not remain for life. All the other 'secular' peers in the Lords are called **Lords Temporal**.

Also in the Upper House are the most senior judges in the country, known as Lords of Appeal in Ordinary or **Law Lords**. However, they are to be separated from the House of Lords in 2009.

At the heart of the Lords for centuries was the Lord Chancellor. The office existed for 1,200 years and, until very recently, had a unique position constitutionally as, simultaneously, the Speaker of the House of Lords, a Cabinet minister with departmental responsibilities and the head of the judiciary in England and Wales. This was a major breach of the principle of separation of powers, and the Labour Government in 2007 abolished the office of Lord Chancellor and separated out the three roles (see below). Prior to reform, the Lord Chancellor was the highest paid minister in government on £214,000 (against the PM's £184,000).

Most peers are members of the main parties. However, there are around 200 **cross-benchers** (so-called because of the chamber's seating arrangements), that is, independent peers without any party affiliation, who include the Law Lords and bishops. These provide a relatively independent element which is absent from the Commons. In 2005, for example, the government was heavily defeated by support for a cross-bench amendment which sought to add freedom of speech safeguards to the controversial Racial and Religious Hatred Bill.

As long ago as 1909, Liberal Prime Minister, Lloyd George, criticised the hereditary peers in the following terms: 'They do not even need a medical certificate. They need not be sound in either body or mind. They only require a certificate of birth – just to prove that they were the first of the litter. You would not choose a spaniel on those principles.'

Labour Prime Minister, Harold Wilson, said in 1964 that he would create no more new hereditary peerages. Prime Ministers Heath

(Conservative) and Callaghan (Labour) followed suit and it was widely assumed that new hereditary peerages were a thing of the past. However, Margaret Thatcher (Conservative) reintroduced the practice as a signal honour for a few of her favoured colleagues (such as Harold Macmillan and William Whitelaw). She was the last Prime Minister to do so.

The 1997 Labour Government came to power with a manifesto commitment to abolish all of the hereditary peers, stating: 'This will be the first stage in a process of reform to make the House of Lords more democratic and representative'. Most of the hereditary peers were abolished (that is, excluded from the chamber, rather than losing their titles) in 1999. Lord Cranborne, then leader of the Conservatives in the Lords, did a secret deal with the Labour Government to keep ninety-two hereditary peers in return for the smooth passage of government legislation. Much to the government's irritation, however, the Lords have since been more obstructive than ever, asserting a new degree of legitimacy since reform. There were, for example, eighty-eight government defeats in the Lords in 2002–3, the highest number since 1976. Only eight of them would have happened without the votes of the ninety-two, mainly Conservative, hereditary peers.

Meanwhile, in his first three years in office, former Prime Minister, Tony Blair, created more new life peers (over 200) than Margaret Thatcher did in her entire eleven years as Prime Minister. By the end of 2005, Blair had created 292 new peers, compared with 216 by Thatcher in her eleven years as PM and 171 by John Major in seven years. Thus, the Labour Party now has more peers than the Conservatives, for the first time ever (though still not an overall majority in the House). Blair also included more peers in his governing team than any Prime Minister for over a century – including prime ministerial advisers such as Baroness Morgan and Lord Birt. Thus, they avoided the inconvenience of election and Commons scrutiny. For example, Lord Birt – formerly Blair's 'blue-skies' strategic policy adviser on transport – simply refused to appear before the Commons Transport Select Committee in 2002, on the grounds that he was a peer.

In 2001, fifteen new 'people's peers' (a Labour spin doctor's construction) were appointed by an independent commission from 3,000 public nominations, in an attempt to make the chamber look more socially representative. However, there was widespread criticism that the people chosen were not truck drivers or hairdressers but were, as usual, the 'great and good'. Of the fifteen, six had already gained knighthoods, three had OBEs and two had CBEs. There was further criticism about their low voting records in the House. The experiment was not repeated.

Cash for peerages

The 'cash for honours' police inquiry (2006–7) probed into loans made to political parties before the 2005 general election. To fund this campaign, Labour was secretly loaned nearly £14 million, the Conservatives £16 million and the Liberal Democrats £850,000. It then emerged that some of these wealthy donors had been nominated for peerages or other honours. The implication was that the money was being rewarded with honours, in contravention of the Honours (Prevention of Abuses) Act 1925.

Almost 10 per cent of the life peers created by former PM Blair were Labour Party donors who, between them, contributed £25 million to the party. As noted in *The Times*: 'Blair has been the biggest dispenser of political patronage in the Lords since life peerages were created in 1958.'[2] Some examples include music industry tycoon Michael Levy, David Sainsbury (who was also made a minister), crime writer Ruth Rendell, film director David Puttnam, TV presenter Melvyn Bragg and Paul Drayson (whose company won a £32 million smallpox vaccination contract from the government after his first party donation, and who was later appointed as a government minister).

Prime Minister Tony Blair himself was questioned three times by the police during the 'cash for honours' inquiry – an unprecedented event in UK politics. However, he was not questioned under caution – otherwise, he probably could not have remained in office.

The police inquiry lasted for 16 months, interviewed 136 people, arrested four people, cost £1 million and probably hastened Blair's premature exit from office but, in July 2007 the Crown Prosecution Service announced that it would not be bringing any charges.

One solution to such perceived corruption, suggested by veteran political commentator Anthony Howard, is more state funding of political parties, as recommended by the Houghton Committee thirty years ago and by the Phillips Inquiry in 2007. As Howard said: 'Can it really be suggested that a method of open public funding is any more improper than our present system of tickling the tummies of fat cats so that, in return for cash delivered, they become peers of the realm?'[3]

However, the 'cash for honours' row is nothing new. King James II began it all by putting a price on baronetcies in the seventeenth century. This, however, was nothing compared with the blatant corruption of the early 1900s when Liberal PM, David Lloyd George, sold honours like used cars. One contemporary wrote: 'Anyone could buy a barony for £50,000, a baronetcy for £25,000 or a knighthood for £15,000.' It was this ongoing climate of corruption which prompted the passing of the 1925 Act.

The powers and functions of the House of Lords

As a wholly non-elected chamber, the Lords' powers are much more limited than those of the Commons. The Lords can play a useful role in amending and revising legislation, but they cannot touch money bills, that is, Bills which are largely about the raising and spending of government money. They have the power to delay other Bills for a maximum of one year, after which the Commons can invoke the Parliament Act 1949 and simply override the Lords. The only significant type of Bill which the Lords can block entirely is any Bill seeking to extend the life of Parliament beyond its five-year maximum legal term – in effect, that means any Bill which seeks to postpone or cancel a general election. The Lords have never, yet, had to use this power.

If amendments by the Lords are not accepted by the Commons, usually the Lords will back down – but not always. They have, for example, repeatedly blocked curbs on the right to jury trial. By the end of 2005, the Lords had inflicted over 100 significant defeats on the government since reform of the Lords in 1999; but the government was determined to overturn all of them – further examples of 'elective dictatorship'. For example, the Labour Government invoked the rarely-used Parliament Act 1949 to override the Lords and push through the introduction of closed lists for EU elections, the lowering of the gay age of consent to sixteen and the ban on fox hunting. A ruling by the European Court of Human Rights required the United

Box 3.2 The Salisbury Convention

A historical footnote: the Salisbury Convention is usually presented in textbooks as asserting the democratic principle that the Lords should not obstruct manifesto commitments. In fact, it began the opposite way round: in the late nineteenth century the Conservative majority in the Lords, guided by the third Marquess of Salisbury, developed the 'Referendal Theory' – applied solely to Liberal legislation – by which they could obstruct government legislation unless and until it had received majority approval at a general election. The fifth Marquess of Salisbury was Conservative leader in the Lords during the time of the first majority Labour Government in 1945–51. Despite the Conservatives' large majority in the Lords, they were wary of obstructing a government with such a decisive mandate, so Salisbury announced that the Lords 'would not seek to thwart the main lines of Labour's legislation provided it derived from the party's manifesto for the previous election.'[4] However, Bills could be 'improved' in committee, and the Lords continued to assert free reign over non-manifesto Bills.

Kingdom to cease discrimination on the ages of consent. The government felt justified in using the Parliament Act to push through reform of the EU voting system and the hunt ban because these proposals were in its manifesto and, under the Salisbury Convention (see above), the House of Lords is expected not to obstruct such commitments because they have a mandate from the voters.

In 2005, a pro-hunting pressure group, the Countryside Alliance, tried to argue in court that the hunt ban was invalid because the 1949 Parliament Act was, itself, invalid because it was passed using the 1911 Parliament Act, that is, it had not received the approval of the Lords. However, their case failed.

The Lords' legislative powers

Revision of Commons legislation takes about two-fifths of the Lords' time, and this is the most important and controversial function of the Lords.

Early in 2005, for example, the government got its new Terrorism Bill through Parliament only after a day of high parliamentary drama involving a rare all-night sitting, repeated legislative 'ping-pong' between the Commons and the Lords and some significant government concessions, including the surrender of decision-making powers on control orders from the executive to the courts and the promise of a 'sunset clause' requiring a lapse or parliamentary renewal of the new law within a year. Even former Lord Chancellor, Lord Irvine, joined the sunset clause revolt.

Most Lords' amendments of government Bills, however, are actually suggested by the government, and critics, therefore, accuse the government of manipulating and misusing the Lords' time to improve poorly drafted bills. About one quarter of government Bills actually begin their passage in the Lords rather than in the Commons.

The Lords also devotes more time than the Commons to the scrutiny of delegated legislation and Private Bills, freeing up Commons time and adding an element of detailed expertise to the scrutiny process. Some thirty new Private Bills are presented to Parliament each year and the Lords has equal powers with the Commons on such Bills: thus, it can reject them entirely, as it can with delegated legislation.

Peers, like MPs, can also introduce their own Private Members' Bills. For example, in 2005, cross-bench peer (and former human rights lawyer) Lord Joffe introduced a Bill advocating assisted dying, whereby doctors could prescribe a lethal dose of medication which patients could self-administer. The Bill was strongly opposed by the Lords Spiritual – who tend to turn out in force for 'moral' issues such as this – and it was defeated.

The House has a permanent Select Committee on the European Communities which scrutinises EU legislation. Its reports are given detailed attention by interested MPs, Whitehall and the media, and are widely regarded as more thorough and authoritative than their Commons equivalents.

Like the Commons, the Lords has the protection of parliamentary privilege, that is, freedom from the laws of defamation for words spoken in Parliament. In 2007, Ulster Unionist peer Lord Laird of Artigarvan used this privilege to name several Provisional IRA men whom he believed were responsible for the murder of a young man in a local dispute. The media were then free to quote his comments – and the names – under the rules of privilege.

The Lords' powers of scrutiny

There is no exact equivalent of Commons Question Time in the Lords. Instead, the first thirty minutes of each sitting are spent on four oral questions, with supplementaries, to ministers who are peers.

Debates in the Lords are conspicuously less partisan and rancorous than in the Commons. They are widely presented as being of higher quality, reflecting the Lords' expertise and status. However, this can be overstated. One anecdote has it that peers called to a quietly spoken member to speak up during a debate, to which he replied: 'I'm so sorry, I had no idea that anyone was listening'. This story reinforces the contrasting stereotype of peers as bumbling old duffers out of touch with the modern world.

Many Lords' committees, such as the Science and Technology Committee, are, however, internationally renowned for their expertise. In 2007, the Committee produced a report on e-crime which said that the internet was now 'the playground of criminals' and that the government must do more to protect internet users from hacking, phishing and identity theft. The Lords Constitution Committee also attracts attention for its consideration of significant political issues. In 2005, for example, it produced a critical report on the government's plans for compulsory national ID cards, warning that 'contrary to the government's assertions, the Bill fundamentally alters the relationship between citizens and the state'.

There are also joint committees of MPs and peers combined, such as the Joint Committee on Climate Change which, in 2007, criticised the adequacy of the government's targets on cuts in carbon emissions.

The government can, of course, simply ignore or reject all such proceedings – and it usually does. This highlights the chronic imbalance of power between Parliament and government which runs like a fault line through the entire UK political system.

The judicial powers of the Lords

At the time of writing (2008) the House of Lords is the supreme court of appeal for civil and criminal law in the United Kingdom. Its judicial functions are carried out separately from its legislative and scrutiny functions, by the Law Lords (Lords of Appeal in Ordinary). About seventy cases are heard each year.

Law Lords can and do participate in the legislative and scrutiny work of the Commons, lending their weight to discussions on the legal implications of Bills and wider issues of criminal and civil justice. Notwithstanding their legal expertise, this does constitute a major breach of the liberal democratic principle of the separation of powers. The Law Lords will, therefore, be removed from the House of Lords to a separate 'supreme court' in 2009 (see below).

Arguments for and against the House of Lords

Defence of the Lords

One possible argument in defence of an unelected chamber is that its members gain valuable knowledge and experience over their many years of service and that they add stability and continuity to the law-making process. Since they have total job security (short of outright abolition), they are less beholden to their party and to the government than are MPs, and so peers may be more independent-minded and less vulnerable to party pressure.

People who have distinguished themselves in wider public life, such as in industry, the trades unions, education, science, the arts and local government, are often brought into the House of Lords. 'Expertise' is also, therefore, often cited as a merit of the Lords: examples include former Prime Ministers such as Thatcher and Callaghan; former Foreign Secretaries such as Hurd and Carrington; Law Lords such as Nolan and Neill; businessmen such as the banker Lord Williams of Elvel; and media people such as Lord Melvyn Bragg. Lord Hives was an expert on beekeeping, and contributed usefully to the Bees Act 1980! Following a positive report by the prestigious Lords Science and Technology Committee, medical trials for cannabis use began in 1999.

One staunch defender of the unelected chamber, Conservative peer Lord Howe, has pointed out that, while the Commons was unable to secure a debate on Iraq or Afghanistan for months in 2005, the Lords did so 'with participation by four former foreign or defence secretaries, four chiefs of defence staff, two former chairmen of the Commons Foreign Affairs Committee and plenty more'. He argued that, since the removal of most of the hereditary peers, the party balance in the Lords is much more equitable 'and the bulk of the membership of the entire House is dominated by diversity, expertise, experience and independence'.[5] (Of course, the Commons also contains experts in many diverse fields; that is, election does not preclude expertise, although it may render it less permanent.)

The Lords sometimes like to see themselves as 'the guardians of the UK constitution' – as the last bulwark against the Commons seeking to extend the life of Parliament or to pass some other law which could threaten the basic principles of the UK political system or civil liberties. The Lords often claim that they represent stability and tradition in a relatively detached way, especially against strong majority governments in the Commons whose claim to a 'mandate' is tenuous. In the decades since the 1950s, the Lords has, in some ways, grown to reflect the social composition of the public better than the Commons and it combines this with an apparent concern for the public interest.

Criticisms of the Lords

It is, however, hard to defend a wholly non-elected legislative chamber in a twenty-first century liberal democracy. The House of Lords is undemocratic, unrepresentative and unaccountable. It is often dubbed the 'best gentlemen's club in London' and has been described as 'the perfect eventide home' (Baroness Stocks). This highlights its unflattering image as a singularly privileged old folks' home, or, as one particularly harsh critic has put it, 'a meek, elderly Quango of the Dead'.[6]

The Lords are also not immune from allegations of 'sleaze'. In 2001, Labour Lord Chancellor, Lord Irvine, was accused of seeking 'cash for wigs' when he urged lawyers to give donations to the Labour Party. This was widely seen as improper pressure since he played a key role in appointing new judges from the ranks of the lawyers. The 'cash for peerages' controversy has already been documented.

Peers are paid only an attendance allowance and expenses for their work. By 2008 they could claim up to £308 per day, untaxed and with no receipts required. If a peer claimed the full amount for all 120 sitting days a year – and the majority do – he or she would take home the same amount as someone with a taxable salary of about £50,000. Peers' expenses cost the taxpayer £18 million in 2007, representing

18 per cent of the running cost of the Lords. The Lords' rulebook states:

> All amounts paid in settlement of claims represent reimbursement of actual expenses arising out of unpaid parliamentary duty, rather than income from employment. Consequently, they are not subject to income tax . . . Receipts are not required but the member's signature effectively certifies that the amount claimed has been spent for the purposes of parliamentary duties.

According to hereditary Conservative peer Lord Onslow, 'This is not corruption and you are dealing with honest men [sic] doing an honest job for a combination of seeing their friends, public duty, contributing to the public weal and a bit of pocket money'.[7]

The main problem with regard to further reform of the Lords is the lack of consensus among the main parties and politicians.

Reform of the House of Lords

Past proposals for reform of the Lords include:

- complete abolition of the House of Lords (in the radical 'old' Labour manifesto of 1983);
- 'functional representation' based upon pressure and interest groups, rather than upon a party system;
- indirect election of representatives from regional bodies (in the Liberal/SDP Alliance manifesto of 1987);
- a directly elected second chamber based on proportional representation (suggested by Lord Hailsham in his 1976 lecture 'Elective Dictatorship').

The Labour Government's plans for further reform of the Lords

In the 2003 Queen's Speech, the Labour Government announced that it would legislate on the following changes:

- abolishing the office of Lord Chancellor;
- creating a 'supreme court' of senior judges separate from the House of Lords;
- creating an independent judicial appointments commission;

- abolishing the remaining ninety-two hereditary peers;
- retrospectively barring convicted criminals from sitting in the House of Lords (apparently targeted at former Conservative Lord Jeffrey Archer).

The Prime Minister announced the abolition of the post of Lord Chancellor in a 2003 Cabinet reshuffle, without any prior consultation on the issue. (The incumbent, Lord Falconer, was given the new title of Secretary of State for Constitutional Affairs.) This provoked fury in the House of Lords – what Opposition Leader, Lord Strathclyde, described as 'the worst atmosphere here that I can recall' – and a flurry of government defeats.

In 2004, the government's Constitutional Reform Bill – containing the first three of the changes listed above – was defeated in the Lords. The government dropped a separate Bill seeking to abolish the remaining ninety-two hereditary peers and to bar convicted criminals from the Lords in the face of its possible defeat in Parliament. Peers, Labour and Liberal Democrat MPs were all angry because it was not accompanied by any process of democratisation of the second chamber, as had originally been promised by the government.

These two events demonstrate that the power of the Lords, although limited, should not be underestimated.

At the end of 2007, following the conviction and imprisonment of Lord Conrad Black for fraud, the government resurrected its promise to bar, retrospectively, convicted criminals from sitting in the Lords.

Composition

It was widely expected that the 'second stage' reform of the Lords would include a substantial elected element. In 2003, MPs were given seven free votes on options ranging from no elected members to 100 per cent elected members of the second chamber; this successfully confused them so much that they voted against all of the options, leaving the United Kingdom with a wholly unelected second chamber: an option explicitly favoured by then Prime Minister Blair.

The government was accused by its critics of seeking simply to create a chamber which Blair could pack with his own appointees, such as his former flatmate Charlie, now Lord Falconer of Thoroton. As former Conservative leader Michael Howard said, 'What of the

---

Box 3.3 Off message MPs (2007 vote)

- 153 Labour MPs, including ministers Margaret Beckett and Hazel Blears, voted to abolish the Lords altogether.
- 110 Conservative MPs voted to keep hereditary peers. No Labour or Liberal Democrat MPs did so. Only sixteen Conservative MPs supported the removal of the hereditary peers.
- Ninety-eight Conservative MPs voted against their party's policy of 80 per cent elected members, with only eighty voting in favour.

---

pledge in the 1997 Labour manifesto to "make the House of Lords more democratic"? Well, we now know exactly what the Prime Minister means by democracy. One flatmate, one vote.'[8]

In 2007, the Commons voted once more on several options on the future composition of the Lords, again ranging from wholly unelected to all elected members. This time, they voted for an all-elected chamber by a substantial majority – although some traditionalist Conservative MPs apparently voted for this option to scupper reform entirely. Sure enough, a week later, the Lords voted, by an even more substantial majority, to keep a fully appointed House. The Commons also backed an 80 per cent elected second chamber by 305 to 267 – a smaller but, probably, truer and ultimately more significant majority. Both Houses rejected the government's preferred 50/50 option. None of these White Paper (consultative) votes was binding, since no reform Bill had even been drafted. Stalemate again.

Powers

The effective powers of a future second chamber are, constitutionally, more important than its method of selection or composition; but this aspect of reform has been widely neglected by commentators, including the Commons itself:

> The Commons vote was simple-minded because a wholly elected second chamber in a legislature is meaningless without a parallel statement about the respective powers of the two, but it was widely seen to have made the *status quo* even less acceptable.[9]

The Labour Government wants to curtail the powers of the Lords radically by:

- reducing the Lords' one-year power of legislative delay to sixty sitting days – a proposal outlined in Labour's 2005 manifesto;
- entrenchment of the Salisbury Convention that the Lords should not obstruct manifesto commitments of an elected government;
- a clampdown on the practice of parliamentary 'ping-pong' at the end of a session, when the Lords and Commons pass amendments to controversial Bills to and fro until one House gives way;
- a curb on the Lords' power of veto over secondary legislation.

To many observers, the prospect of a more democratic but even less powerful second chamber is quite illogical.

Reform of the office of Lord Chancellor

In 2005, the government was forced to do a U-turn on abolishing the title of Lord Chancellor in order to get the creation of a separate 'supreme court' through Parliament (see below). Lord Falconer, therefore, combined the job and title of Lord Chancellor with that of Secretary of State for Constitutional Affairs in charge of areas such as devolution, human rights and data protection: hence 'two titles' Falconer. However, since 2006 the Lord Chancellor is no longer head of the judiciary (that role has passed to his former second-in-command, the Lord Chief Justice) and he no longer appoints senior judges. An independent appointments commission has been created.

The Lord Chancellor was also replaced in 2006 as the presiding officer of the upper house by the first Speaker of the Lords to be elected by fellow peers, former Labour minister, Baroness Hayman. This new job comes with a five-year tenure, a salary of over £100,000 a year, an apartment in the Palace of Westminster and a £10,000 gold and silk robe, but no wig. Unlike the Commons Speaker, she does not call peers to speak or rule on points of order; by convention, peers regulate their own proceedings. Like the Commons Speaker, however, she is expected to put aside party affiliation.

However, the Lord Chancellor still had a key role in both the executive and the legislature and – said Lord Falconer in 2006 – he still had a role to play in defending the independence of the judiciary and the rule of law: for example, in warning government ministers against publicly criticising judges' decisions. Lord Falconer also warned judges against straying into politics by publicly criticising government policies.

In 2007, in a major restructuring of the government machine, the Home Office was split into two separate departments: a security department dealing with policing, immigration, asylum and anti-terrorism; and a justice department responsible for criminal law, sentencing, jails and probation. Since the formation of PM Gordon Brown's first Cabinet, the Lord Chancellor is no longer even a lord. Instead, Labour MP Jack Straw combined the offices of Secretary of State for Justice and Lord Chancellor.

A 'supreme court' for the United Kingdom

In 2005, the government finally succeeded in passing a Bill to remove the Law Lords from the House of Lords and establish them as a separate 'supreme court' by 2009, to be located in a redesigned and renovated Middlesex Guildhall in Parliament Square. This further enhances the liberal democratic principle of the separation of powers. However, it is an expensive process: the renovation of the new building alone is costing at least £30 million.

The label 'supreme court' may also be misleading. The new court, like the Law Lords before it, will have constitutional responsibilities in overseeing the relationship between the devolved administrations and the centre, as well as its adjudication of the Human Rights Act 1998. However, the court will have no new powers; unlike the American Supreme Court, for example, it will not be able to veto parliamentary legislation. Hence the Conservative Party's opposition to the change: 'The name and notion of a Supreme Court are alien and add nothing to the system we have'.[10]

The future of the House of Lords

Examination questions often ask which reforms of the Lords you would recommend, and why. Consider the following points:

* The first issue to consider is what roles and powers should the second chamber have, that is, how strong should it be as a check upon the first chamber? For example, should its delaying power

be extended? Should it be allowed to amend government money bills? If you want a substantially stronger and more effective second chamber than the present House of Lords, then it should be democratised to ensure that its powers are legitimate.

- How many members should there be in the second chamber?
- Should they all be elected or should some be appointed?
- Who should appoint the appointed members?
- By what system should the elected members be elected?
- What term of office should the elected members have?
- Should the upper chamber be elected on different constituencies from the Commons?
- Should the term of office coincide with that of the Commons or, like the American system, overlap?
- Should any such changes require a referendum?

✔ What you should have learnt from reading this chapter

- This chapter has outlined the political history of the House of Lords, including the origins and uses of the Parliament Acts which have substantially limited its powers.

- It has described the changing composition of the House and highlighted some of the reasons why reform is widely seen as necessary – including the 'cash for honours' controversy after the 2005 general election.

- It has outlined the legislative, scrutiny and judicial powers of the Lords – the latter soon to be removed.

- It has also assessed the arguments in favour of the current composition and powers of the Lords and has found them wanting – but, as outlined, recent attempts to reform the Lords have been hampered by a lack of consensus both within and across the main parties. Only the office of Lord Chancellor has been fundamentally transformed.

- Finally, you are asked to ponder some of the issues surrounding Lords' reform which the politicians must, eventually, resolve.

🔍 Glossary of key terms

Cross-benchers Peers in the Lords who are independent of any party.
Delegated legislation Law made by bodies other than Parliament (for

example, local authority by-laws) under power passed down by the sovereign Parliament.

Hereditary peers Lords whose right to sit and vote in the upper chamber derives purely from a title inherited within the family.

Law Lords The most senior judges in the United Kingdom.

Life peers Members of the upper chamber appointed by the Prime Minister of the day, for their lifetime only, whose titles are not hereditary.

Lords Spiritual Senior bishops of the Church of England (including the archbishops), who are entitled to sit and vote in the House of Lords.

Lords Temporal All peers other than the Lords Spiritual.

Money Bills Government financial and tax laws (as certified by the Speaker of the Commons).

Private Bills Bills which affect only specific individual or group interests rather than the general public.

? Likely examination questions

Short questions:

- Outline the composition of the House of Lords.

- Outline the functions and powers of the House of Lords.

- Outline differences in the composition of the House of Commons and the House of Lords.

- Distinguish between: (a) the power and influence of the House of Commons; and (b) the power and influence of the House of Lords.

Essay questions:

- Is there a role for a second chamber in the UK political system?

- Outline a case for, and a case against, the reform of the House of Lords.

- Discuss the implications of a fully elected second chamber.

- Describe and assess the balance of power between the House of Commons and the House of Lords.

Helpful websites

http://news.bbc.co.uk

http://www.parliament.uk

http://www.parliament.uk/lords

http://www.parliament.the-stationery-office.co.uk/pa/ld/ldhansrd.htm

Suggestions for further reading

Crewe, E., *Lords of Parliament: Manners, Rituals and Politics*, Manchester: Manchester University Press, 2005.

Rosenburg, P., *House of Lords*, New York: HarperCollins, 2003.

Russell, M., *Reforming the House of Lords: Lessons from Overseas*, Oxford: Oxford University Press, 2000.

CHAPTER 4

The House of Commons: Making the Law

Overview

This chapter examines the roles of MPs, parliamentary parties and **whips**, and explains the timetable and procedures of the House of Commons. It outlines the law-making processes at Westminster: the different types of bills, including **Private Members' Bills** and delegated legislation, the legislative stages and legislative debates.

Key issues to be covered in this chapter

- The roles of MPs, parties and whips
- The timetable of the Commons
- Making the law
- Banned by statute law
- Challenges to Parliament's law-making role

The roles of MPs, parties and whips

MPs

Westminster is the United Kingdom's sovereign legislature and, therefore, MPs are elected as lawmakers to a national legislative assembly. **Backbenchers** are MPs in the House of Commons who are not, in addition, members of the government or of the shadow government, that is, they are not members of Cabinet, junior government ministers or Opposition shadow ministers. The main roles of backbenchers, of any party or of none in the Commons, are to legislate, to scrutinise the executive and to represent their voters as elected representatives.

There is no formal job description for a backbench MP. They have several roles and are subject to a – sometimes conflicting – range of pressures and calls upon their loyalty. Different MPs perceive their multiplicity of functions in different ways and choose to focus upon different aspects of them.

The influential and conservative-minded politician Edmund Burke argued, in 1774, that an MP was a member of 'a deliberate assembly of one nation with one interest, that of the whole', and that MPs should pursue the 'general good' according to their personal judgement. The concept of a 'national interest' is central to the philosophy of traditional political conservatism, but is denied by liberals (who perceive diverse individual interests) and by socialists (who perceive conflicting class interests). However, all governments bring the concept into play when it suits their policy objectives.

By contrast, in the nineteenth century Prime Minister Disraeli said to his MPs, 'Damn your principles! Stick to your party.' The 'doctrine of the mandate' suggests that electors vote for a package of party policies as outlined in a manifesto and, therefore, that MPs are most effectively representing the voters' wishes if they toe the party line. But what if the party breaks its manifesto promises? Contemporary MPs are, nevertheless, increasingly careerist and hence more likely to heed their party leadership and toe the party line, since their jobs usually depend upon their party. Thus, they may be less independent-minded, less likely to revolt and more likely to be 'lobby fodder' for the national and/or local party, which may mean that they are less likely to accurately represent voters' views or interests on controversial issues.

However, some MPs are 'confirmed backbenchers' who have either rejected or abandoned the prospect of promotion to the front benches, and they play an important role as executive scrutineers holding the government to account, often doing a sterling job on the select committees of the Commons (see Chapter 6). They are what the whips often call 'the awkward squad' or worse. Other MPs may have some subject specialism or area of legislative expertise, while still others may focus primarily on their role as local party representative. The local party selects the MP and provides the electoral campaign back-up; rank-and-file activists may also have a good understanding of constituency needs. The local party can also deselect the MP, that is, they may decide not to choose that person as their party candidate at the next election. For example, Jane Griffiths, Labour MP for Reading East, in 2004 became the first MP to be deselected by her constituency party in ten years (despite – or perhaps because of – being a Blair loyalist). This usually terminates an MP's political career. Many MPs, therefore, pay particular heed to the local party, even where this may jeopardise their standing with the national leadership.

However, the local party's views may conflict with those of local voters. When his local party executive tried (unsuccessfully) to deselect long-standing Conservative MP, Sir Patrick Cormack, in 2007 for – apparently – being too old and old-fashioned, Sir Patrick said, 'I've had masses of letters from people who say they vote for me not because I'm Conservative but because they think I'm an independent-minded local parliamentarian. I've always taken the line it's country-constituency-party, in that order.'[1]

Some MPs' roles are controversial. Their growing personal and financial links with outside interests – especially private and commercial businesses – fuelled the 'cash for questions' scandals of the 1990s which led to the resignations of some senior Conservative ministers and prompted the Nolan Inquiry and subsequent curbs on paid advocacy by MPs. Heavy lobbying of MPs by outside interests, whether commercial or voluntary, may distract MPs from focusing on their own constituents' interests.

Finally, MPs may occasionally decide to obey their own consciences. This is the second feature of Burke's theory of the role of an MP: 'Your representative owes you not his industry only, but his judgement; and he betrays instead of serving you, if he sacrifices it to your opinion'. Private conscience for MPs is given expression, particularly in free votes in the Commons (for example, on moral issues such as capital punishment, abortion and homosexuality laws), in Private Members' Bills and in backbench revolts. It may obviously conflict with party, constituency and other interests outlined above.

MPs debate and vote on parliamentary Bills in the House and in **standing committees**. They are constrained by party discipline from speaking or voting against the party line on a two- or three-line whip (see below), on pain of suspension from the party. Shared political ideology and natural party loyalty – together with ambition for higher public office and ruthless party discipline – usually combine to ensure that most backbenchers toe the party line and vote in support of their leadership. This usually means that the majority of MPs in the Commons support the actions and policies of the government of the day. However, backbenchers may assert themselves by rebelling collectively against a Bill. This usually happens when MPs see the Bill as contrary to the basic principles of their party.

Backbenchers may also introduce their own legislation in the form of Private Members' Bills. However, there is usually little time set aside for these and in procedural terms they are easily defeated, especially if the government of the day does not support them. Therefore, few are passed (though good publicity may be won for the issue involved): on average, over fifty are introduced in each parliamentary session but only about six are passed.

MPs in the United Kingdom must be UK subjects and over 18 years of age (lowered from 21 in 2006). Those disqualified from membership of the Commons include: those disqualified from voting (see Chapter 5); undischarged bankrupts; clergy of the established Churches; judges; civil servants and other Crown officials; heads of nationalised industries and directors of the Bank of England; and those convicted of corrupt practices at elections. In summary, the disqualifications seek to exclude the underage, the outsiders, the inept, the corrupt and those who should be politically impartial.

The parties

Most Bills which go through the Commons are government Bills. Many will have been in the government's election manifesto and most will have been announced in the Queen's Speech at the opening of Parliament. The Bills are drafted by lawyers for the government – the Parliamentary Counsel – which the responsible ministers then steer through the various legislative stages with the aid of the whips (see below).

The second largest party in the Commons is known as Her Majesty's Opposition. The Opposition Leader and Chief Whip get an official salary, the Leader gets an official car and the party gets special time and opportunities in Commons debates, Question Times and committees not afforded to the other opposition parties. It is often said that such an institution, formally recognised and protected by the constitution, is one of the hallmarks of a pluralist, liberal democracy. It is also often said that it is the function of the Opposition to oppose the government, that is, to 'nay say' on principle in order to provide voters with a constructive critique of the government's laws and policies and, ultimately, to provide an alternative 'government in waiting'. This assumption has been undermined in recent years as the Conservative Party under David Cameron have, more than once, been instructed in the Commons to vote in support of government legislation. The Education Act 2006 and the renewal of the UK's Trident nuclear weapons system in 2007, provoked big Labour rebellions in the Commons and only passed thanks to Conservative support. This raised difficult constitutional and practical questions about the role of the Opposition – not least for the Conservative Party, who will find it hard to criticise any future problems which may arise with these policies.

Whips

The term 'party whip' was used – perhaps invented – by Whig Party MP, Edmund Burke, as long ago as 1769. He likened the disciplining of MPs on voting to the process of 'whipping in the hounds' during a fox hunt. Party whips are senior MPs in the Commons or peers in the Lords who have been selected by the leadership of their party to act as a channel of communication, that is, information, guidance and party discipline, between the leadership and the party members in each House. The Chief Whip is the most important whip in each party: an MP of substantial power and authority: 'The word sounds aggressive, tyrannical and even physically painful. Doubtless this adds to the feeling that the Whips are more terrible people than they are.'[2]

The term 'whip' is now applied both to these senior MPs and to the written weekly notice which they issue to fellow party MPs informing them of the programme of parliamentary business and instructing them how to vote. They indicate how important each item is by underlining it once, twice or three times. If an item is underlined three times, that is, a 'three-line whip', this shows that the party expects their MPs to be present and to vote as instructed.

It is a serious matter for MPs to defy a three-line whip and, therefore, it happens quite rarely. When it does occur, it can lead to the whip being 'withdrawn' from an MP. Withdrawal of the whip means expulsion from the party, although this may be temporary. For example, several MPs were expelled from the Conservative Party in 1993 because of their rebellion against the EU Maastricht Treaty (and they briefly became renowned as the 'whipless wonders'); but Prime Minister John Major's majority in the Commons became so small that he ignominiously had to accept them back into the party five months later. Labour's George Galloway was permanently expelled from the party in 2003, for the way in which he expressed opposition to the invasion of Iraq. He went on to win election to the Commons as the only MP for the new Respect (anti-war) Party. (However, although MPs can be sacked from their party, they cannot be sacked from Parliament by their parties, because liberal democratic theory suggests that only the voters should have the power to select or reject an MP.)

When the Labour Government planned in 2008 to impose a three-line whip on the Human Fertilisation and Embryology Bill (which included allowing scientists to create embryos with human DNA and animal cells), Catholic Church leaders urged MPs and Cabinet ministers of the faith to follow their consciences and rebel, forcing PM Gordon Brown to climb down and offer a free vote on the most controversial clauses of the Bill.

MPs, too, are not without their own weapons against the whips. In the Commons vote on the Racial and Religious Hatred Bill in 2006, Labour rebels knew that it would be a very close vote, so they used stealth and subterfuge to lull their whips into a false sense of complacency, restraining potential rebels from overt protest while quietly

MONDAY, 28th OCTOBER
Tabling: To be announced
House meets at 2.30pm for: **Home Office Questions**

Main Business
OPPOSITION DAY (20th Allotted Day)
Debate on **'Implications of the Human Rights Act'** on an Opposition Motion.
Thereafter, Debate on **'Access to facilities of the House'** on an Opposition Motion.

Your attendance in the Chamber for the Opening Speeches is essential.

Important divisions will take place and your attendance at 6.30pm for 7.00pm and 9.30pm for

10.00pm is essential.

TUESDAY, 29th OCTOBER
Tabling: To be announced
House meets at 2.30pm for: **Health Questions**

Main Business
1. 10 Minute Rule Bill: **Air Weapons** (Jonathan Shaw)
2. Debate on Motions relating to the **Modernisation Committee Report on Reforming the House of Commons** and the **Procedure Committee Report on Parliamentary Questions**.

Important Divisions will take place at 10.00pm.

All Divisions will be **Free Votes**.

WEDNESDAY, 30th OCTOBER
Tabling: To be announced
House meets at 2.30pm for: **Wales Office Questions**
Prime Minister's Questions

Deferred Divisions (voting between 3.30pm and 5.00pm)
Colleagues should be prepared to respond to a 3-line Whip for any **Deferred Divisions**.

Main Business
1. 10 Minute Rule Bill: **Patient Choice** (Peter Lilley)
2. Motion to **approve a Statutory Instrument relating to the Provisions of the Terrorism Act 2000**.

Figure 4.1 The Conservative Whip

Box 4.1 Functions of the whips

- *Management*: The whips keep MPs informed of parliamentary business (through the written whip); and arrange business (through the 'usual channels', that is, consultation between the whips' offices of the main parties).
- *Communications*: They keep MPs and party leaders informed of each others' views. They are said to be the 'eyes and ears' of the party leadership.
- *Assistance*: The whips may take it upon themselves to help MPs with both political and personal matters, such as financial difficulties or even sexual scandals.
- *Persuasion and discipline*: Methods of influencing MPs can range from gentle exhortation, through reproach, to genuine bullying and, ultimately, punishment. One infamous occasion was the ratification of the EU Maastricht Treaty in 1993 when, in full view of the TV cameras, Conservative whips were literally pinning recalcitrant MPs against walls and pushing them into the 'Aye' lobby. They self-confessedly made use of their 'black book', containing details of MPs' sexual and financial peccadilloes, to blackmail them into compliance. Nevertheless, the scale of the revolt was such that the Conservative Government would have been defeated without a deal with the Ulster Unionists. This episode demonstrated both the power of the whips and the limits of their power.

---

lobbying and mobilising the other parties. The Conservatives, likewise, imposed a two-line whip – which allowed MPs to be absent with permission – and then discreetly called in far more MPs than the Labour whips had expected. The government was spectacularly outmanoeuvred and defeated on two key clauses – the second time, by just one vote because the Labour whips assured then Prime Minister, Tony Blair, that he could safely leave the House. One unnamed Labour rebel said, 'We could never surprise them again like this, I don't see, for at least a decade. Whips should watch *The West Wing*. On Sunday night the Democrats were trying to get something through Congress and used exactly the same tactics – low profile.'[3] Labour's Chief Whip, Hilary Armstrong, lost her job in a Cabinet reshuffle three months later.

The Commons timetable

The timetable of Parliament is divided into annual sessions which run from October to October. Legislative processes are usually completed by the end of July, but Parliament is not prorogued (meaning the formal end of the parliamentary session) until the autumn, to allow for the possible recall of Parliament in the event of an emergency and for the conclusion of any unfinished business.

The government largely controls the Commons timetable and its business usually takes precedence, with the exception of: twenty Opposition Days each year when the opposition parties choose the topics of debate; three days allocated to the select committees; and certain times set aside for backbench concerns such as Private Members' Bills. About one-third of Commons time is devoted to government Bills and about one-twentieth to Private Members' Bills. The rest is spent debating the policies and activities of the government. Government control of the Lords timetable is weaker and not entrenched through Standing Orders as it is in the Commons.

In 2002, MPs voted to reform the working hours of the Commons and end the centuries-old tradition of late night sittings, to make the chamber more family-friendly especially for the growing number of women MPs, better suited to television coverage and to make it seem more relevant and up-to-date to voters. Only Mondays retained the traditional late start to allow MPs to return from their constituencies. Opponents claimed that the new hours would disrupt morning sittings of select committees and voters' tours of the Commons, would make MPs look lazy and prevent them from gaining valuable experience by doing other jobs in the mornings. Suspicions were expressed, however, that some more traditional MPs did not want to abandon the drink-fuelled camaraderie and old boys' club ethos of late sittings.

One consequence of the new hours was that the many bars, cafes and restaurants in the Palace of Westminster lost substantial revenue. Previously well-subsidised prices went up and some catering staff were made redundant. Critics also argued that the new hours actually hindered the capacity of MPs to scrutinise the government and gave them less time for committee and constituency work. In 2005, MPs voted to restore late starts and late sittings on Tuesdays, and to start an hour earlier on Thursdays. Some cynics have cruelly suggested that the Commons still starts 'at the crack of lunch'.

In 2002 MPs also backed a general time limit of ten minutes for speeches, and a shorter timescale for tabling questions to produce more topical Question Times. Prime Minister's Question Time moved from 3pm to noon each Wednesday and ministerial statements on key issues shifted from 3.30pm to 12.30am, mainly to catch the lunchtime news bulletins. The changes came into effect at the beginning of 2003.

In 2007, MPs voted for longer recesses (holidays), increasing their time away from Westminster to eighteen weeks in each year. MPs and ministers have pointed out that, just because Parliament is not sitting, that does not mean that politicians are idle; MPs have constituency work and ministers have departmental work to do. However, some MPs were unhappy about the impression their long holidays may make on hard-working voters, especially since they have also been awarding themselves higher pay and larger pensions. Other MPs blamed a front-bench conspiracy to keep MPs out of Westminster for as long as possible. One said, 'They don't really like us being around and together. That's when trouble usually starts for them.'[4]

Making the law

About one-third of Parliament's time is now taken up with the processes of making and amending legislation. It is Parliament's most time-consuming function, and modern Bills are increasingly long and complex. Over 2,000 pages of legislation are now passed each year, three times the number passed in the 1950s.

Types of Bills
There are two broad types of parliamentary Bills:

Public Bills: which concern the general public interest. These, in turn can be sub-divided into:

1. government Bills;
2. money bills (a special type of government Bill, which cannot be amended by the Lords); and
3. **Private Members' Bills** (usually public Bills).

Private Members' Bills (PMBs)

There are three ways of introducing Private Members' Bills in the House of Commons: the ballot; the ten-minute rule; and presentation.

Ballot Bills have the best chance of becoming law, as they get priority for the limited amount of debating time available. The names of MPs applying for a Bill are drawn in a ballot held at the beginning of the parliamentary year. MPs may have little or no idea, at the time of the ballot, what Bill they want to put forward; but also present in the room are representatives of various interest and pressure groups, often ready with their own draft Bills for their own pet causes in hand, which they will press upon any seemingly sympathetic MP who is drawn early in the ballot. Usually only the first six names chosen have a serious chance of getting their Bills through Parliament because of shortage of time in the parliamentary year.

Ten-minute rule Bills are often an opportunity for MPs to voice an opinion on a subject or an aspect of existing legislation, rather than a serious attempt to get a Bill passed. MPs make speeches of no more than ten minutes outlining their position, which another MP may oppose in a similar short statement. It is a good opportunity to raise the profile of an issue and to see whether it has support among fellow MPs.

Under 'presentation', any MP may introduce a Bill as long as he or she has previously given notice of their intention to do so. MPs formally introduce the title of the Bill but do not speak in support of it. These very rarely become law.

Significant Private Members' Bills previously passed include Sidney Silverman's Abolition of Capital Punishment Act 1965 and David Steel's Legalisation of Abortion Act 1967. (PMBs often address moral issues which are deemed matters of individual conscience for MPs and tend to cut across party lines.) Hence, votes on PMBs are usually free (that is, non-whipped); but Conservative MP Richard Shepherd's Bill to reform the Official Secrets Act in 1987 was notable because a three-line whip was imposed against it, for the only time in the twentieth century. The Bill failed. In 2005, former Cabinet minister Clare Short (who resigned from the government over the invasion of Iraq) introduced a Private Member's Bill to give MPs the final say over committing troops to war. However, Commons Leader Geoff Hoon – a Cabinet minister – filibustered to prevent a vote being taken, and effectively killed the Bill – a manoeuvre which some MPs described as disgraceful.

Private Bills: which concern specific individual or group interests (for example, the Whitehaven Harbour Act 2007 which created a new body of commissioners to run the harbour). Because such Bills, by definition, do not treat everybody equally under the law – that is, they breach the 'rule of law' and the principle of legal equality – they are subject to special parliamentary procedures and scrutiny, notably by the Lords, who have the power to reject such bills outright.

Stages of legislation
The stages of parliamentary legislation are usually quite lengthy and complicated:

- *Preparation and consultation*: government Bills are drafted by lawyers and civil servants, and may be preceded by a consultation paper (**Green Paper**) and/or a draft proposal (**White Paper**) – so-called simply because of the colour of paper upon which they are printed.
- *First reading*: a purely formal reading of the Bill's title to alert the MPs, pressure groups and business interests concerned (a necessary process before the invention of printing, and it has lived on by tradition).
- *Second reading*: this is the really important stage of the Bill, when it is outlined by the relevant minister and debated in detail and voted upon in the Commons chamber.
- *Committee stage*: the Bill goes to a standing committee of Commons backbench MPs (proportionally reflecting the parties' strength in the Commons) who scrutinise and amend the details of the Bill, clause by clause. The whips have substantial control of the memberships of these committees; thus, on average, only 5 per cent of committee amendments have not been previously agreed with the government and, of these, only 1 per cent succeed.
- *Report stage*: the amended Bill is reported back to the whole House of Commons.
- *Third reading*: only minor amendments to grammar and wording can be made at this stage, and the whole Bill is then passed or rejected by the Commons.

When a Bill has been passed by the Commons, it goes to 'another place' – the Commons' quaint name for the House of Lords because, traditionally, the two Houses cannot name each other.

- The Bill now goes through similar stages in the Lords.
- Then it is returned to the Commons, where Lords' amendments are debated and either accepted or rejected. A controversial Bill may go back and forth between the two Houses several times in a process commonly known as 'parliamentary ping-pong', until one House backs down.
- *Royal assent*: nowadays a formality.

For MPs to vote on each part of a Bill, they must walk into two small rooms on either side of the chamber – the 'Aye' and 'No' lobbies – where they are locked in. As they leave, their names are taken and the votes are counted by whips known as 'tellers'. This arcane and time-consuming process is often critically contrasted with other legislatures where electronic push-button voting means MPs do not have to leave their seats. However, the whips favour the Commons process of voting because they can maintain more control – sometimes literally physical

---

Box 4.2 Principal stages in the legislative process for government Bills

- Bill enters House of Commons.
- First reading (no debate).
- Second reading (principles debated on the floor of the Commons).
- Committee stage (clause by clause scrutiny in standing committee).
- Report (amendments considered on the floor of the Commons).
- Third reading (final version debated on the floor).
- Bill passes to the House of Lords.
- Stages similar to House of Commons.
- Reconciliation of texts between Lords and Commons.
- Royal Assent
- Implementation

See http://www.pacts.org.uk/bills-and-acts.php?id=16: accessed on 23 April 2008.

control – over MPs' movements and steer them towards the right lobby. It should be said, however, that MPs also value this process because it enables them to button-hole otherwise often inaccessible ministers or shadow ministers in the lobbies for a quiet word.

It is, absurdly, possible for MPs to vote both 'yes' and 'no' on a single clause or Bill by going quickly through the first lobby and then nipping round into the other (since MPs have precisely eight minutes in which to vote). Labour's David Taylor has done this twenty-five times in his parliamentary career because, he says, it is the only way of registering a 'positive abstention' rather than simply looking as if he was absent. There is no rule against doing this although, as one official put it, it is not encouraged.

Students sometimes ask why MPs' votes are not secret. The simple answer is that MPs are voting on behalf of their constituents, as their representatives. Voters should, therefore, know how their MPs have voted on key Bills so that, if they are unhappy with their MP's record, they can vote him or her out at the next election.

Pairing is a process by which government and Opposition back-benchers arrange permanent 'pairs' at the beginning of each Parliament; they can then be mutually absent on important votes (with the permission of the whips). This gives MPs a break from long attendance in the House, especially when the government has a safe majority and the result of most votes is, anyway, a foregone conclusion. However, if a government has little or no majority, or if relations between the two main parties are particularly fractious, pairing may be suspended, making life uncomfortable for all concerned. (This helps to answer another common student question: why don't MPs cheat at pairing? Answer: they could only get away with it once, and their life in the House thereafter would be tedious and inconvenient, to say the least.)

Law-making is Parliament's most time-consuming role, and one at which it is notably inefficient. The adversarial ethos of the Commons discourages cross-party co-operation and, therefore, early consultation and scrutiny of draft legislation is limited and inadequate. Because Bills are often poorly drafted, the government itself often has to introduce a mass of amendments as the Bill is going through Parliament; for example, there were 500 amendments to the Financial Services Act 1986 while it was going through the Lords. *Post hoc* study of the consequences of legislation is even more scanty, as illustrated by some famously 'bad laws' which proved to be more or less unworkable, such as the poll tax, the Dangerous Dogs Act 1991 and the hunt ban.

In response to such criticisms, the 1997 Labour government promised more publication of draft Bills for scrutiny. They set up a Modernisation Committee, chaired by the Leader of the House – a senior government minister – to consider a whole range of reforms of Commons procedures. Its first report made the following recommendations:

- increased consultation on draft Bills;
- more pre-legislative scrutiny, including by appropriate Commons select committees;
- carry over of Bills from one session to the next;
- more effective use of standing committees;
- a more open and systematic approach to the timetabling of Bills.

Since 2004, it has been possible for Bills to be carried over from one session to the next when time is short, and this has discouraged the government from using the unpopular guillotine procedure whereby debating time is cut short, often with whole clauses not considered at all. Departmental select committees (see Chapter 6) now take more interest in both pre- and post-legislative scrutiny, allowing more efficient drafting and better feedback of voters' views to the government.

However, the government allows pre-legislative scrutiny of Bills only where there is already broad cross-party agreement on the general principles. Controversial Bills are excluded from the process, and these, of course, are likely to be those that are the most troublesome. Some commentators are, moreover, sceptical of the motives behind such modernising reforms:

> There are always tensions between even cautious advocates of reform . . . and the desire of party whips not to surrender control. Parliamentary reform has always turned on the balance between procedural changes that make it easier for MPs to call ministers to account . . . and those that enable the government to conduct its business more smoothly and predictably.[5]

Although the parliamentary law-making process is usually slow and cumbersome, occasionally it may move very fast. On such occasions, however, the resulting statute is sometimes badly written and, more often than not, illiberal. For example, draconian new anti-terrorism laws were passed through Parliament in a single day in 1998, despite a significant backbench revolt.

Plain English

Centuries of parliamentary tradition were swept away in 2006 with the publication of a 'plain English' translation of a Bill – the Coroner Reform Bill – alongside the usual format with its customary, impenetrable, legal language. Bills regularly refer to previous statutes, by numbered and lettered clauses and sub-clauses, without any further explanation, making them impossible to understand for anyone without specialist legal knowledge or access to legal publications. The parallel translation of the Coroner Reform Bill pares down the eighty-one clauses and ten schedules of the 128-page Bill, spelling out all the relevant sections of previous legislation and clarifying how the coroners' system is to be reformed (with, for example, a new right of appeal for families who contest the court's verdict). How far this laudable experiment may be extended to the wider legislative process remains to be seen.

A statute law revision team – a department of the Law Commission – constantly reviews and culls obsolete legislation, with the approval of the House of Lords. It has abolished over 2,000 statutes in the last forty years, including: in 2008, the Land of Idiots Act 1324 (allowing the seizure of land of people deemed insane); the Making of Hats Act 1551; and the Clapboard Act 1592. The team may be kept busy as parliamentary researchers estimate that 3,679 Acts of Parliament have been passed since 1801, with 12 per cent of those being passed by 'new' Labour since 1997.

Challenges to Parliament's law-making role

The European Union

A major challenge to Westminster's law-making function has come from the United Kingdom's membership of the European Union, whose legislation takes precedence over the laws of member states.

Box 4.3 Examples of activities banned by statute law

- Wearing armour to Parliament (Royal Prerogative 1279). Not repealed.
- Christmas, 1652–60: by Puritans who said it was a Catholic superstition. It was reinstated when the monarchy was restored.
- Monarchs marrying Catholics: banned under the Act of Settlement 1701 to ensure a Protestant succession. Not repealed.
- Kilts, 1746–82: after the Battle of Culloden in which the English Army defeated Bonnie Prince Charlie's Scots.
- Slavery, 1833.
- Firing a cannon close to a dwelling house, or baiting or fighting lions or bears (Metropolitan Police Act 1839). Not repealed.
- Hanging washing in the street, beating a carpet, flying a kite or using any slide upon ice or snow (Town Police Clauses Act 1847). Not repealed.
- Child chimney sweeps, 1864: effectively banned by a £10 fine.
- Speeding: the Locomotive Act 1865 restricted motor vehicles to 2–4mph and required someone to walk ahead carrying a red flag. Modified in 1896.
- Driving cattle through the streets of London (Metropolitan Streets Act 1867). Not repealed.
- Being drunk in charge of a horse, cow or steam engine (Licensing Act 1872). Not repealed.
- Homosexuality, 1885–1967: used to convict Oscar Wilde to two years' hard labour in 1895.
- Child labour, 1920: with regulated exceptions such as newspaper deliveries.
- Cocaine, 1920: following stories of crazed First World War soldiers. Not repealed.
- Capital punishment, 1965: with exceptions for treason, piracy with violence and arson in royal dockyards (never since applied, and all abolished by 1998).

The assent of the UK Parliament is not required. This effectively negates parliamentary sovereignty; although, technically, the UK Parliament could legislate to withdraw from the EU at any time, in practice this is unlikely. The more policy areas that are transferred to the decision-making of the EU – for example, by the Single European Act 1986 and the Maastricht Treaty 1993 – the less law-making power rests with Westminster (see Chapter 7).

Devolution

The delegating of some legislative powers from central to regional bodies – and especially the creation of a fairly powerful Scottish Parliament – has lightened the load of Westminster considerably but may ultimately threaten its national sovereignty (see Chapter 8).

Delegated legislation

This is also known as indirect, subordinate or secondary legislation, because it allows ministers, local authorities and civil servants to make detailed regulations under powers delegated by Parliament in a parent Act. The most common forms are Statutory Instruments and Orders in Council. They are generally used for detailed and specialised matters about which MPs have little expertise. About 3,000 Statutory Instruments are brought before Parliament every year. Only a small number of these are debated in Parliament. However, they can turn ministers into lawmakers, breaching the principle of 'separation of powers', and they are subject to little parliamentary oversight. They may be debated on the floor of the House or in a Statutory Instrument Committee for up to one and a half hours. MPs can vote to reject Statutory Instruments wholesale but they cannot amend them. Governments, therefore, sometimes use them to enact controversial legislation which would be seriously impeded by the normal parliamentary processes – a device which often alarms human rights lawyers and civil liberties groups.

One such example was the Regulation of Investigatory Powers Act 2000, which gave certain organisations the right to find out specific information about how people use technology. Under this parent Act, a Statutory Instrument was introduced in 2003 which gave a range of bodies the authority to view private internet, e-mail and mobile phone records, including the emergency ambulance services, fire authorities, the Maritime and Coastguard Agency, the Scottish Drugs Enforcement Agency and the Atomic Energy Authority police, as well as, of course, employers and college authorities, among others.

✔ What you should have learnt from reading this chapter

- This chapter has outlined the diverse roles of MPs and conflicting calls upon their loyalties, which have sometimes generated distraction from their representative role, or outright corruption.

- It has summarised the function of the Opposition as an alternative 'government in waiting' – a role which is occasionally neglected or negated in the recent climate of consensus politics.

- It has explained the functions of the party whips – MPs of substantial power and authority, but not infallible.

- It has described the timetable of the House of Commons (the subject of limited reform in recent years), the different types of Bills and the stages of legislation by which they process through Parliament.

- It has highlighted the weaknesses of Commons standing committees and explained why the arcane process of voting in the House has never been updated.

- It has concluded that law-making – Parliament's most time-consuming role – is not an efficient process, despite recent reforms.

- Finally, it has identified the main challenges to Parliament's law-making role as the EU, the devolved assemblies and delegated legislation – all assessed in detail in later chapters.

🔎 Glossary of key terms

Backbenchers MPs in the House of Commons who are not, in addition, members of the government or of the shadow government.
Devolution The passing down of limited executive or legislative powers from the sovereign centre to subordinate local bodies.
Green Paper A consultative document of diverse ideas and options published by the government prior to a Bill.
Pairing A process by which government and Opposition backbenchers can be mutually absent on important votes (with the permission of the whips).
Private Bill A Bill which affects only specific individual or group interests rather than the general public.
Private Member's Bill A Bill introduced by an individual backbench MP (of any party) rather than by the government.
Public Bill A Bill which concerns the general public interest.
Standing committee A Commons committee of backbenchers which scrutinises and amends Bills.
Whip An MP or peer appointed by the leaders of each party in

Parliament to help organise and control their party's parliamentary business.

White Paper A draft Bill for public and parliamentary consultation.

? Likely examination questions

Short questions:

- Outline the role of backbench MPs.

- Describe the role and powers of Her Majesty's Opposition.

- Explain the role of the whips in the House of Commons.

- Distinguish between a private Bill and a Private Member's Bill.

Essay questions:

- How representative is the House of Commons?

- 'There is too much party discipline in the House of Commons.' Discuss.

- Outline and assess the challenges to Parliament's law-making supremacy.

- 'Law-making procedures in the House of Commons could, and should, be improved.' Discuss.

Helpful websites

http://news.bbc.co.uk

http://www.parliament.uk

http://www.publicwhip.org.uk

http://news.bbc.co.uk/1/hi/uk_politics/political_links/81344.stm

Suggestions for further reading

Brandreth, G., *Breaking the Code: Westminster Diaries 1992–97*, London: Weidenfeld and Nicolson, 1999.

Rush, M., *The Role of the MP from 1868: From Gentlemen to Players*, Oxford: Oxford University Press, 2001.

Walters, R. and Rogers, R., *How Parliament Works*, London: Longman, 2006.

CHAPTER 5

The House of Commons: Representing the People

Overview

This chapter explains the diverse interpretations of 'representation' and assesses how far the Commons addresses them, given: (1) the consequences of the first-past-the-post electoral system, including its impact upon the **party system**; (2) the social composition of MPs and their relations with their constituents; (3) MPs' connections with external interests, including analysis of allegations of 'sleaze'; (4) and the use and abuse of parliamentary privilege.

Key issues to be covered in this chapter

- Representation
- The electoral system
- The party system
- The social composition of MPs
- MPs and voters
- MPs and external interests
- The use and abuse of parliamentary privilege

Representation

Democracy – from the Greek *demos kratos* – literally means 'people power', or self-government of the people, by the people, for the people. In its original form, it meant the right of all qualified citizens to decide directly upon matters of general concern. This form of government began in the ancient Greek city-state of Athens in the fifth century BC, where all qualified citizens would gather regularly to vote directly on issues of concern. (It should be noted, however, that only adult, free men were qualified citizens – women, slaves and non-Athenians were excluded.)

Any form of direct decision making or direct action by the people that increases their own control over their own lives may, therefore, be 'democratic' in this literal sense – be it a vote on an issue at local, workplace or national level, a boycott, a strike, a riot or a revolution. 'People power' may thus be legal or illegal, peaceful or violent.

It is widely argued that most modern industrial states are too big and complex for such 'direct democracy' to be possible. This is debatable as large states can be sub-divided into small political units, and modern technology could, in theory, enhance the capacity for direct political participation. Interactive TV and internet websites are now commonplace. This two-way media facility could be applied easily to the process of political decision making if the political will was there. Perhaps, however, political leaders are too reluctant to surrender their power, and/or most people are too apathetic to take it, for the possibility of more direct democracy to be considered seriously.

The United Kingdom is not, therefore, a direct democracy. Like most other modern states, the United Kingdom claims to be an indirect or **representative democracy**. This involves the election by qualified citizens of representatives who govern over, and on behalf of, the people. Mere vote casting is, obviously, a limited form of 'people power' and participation. All representative democracy, therefore, entails **oligarchy** or elitism, that is, rule by the few.

In the United Kingdom, representative democracy – the extension of the franchise – developed in the nineteenth and twentieth centuries under pressure from popular movements such as Chartism, the trades unions and suffragettes, and was, in part, a conscious effort on the part of the holders of political power to forestall radical demands for more direct or extensive political democracy. In the words of the Conservative politician Lord Hailsham: 'If you don't give them reform, they will give you social revolution.'

The extent to which Parliament represents the people of the United Kingdom depends, first, upon what is meant by the concept of a 'representative'. A political 'representative' may:

- reflect the views and wishes of the voters;
- reflect the interests of the voters as the representative sees them; or
- reflect the social background and typicality of the voters.

The strongest interpretation of the concept of 'representative' is that of a delegate: an elected power-holder who acts as instructed by his or her voters, thus reflecting and implementing the voters' wishes on every issue. This does not apply to UK MPs, and it would be difficult for them, in practice, to consult all their voters on every issue.

Alternatively, representation can mean the reflection of voters' interests, even if the decisions are not popular (this form of representation is commonly claimed by politicians when they are increasing taxes or closing hospitals). This has been the predominant constitutional interpretation of MPs' representative role for over two centuries, since Edmund Burke set out his views in a speech to his Bristol voters in 1774: 'Your representative owes you, not his industry only, but his judgement; and he betrays, instead of serving you, if he sacrifices it to your opinion.' In other words, MPs have the 'enlightened conscience' and 'mature judgement' to decide what is in voters' best interests, not just at constituency but at national level. 'Parliament is a deliberative assembly of one nation, with one interest, that of the whole', said Burke. This is a clear example of the traditional conservative perception of an organic national interest which the educated elite of 'natural governors' are best able to determine. It may sometimes still apply to UK MPs in modern practice – particularly when they use their independent judgement and conscience in free votes or backbench revolts – as, for example, in the repeated rejection of the death penalty by Parliament since the 1960s, apparently contrary to majority public opinion. However, MPs are more often closely tied to the aims and interests of their parties.

Finally, it can mean the reflection of voters' social backgrounds and typicality by the political representatives, for example, the percentage of female, ethnic minority, young or gay MPs in Parliament. UK MPs are now more representative of the wider public in this sense than ever before, but they are still quite atypical (see below).

The franchise

Democracy in the United Kingdom is usually said to originate from 1832 when the franchise, that is, the vote, began to be extended to more and more people: from male property holders and then male householders to most adult men and, in 1918, to older women (over 30). In 1928, most men and women aged twenty-one were allowed to vote; this established the principle of 'universal adult suffrage'. The voting age was lowered to eighteen in 1969. Those still not allowed to vote are members of the House of Lords, non-UK citizens, those under eighteen, certified mental patients, prisoners under sentence and people disqualified for corrupt electoral practices (such as bribery).

The right of all adults to vote for elected representatives in free, fair, secret and competitive elections is widely regarded as the defining feature of a liberal democracy, such as the United Kingdom claims to be. However, even this apparently basic criterion begs questions: for

Table 5.1 The right to vote: number of persons per 100 adults	
Date	Number of persons per 100 adults having the right to vote in the UK
1800	3
1832	5
1867	13
1884	25
1918	75
1928	100

example, who is defined as an 'adult'? At present, most people over the age of eighteen can vote in the United Kingdom, but those aged sixteen may work, pay taxes, get married and join the Army, yet cannot vote. Voting at sixteen is already the official policy of the Liberal Democrats, the Scottish and Welsh Nationalists and the Green Party, while the Labour Government began to consider this idea at the end of 2003. This was mainly because of declining turn outs in recent elections. In the 2001 **general election**, only 59 per cent of qualified voters actually voted: the lowest turn out since the 1920s. If voting numbers continue to decline, it could damage any future government's claim to democratic legitimacy.

Table 5.2 The right to vote: voting age	
State	**Voting age**
Japan	20
Australia	18
United Kingdom	18
USA	18
Yugoslavia	16 if employed, otherwise 18
Bosnia-Herzegovina	16 if employed, otherwise 18
Brazil	16; compulsory from 18
Seychelles	17
Sudan	17
Indonesia	17
East Timor	17
North Korea	17
Austria	16
Nicaragua	16
Cuba	16
Isle of Man	16
Iran	15

A general election, involving all UK constituencies, must be held when Parliament has run its full five-year term (under the Parliament Act 1911) or is dissolved earlier when the Prime Minister of the day calls for a general election.

A **by-election** takes place in a single constituency when the MP dies, loses the seat through disqualification (for example, for corrupt electoral practice or by being granted a peerage) or resigns for other reasons. By-elections are inevitably used as pointers to the current popularity of the government and other parties but they are, by definition, singular events where factors come into play which do not feature in general elections. Very few seats are 'safe' in by-elections. The Conservatives did not win a single by-election while they were in power between 1988 and 1997 – a factor which helped PM John Major to lose his slim majority entirely by the time of the 1997 general election. In 2003 the Liberal Democrats inflicted Labour's first by-election defeat for fifteen years in Brent East, and in 2004 they won Leicester South from Labour, a victory largely attributed to Muslim voters switching from Labour in protest at the invasion of Iraq.

Why is voting behaviour often so different in by-elections from general elections? This can be for a number of reasons, including:

- voters know that they are not voting for a whole new government, therefore, their voting behaviour often changes;
- turn outs also, therefore, usually fall quite sharply;
- local issues may matter more than in a general election;
- the individual candidates and their personalities may matter more;
- media attention is focused on a single constituency, therefore, many more small parties may stand candidates for sheer publicity, and the voters may have much more choice;
- voters often use a by-election to register a protest vote against the government;
- support for third and smaller parties often increases markedly – if only temporarily.

In sum, by-election results are not a good basis for predicting the results of general elections.

Political equality in a liberal democracy should mean one person, one vote, one value – which implies a proportional system of voting, where the percentage of votes received by a party equates to the percentage of political seats granted to them. This is not the case with the Westminster voting system of first-past-the-post (see below).

Moreover, at the 2005 general election, the average size of an English constituency was 70,000 people, in Northern Ireland it was just over 66,000, in Wales just over 59,000 and in Scotland 53,000. Even within England it varied from about 51,000 voters in Sheffield Brightside (David Blunkett's seat) to 103,480 in the Isle of Wight. Political equality, not.

Political equality also implies equal opportunity to stand for office and equal opportunity to be elected to office. There are, however, always restrictions on those qualified to stand for office: in the United Kingdom, to stand as a Westminster MP, a person must pay a deposit of £500. This is intended to discourage 'frivolous' candidates, but it effectively excludes many serious contenders who do not have the financial backing of a large party.

The electoral system

First-past-the-post

This is the system used for elections to the Westminster Parliament. It entails one vote per person in single-member constituencies, that is, one MP is elected to represent a single local area; and the candidate with the most votes wins the constituency, with or without an 'absolute majority' of over 50 per cent of the votes cast.

Advantages of the first-past-the-post

The advantages of the first-past-the-post system include:

- The first-past-the-post system is simple, quick and cheap.
- One person, one vote is a basic form of political equality.
- It is said to favour the two-party system as it usually produces a single-party, majority government and a second, strong Opposition party in the House of Commons; hence strong and stable government which is clearly accountable to the voters. However, this must be qualified: the system has produced minority governments – with under 50 per cent of the seats in the Commons – in the

1970s; and a two-party system has both advantages and disadvantages – the latter including lack of choice and diversity (especially in **safe seats** where one particular party is virtually certain to win every time), unfair representation of minority parties and their voters, and a majority-seat government with a minority of votes cast. The rise of the Liberals – now Liberal Democrats – since the 1970s has undermined the two-party system; as have the marked regional differences in party support, for example, in Scotland.

- It is also sometimes said that the two-party system created by the first-past-the-post electoral system reflects a 'natural' political divide between conservatism and radicalism. However, the substantial third-party vote since the 1970s belies this argument, as do the substantial policy similarities between the two main parties in recent years.

- Finally, it is said that contact between MP and constituents is closer than in large, multi-member constituencies. In principle there is, indeed, a one-to-one relationship; but, in practice, MPs need not even live in their constituencies and contact with voters is often negligible, especially in safe seats (though these are now declining as voters become more volatile). Do you know the name of your own MP?

Disadvantages of the first-past-the-post

The disadvantages of the first-past-the-post system include:

- Since any vote for a losing candidate is 'wasted', that is, not directly represented at all in the Commons, not all votes carry equal weight, that is, the system does not grant one person, one vote, one value, and political equality is denied. Voters may, therefore, be discouraged from voting for minority parties, or from voting at all.

- Because most MPs have fewer than 50 per cent of the votes cast in their constituencies, no government since the 1930s has had an absolute majority (over 50 per cent) of votes cast in the country, although most have had an absolute majority of seats in the Commons. This usually produces a powerful government which the majority of people voted against – arguably an 'elective dictatorship' (to use Lord Hailsham's phrase) of an unrepresentative

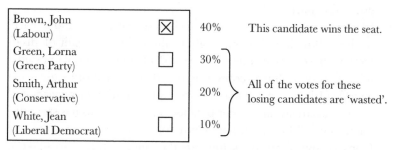

Figure 5.1 A first-past-the-post ballot paper

kind. Opinion polls suggest that around 60 per cent of voters now favour a system of proportional representation (PR).

- Until 1997 onwards when the Conservatives were under-represented in the Commons, the two main parties had both been consistently over-represented, while the Liberal Democrats in particular – because of the geographical dispersal of their votes – have been consistently under-represented.

- Occasionally, a government may have more seats but fewer votes than the 'losing' party: for example, the Conservatives in 1951 and Labour in February 1974 (because of unequal constituency sizes and winning margins). The party with the most votes does not always win.

- Independent candidates (with no party attachment) have very little chance of success. This may exclude quality and diversity from the system.

- Finally, in the period of economic boom from the 1950s to the mid-1970s, the two-party system was based on '**consensus politics**', when the two main parties shared very similar, centrist policies in support of the mixed economy, welfare state, full employment and nuclear defence. This was praised by some for producing moderation and stability, but was criticised by others for its lack of innovation and choice. Conversely, the recessions of the 1980s were said to have produced '**adversary politics**' with more right-wing Conservative governments and a more influential left wing in the Labour Party. The opposite pros and cons were advanced: more diversity and choice, but also more risk of a 'pendulum swing', that is, sharp policy reversals between different governing parties.

- However, after four successive election defeats, the Labour Party in the 1990s shifted increasingly to the right in pursuit of disaffected Conservative voters. The post-1997 period has witnessed a new kind of political consensus based upon a more right-wing agenda of low taxation and inflation, privatisation of services and authoritarian law and order policies. This consensus has strengthened since 2005 as David Cameron has sought to steer the Conservative Party back towards the centre ground to make it more electable.

Table 5.3 The 2005 general election results			
	Labour	Conservative	Liberal Democrats
% Votes	35.2	32.4	22.0
Number of seats	356	198	62
% of seats	55.1	30.7	9.6

Labour won only 35 per cent of the votes cast in 2005, the lowest support for a government since the Great Reform Act 1832. Not a single MP won 50 per cent of the votes cast in any constituency and only two MPs won more than 40 per cent. It took just 26,858 votes to elect a Labour MP, 44,241 to elect a Conservative MP and 98,484 to elect a Liberal Democrat MP.

The 2005 turn out was 2 per cent higher than the 2001 turn out, largely because of an increased provision for postal voting. However, applications for postal votes rose by up to 500 per cent in some marginal seats, sparking concerns about electoral fraud – especially since a number of local councillors were found guilty of fraud in the 2004 all-postal ballot pilot schemes in some local council elections (which the judge declared 'would disgrace a banana republic'). The

2005 election generated seventeen police investigations into alleged electoral fraud. The government was furious when the independent Electoral Commission advised against all postal voting in future elections, and decided to ignore the advice. Instead, the Electoral Administration Act 2006 requires postal voters to give their signature and date of birth both when they register to vote and when they send in their ballot papers. The delays caused by checking these may mean an end to the traditional – and usually decisive – election night count. Voters will also have to sign for their ballot papers at polling stations 'to deter fraud' – an amendment forced upon the government by the Lords. This law also lowered the minimum age for election candidates from twenty-one to eighteen.

However, in 2008 the Council of Europe condemned the UK system of postal voting as still 'childishly simple' to rig. If the system is not improved, Britain may suffer the ignominy of being placed under full monitoring by the Council, whose recent targets have included President Putin's Russia.

The party system

A **party system** implies political decision making and representation on the basis of formal, organised groups of (more or less) like-minded people who stand candidates for election on a common policy programme. A party system may contain only one party – which would widely be seen as a dictatorship – or two, or many. A party system, of any type, has merits and demerits as compared with, for example, representation and political decision making by independent individuals. The issues involved include representative and responsible government, pluralism and 'elective dictatorship'.

There are (in 2008) ten parties in the House of Commons (including the Scottish and Welsh nationalists and the Northern Irish parties) and around 170 'parties' stood candidates in the 2005 general election! Many of them, of course, were very small groups indeed – often more like pressure groups pursuing a single cause and standing candidates merely for publicity. Some of them were clearly frivolous, but even these served a valuable function in a pluralist democracy by providing a channel for political participation and protest.

Box 5.1 The major and minor parties which took part in the 2005 general election

Conservative, **C**; Labour, **Lab**; Labour and Co-operative, **Lab Co-op**; Liberal Democrat, **LD**; Plaid Cymru, **PC**; Scottish National Party, **SNP**; Green Party, **Green**; Ulster Unionist Party, **UUP**; Democratic Unionist Party, **DUP**; Social Democratic and Labour Party, **SDLP**; Sinn Féin, **SF**; Alliance, **Alliance**; Workers' Party, **WP**; Alliance for Change, **AFC**; Alliance for Green Socialism, **Green Soc**; Alternative Party, **AP**; Anti-Corruption Forum, **Anti-Corrupt**; Asian League, **AL**; Blair Must Go Party, **BMG**; British National Party, **BNP**; British Public Party, **BPP**; Build Duddon and Morecombe Bridges, **Bridges**; Burnley First Independent, **Burnley**; Campaigning for Real Democracy, **CRD**; Chairman of Sunrise Radio, **Sunrise**; Christian Democrat, **Ch D**; Christian Peoples Alliance, **CPA**; Church of the Militant Elvis Party, **Elvis**; Civilisation Party, **CP**; Clause 28 Children's Protection Christian Democrats, **Clause 28**; Communist Party, **Comm**; Communist Party of Britain, **Comm Brit**; Community, **Community**; Community Action Party, **CAP**; Community Group, **CG**; Countryside Party, **Country**; Croydon Pensions Alliance, **Croydon**; Death Dungeons & Taxes Party, **DDTP**; Defend the Welfare State Against Blairism, **Def Welfare**; Demanding Honesty in Politics and Whitehall, **Honesty**; Democratic Labour Party, **Dem Lab**; Democratic Socialist Alliance – People Before Profit, **Dem Soc All**; Direct Customer Service Party, **Customer**; English Democratic Party, **EDP**; English Democrats – Putting England First, **England**; English Democrats Party, **Eng Dem**; English Independence Party, **Eng Ind**; English Parliamentary Party, **EEP**; Extinction Club, **Ext Club**; Fancy Dress Party, **FDP**; Fathers-4-Justice, **Fathers**; Fit Party for Integrity and Trust, **Fit**; Forward Wales Party, **FWP**; Free Party, **Free**; Free Scotland Party, **Free Scot**; Freedom Party, **FP**; Get Britain Back Party, **GBB**; Green Party, **Green**; Grey Party, **Grey**; Imperial Party, **IP**; Independent, **Ind**; Independent J, **Ind J**; Independent – Vote for Yourself Party, **Ind Vote**; Independent B, **Ind B**; Independent Batchelor, **Ind Batch**; Independent Bell, **Ind Bell**; Independent Booth, **Ind Booth**; Independent Br, **Ind Br**; Independent Braid, **Ind Braid**; Independent Cam, **Ind Cam**; Independent Community Candidate Empowering Change, **Community**; Independent Green, **Ind Green**; Independent Haines, **Ind Haines**; Independent Hill, **Ind Hill**; Independent Hinkles, **Ind Hinkles**; Independent Hunt, **Ind Hunt**; Independent John, **Ind John**; Independent K, **Ind K**; Independent Keys, **Ind Keys**; Independent Kidderminster Hospital and Health

Concern, **KHHC**; Independent KI, **Ind KI**; Independent Labour, **Ind Lab**; Independent M, **Ind M**; Independent Masters, **Ind Masters**; Independent McBride, **Ind McBride**; Independent N, **Ind N**; Independent Nazir, **Ind Nazir**; Independent P, **Ind P**; Independent Pev, **Ind Pev**; Independent Pr, **Ind Pr**; Independent Prachar, **Ind Prachar**; Independent R, **Ind R**; Independent Sh, **Ind Sh**; Independent Sib, **Ind Sib**; Independent Stone, **Ind Stone**; Independent T, **Ind T**; Independent United Unionist, **Ind UU**; Independent W, **Ind West**; Independent Walsh, **Ind Walsh**; Independent Working Class Association, **IWCS**; Independent X, **Ind X**; 'Iraq War Not in My Name', **Iraq**; Islam Zinda Baad Platform, **IZB**; Isle of Wight Party, **IOW**; Jam Wrestling Party, **Wrestling**; John Lillburne Democratic Party, **JLDP**; Justice Party, **JP**; Left Alliance, **Left All**; Legalise Cannabis Alliance, **LCA**; Liberal, **Lib**; Liberated Party, **LP**; Local Community Party, **Local**; Lower Excise Duty Party, **Low Excise**; Marxist Party, **Marxist**; Max Power Party, **Power**; Mebyon Kernow, **Meb Ker**; Monster Raving Loony Party, **Loony**; Motorcycle News Party, **MNP**; Muslim Party, **Muslim**; National Front, **NF**; New Britain Party, **NBP**; New England Party, **NEP**; New Millennium Bean, **Bean**; Newcastle Academy with Christian Values Party, **NACVP**; No description, **ND**; No description Bardwaj, **ND Bardwaj**; Northern Ireland Unionist, **NI Unionist**; Northern Progress for You, **Northern**; Open-Forum, **Forum**; Operation Christian Vote, **OCV**; Pacifist for Peace, Justice, Cooperation, Environment, **Pacifist**; Pathfinders, **PF**; Peace Party, non-violence, justice, environment, **PPN-V**; Peace and Progress Party, **Progress**; Pensioner Coalition, **Pensioner**; Pensioners Party Scotland, **PPS**; People's Choice, **Choice**; People's Justice Party, **PJP**; Personality and Rational Thinking? Yes! Party, **PRTYP**; Pride in Paisley Party, **Paisley**; Pro Euro Conservative Party, **Pro Euro C**; ProLife Alliance, **ProLife**; Progress Democratic Party Members Decide Policy, **Prog Dem**; Progressive Democratic Party, **PDP**; Progressive Unionist Party, **PUP**; Protest Vote Party, **Protest**; Public Services Not War, **PSNW**; Publican Party – Free to Smoke (Pubs), **Publican**; Qari, **Qari**; Rainbow Dream Ticket Party, **Dream**; Rate Payer, **RP**; Reform 2000, **Reform**; Reform UK, **Ref UK**; Removal of Tetra masts in Cornwall, **Masts**; Residents Association, **RA**; Residents and Motorists of Great Britain, **Res Motor**; Respect the Unity Coalition, **Respect**; Rock & Roll Loony Party, **R&R Loony**; SOS! Voters against Overdevelopment of Northampton, **SOS**; Save the National Health, **SNH**; Save the Bristol North Baths Party, **Baths**; Scottish Freedom Referendum Party, **Scot Ref**; Scottish Independence Party, **Scot Ind**; Scottish Labour, **Scot Lab**; Scottish Senior Citizens Party, **Scot Senior**; Scottish Socialist Party, **SSP**;

Scottish Unionist, **Scot U**; Seeks a Worldwide Online Participatory Directory, **Online**; Senior Citizens Party, **Senior**; Silent Majority Party, **Silent**; Socialist, **Socialist**; Socialist Alliance, **Soc All**; Socialist Alternative Party, **Soc Alt**; Socialist Environmental Alliance, **Soc EA**; Socialist Labour Party, **Soc Lab**; Socialist Party, **Soc**; Socialist Unity Network, **Soc Unity**; St. Albans Party, **St. Albans**; Stuckist, **Stuck**; Tatton Group Independent, **Tatton**; The Common Good, **Common Good**; The Millennium Council, **MC**; The Peace Party – non-violence, justice, environment, **TPP**; The People's Choice Making Politicians Work, **Work**; The Resolutionist Party, **The RP**; The Speaker, **Speaker**; Their Party, **TP**; Third Way, **Third**; Tigers' eye the party for kids, **TEPK**; Truth Party, **Truth**; UK Community Issues Party, **UKC**; UK Independence Party, **UKIP**; UK Pathfinders, **UK Path**; UK Pensioners Party, **UKPP**; United Kingdom Unionist, **UKU**; Unrepresented People's Party, **Unrep**; Veritas, **Veritas**; Virtue Currency Cognitive Appraisal Party, **Currency**; Vote for yourself rainbow dream ticket, **Vote Dream**; WWW.XAT.ORG, **WWW.XAT.ORG**; Wessex Regionalist, **Wessex Reg**; Women for Life on Earth, **WFLOE**; Women's Coalition, **Women's Co**; Workers' Revolutionary Party, **WRP**; World Revolutionary Party, **World Rev**; Xtraordinary People Party, **XPP**; Your Party (Banbury), **YPB**; familiesfirst.uk.net, **FFUK**; telepathicpart-nership.com, **telepath**.

There are several possible ways of describing the party system in the UK, and all of them have some validity, depending upon which part of the political system, and which time period, is under scrutiny.

First, a multi-party system is one where many parties exist and there is a fairly even balance of power between them. Clearly, as shown above, many parties exist in the United Kingdom and even within Parliament. There are also clear regional differences in the parties' strengths: for example, in Scotland and Wales the Scottish Nationalist Party and Plaid Cymru, respectively, are currently (2008) in government. In local government, too, the small parties, such as the Greens and the BNP, do better than at national level. Finally, because of its unique history, there is a completely different party system in Northern Ireland, based upon Nationalist and Unionist parties.

Secondly, a two-and-a-half party system is one where two parties dominate but a third party plays a significant role. The Liberal Democrats won 22 per cent of the votes cast in the 2005 general election; they were in a coalition government with Labour in Scotland from 1999 to 2007; and, in the 2004 local elections, the Liberal Democrats pushed Labour into third place.

Thirdly, a two-party system is one where, although many parties exist, only two dominate the legislature and have any real prospect of winning government power. The first-past-the-post system of election transforms – or deforms – a multi-party system in the country into a two-party system in Westminster. Only the Labour and Conservative Parties have formed (single-party) national governments since 1945; almost 90 per cent of Westminster MPs are Labour or Conservative; the constitution recognises only 'Her Majesty's Government' and 'Her Majesty's Opposition'; and Westminster parliamentary procedures such as pairing and Opposition Days and even the two-sided layout of the Commons' chamber, assume and reinforce the two-party system.

A dominant-party system is one where one particular party is in executive power for significantly longer periods of time than any other party (whether with a small or large majority). The Conservatives, by 1997, had been in power for the previous eighteen years, for two-thirds of the post-war era and, indeed, for over two-thirds of the twentieth century.

The main disadvantages of a dominant party system are:

- the governing party becomes complacent, arrogant and even corrupt;
- government becomes stagnant and runs out of useful ideas;
- alternatively, government casts around for new ideas for their own sake, which may generate policy instability;
- the Opposition lacks information and experience over the long term, especially in a system as secretive as that of the United Kingdom;
- institutions such as the civil service, police and judiciary may become 'politicised';
- large sections of the electorate are excluded for long periods from representation by government and may become apathetic or angry, and may turn to direct action etc. Even supporters of the

governing party may get fed up and develop the 'time for a change' sentiment so evident in the 1997 General Election.

It remains to be seen whether Labour is the new dominant party of the twenty-first century.

'Elective dictatorship' is the phrase used by Lord Hailsham to describe periods of time in the United Kingdom when the governing party has such a large majority in the Commons that they can overwhelmingly dominate it and push through almost any decision they want. Within its first year in office in 1997, Labour had pushed through many unpopular policies which were not in its manifesto, such as benefit cuts for lone parents and disabled people, students' tuition fees, a five-year public sector pay squeeze and increased taxation of pension funds.

Advantages of a party system

- Parties provide the basis for the choice of a prime minister and the formation of a legitimate and unified government.
- Parties provide the basis for a coherent and comprehensive body of policies for government.
- Parties organise and crystallise public opinion into coherent blocks.
- Parties educate public opinion through their activities both inside and outside Parliament and through the media (though they may also try to manipulate and mislead public opinion for party advantage).
- Parties provide effective organisation, financing and campaigning for candidates.
- According to the 'doctrine of the mandate', an elected government is authorised, or even obliged, to implement the policy proposals contained in its party manifesto; the party system is, therefore, essential for representative government.
- The convention of collective responsibility, whereby government is accountable to Parliament and hence to the electorate, assumes an executive united around a common body of policy. The party system is, therefore, essential for responsible government.
- The party system provides stability and consistency of government.

Disadvantages of a party system

- A single-party, majority government based on strong party discipline may amount to 'elective dictatorship'.
- Parties may encourage partisan conflict for its own sake, undermining effective government.
- Voters have no choice between the policies of any one party.
- Voters have no say in the parties' candidates (though 'open primaries' could be introduced as in the United States, and the Conservative Party used this process in 2007 to choose its London mayoral candidate).
- The party system discourages close, personal contact between MPs and voters.
- The party system undermines MPs' independence and individualism.
- The national or local party machines may have excessive power, for example over MPs, at the expense of the voters.
- The party system may permanently exclude some minority views, or may neglect important issues which cut across orthodox party lines (for example, moral issues such as abortion or capital punishment).
- The party system excludes able independents.

Party funding

There were several scandals about party funding in the 1990s: for example, the Conservatives took money from what their critics called 'foreign crooks' such as fugitive businessman Asil Nadir; and Labour had its Ecclestone affair, where the 1997 Labour Government received a £1 million donation from Formula One boss Bernie Ecclestone, which coincided with an exemption for motor racing from a ban on tobacco sponsorship. The Labour Government asked the Committee on Public Standards to establish clear rules about party funding. In 1998 the following rules were proposed:

- foreign donations to be banned;
- blind trusts to be abolished;
- all national donations of more than £5,000 and local donations of more than £1,000 to be made public;
- anonymous donations of £50 or more banned (but how?!);

- a £20-million ceiling on each party's national election campaign spending;
- tax relief on donations up to £500;
- increased state funding for opposition parties;
- shareholders to approve company donations and sponsorship;
- equal state funding for both sides in referenda campaigns, and government should remain neutral;
- an Electoral Commission to oversee the rules with the power to impose heavy fines.

The government almost immediately rejected the idea that it should remain neutral in possible future referenda such as on the single European currency, but legislated on the rest of the proposals in 1999. The Labour Party was also obliged to return Bernie Ecclestone's £1 million donation to him.

The 2005 general election cost over £112 million, with £70 million in administrative costs and the three main parties spending over £40 million on their campaigns – up more than £15 million from 2001. Administrative costs (such as employing returning officers and officials at counts) are met by the taxpayers, but party costs are met by donations. Advertising was the biggest cost for the parties.

Table 5.4 The 2005 general election: spending by the main parties	
Labour	£17.94 million
Conservatives	£17.85 million
Liberal Democrats	£4.32 million
UKIP	£648,397
Respect	£320,716
Ulster Unionists	£251,119
SNP	£193,987
Green Party	£112,068

Each party was allowed to spend, in total, up to £19,380,000 under UK election rules.

The Labour Government had, in effect, made a rod for its own back by legislating for more open government on the issue of party funding, thus generating the 'cash for honours' investigation in 2006 after it was revealed that the Labour Party had been given secret loans

Table 5.5 Loans to parties at the end of 2006	
Conservatives	£35.3 million
Labour	£23.4 million
Liberal Democrats	£1.1 million
SNP	£525,393
Plaid Cymru	£352,000
Respect	£34,878
UKIP	£19,200

Table 5.6 Donations to parties at the end of 2006	
Labour	£3,227,340
Conservatives	£2,867,019
Liberal Democrats	£629,903
Co-operative Party	£142,036
Green Party	£138,396
SNP	£52,430
Scottish Greens	£31,373
UKIP	£17,913
Plaid Cymru	£12,250

before the 2005 general election and that some of those lenders had subsequently been nominated for peerages. Parliamentary and police inquiries were initiated and then widened to include the other main parties. The police inquiry was closed in 2007 with no charges brought.

By the end of 2006 (the first time that parties had to declare all loans as well as donations above £5,000), the main political parties owed a total of £60 million in loans.

Box 5.2 Biggest lenders to political parties at the end of 2006

Allied Irish Bank: £18.45 million (to Conservatives – mortgage)
Co-operative Bank and unions: £15.3 million (to Labour)
Lord Alliance: £250,000 (to Liberal Democrats)
(*Source*: http://news.bbc.co.uk, November 2006.)

'**Short money**': this is the grant provided to help opposition parties in the Commons with their parliamentary running costs and now amounts around £6 million per year from taxpayers. (It is named after Labour MP, Ted Short, who, as Leader of the House at the time, played a part in its introduction in 1975.) There is little guidance on what it should and should not be allowed to subsidise. The amount payable is worked out according to the number of seats a party has and the amount of votes that the party received at the last election.

Some commentators advocate more state funding of political parties to reduce the risks of corruption: 'It is only by giving politicians a safe, clean supply of state funds to run their campaigns that we can wean the Blairs, Camerons and Campbells off their addiction to the electoral crack doled out by billionaires for their own obvious purposes.'[1]

In 2006, Tony Blair commissioned an inquiry into party funding under former civil servant Sir Hayden Phillips. His year-long review recommended that limits be imposed on donations to parties and on campaign spending of £150 million per party for local and national campaigning for each Parliament, including £20 million for a general election, as well as a £25 million rise per year in state funding. The

	General	Travel	Leader of the Opposition	Total
Conservative	£3,655,400.00	£91,669.75	£595,999.00	£4,343,068.75
Liberal Democrats	£1,557,801.00	£39,066.38		£1,596,867.38
DUP	£146,027.00	£3,662.05		£149,689.05
SNP	£129,417.00	£3,245.51		£132,662.51
Plaid Cymru	£60,710.00	£1,522.48		£62,232.48
SDLP	£54,424.00	£1,364.84		£55,788.84

Table 5.7 Short money allocations, 2007–8

parties agreed with the broad principles but not the details. In particular, the Labour Party feared that the recommended £50,000 upper limit on donations from individuals and organisations would jeopardise its trade union funding, and the Conservatives resisted overall limits on spending. The cross-party talks broke down in 2007 amid much recrimination. Opinion polls have also indicated rapidly declining public support for higher taxpayer funding, although voters also dislike big donations by wealthy individuals.

A further flurry of scandals in 2007 about proxy donations and undeclared donations to individual MPs culminated in the resignation of Cabinet minister, Peter Hain, over £100,000 of undeclared donations towards his (unsuccessful) bid for the Labour Party deputy leadership.

The social composition of MPs

Despite significant improvements since 1997, the social backgrounds of parliamentary candidates and MPs are still by no means 'representative' of the electorate; to put it simplistically, they are still predominantly white, male, middle-aged and middle class. This is partly because of discrimination in the process of selection of candidates, and partly because working-class people, young people, women and

Table 5.8 School and university background of Labour and Conservative MPs

	Independent school (%)		Oxbridge (%)	
Current national of all students	7%		2%	
	1983	**2005**	**1983**	**2005**
Labour	14	18	15	17
Conservatives	70	59	48	46

ethnic minorities are slower to come forward as candidates (because of pressures of work, financial constraints, or lack of political background, contacts, interest or self-confidence). In the early 1990s, the Labour Party briefly adopted a policy of all-women short-lists in many constituencies, and a record number of female Labour MPs were elected in 1997. Since the 1997 election, minor 'family friendly' reforms have been introduced in the Commons – such as fewer late-night sittings – which make it slightly easier for women, especially, to serve as MPs. After the 2005 general election, though, still only 19 per cent of MPs were female, and only 15 out of 646 (under 2 per cent) were black or Asian compared with 8 per cent of the wider population.

Sutton Trust Charity chairman, Sir Peter Lampl, said, 'The educational profile of our representatives in Parliament does not reflect society at large. This is symptomatic of a wider issue – the educational apartheid which blights our system and which offers the best life chances to those who can afford to pay for their schooling.'[2]

MPs and voters

A 2006 survey by the Hansard Society (an educational charity to promote parliamentary democracy) found that MPs worked an average of seventy-one hours per week in 2006 compared with sixty-two hours in 1982. They are probably more connected to their constituencies now than they have ever been. A record average of 40 per cent of MPs' time is now spent on constituency issues, and 90 per cent of them say that their constituency is more important to them than party or national interests. This compares favourably with fifty years ago when MPs tended to treat Parliament as a part-time hobby, they had very limited resources to fulfil any of their roles effectively, they rarely lived in their constituencies and they seldom even visited them.

MP versus party

In UK elections for the Westminster Parliament, voters choose one local MP to represent a single constituency and are, therefore, said to have a one-to-one personal, relationship with that MP. For this reason, if an MP defects from one political party to another between general elections, no new by-election is held – on the grounds that the electorate voted for the person and not for the party label. MPs do occasionally leave their own party and 'cross the floor of the House' to join another party. Voters simply wake up to find themselves with the same MP, but of a different party. (The classic example was Winston Churchill who entered Parliament in 1900 as a Conservative, then defected to the Liberals in 1904 and eventually rejoined the Conservatives in 1924. As he said then, 'Anyone can rat, but it takes a certain amount of ingenuity to re-rat.')

However, a wholly contradictory principle of the UK constitution is the 'doctrine of the mandate' (see Chapter 2). This theory rests on the assumption that the electorate are voting, not for the individual candidate, but for a party label and package of party proposals. This theory is, more often than not, true in practice. Voters, therefore, often punish defectors by voting them out at the next general election, unless a very safe seat is found for them.

Hence, there is always controversy when an MP defects from one party to another between elections – not least because of the sense of betrayal which this may generate. Martin Hill, the Conservative leader of Lincolnshire County Council, said of Quentin Davies' defection in 2007: 'I think it's a slap in the face for all of those people who supported and went round for him. I feel very strongly. I don't approve of politicians who stand under one flag and then change to

Box 5.3 Defecting MPs

Quentin Davies	Conservative to Labour 2007	
Robert Jackson	Conservative to Labour 2005	Stood down at next election
Andrew Hunter	Conservative to DUP 2004	Stood down at next election
Paul Marsden	Labour to Liberal Democrats 2001	Stood down at next election
Shaun Woodward	Conservative to Labour 1999	Was found a safe seat in 2001 and is currently a Cabinet minister
Peter Temple-Morris	Conservative to Labour 1998	Stood down at next election and received a life peerage
Sir George Gardiner	Conservative to Referendum Party 1997	Lost seat in 1997 election
Emma Nicolson	Conservative to Liberal Democrats 1995	Received a life peerage in 1997 and became an MEP in 1999
Alan Howarth	Conservative to Labour 1995	Was found a safe seat in 1997 and became a Labour minister

another flag for their own convenience. It is an act of treachery and betrayal, frankly.'[3] (Of course, even the recipient party may not trust a defector who has previously been their political enemy).

MPs' pay
From the thirteenth to the late seventeenth century MPs were paid locally by those who lived in the constituency that they represented, which meant that local voters could hold their MPs directly accountable for their performance. The practice then lapsed and, in the eighteenth and nineteenth centuries, MPs were unpaid. This meant that MPs required substantial personal wealth and leisure time. As the

middle and working classes sought and won election in the late nineteenth century, there were growing calls for MPs to be paid. The Parliament Act 1911 began the process, initially in the form of a £400 annual allowance. MPs' salaries, allowances, expenses and pension rights only began rising exponentially – in the eyes of critics – from the 1960s.

The basic salary for a backbench MP has risen from about £30,000 in the mid-1990s to just over £60,000 in 2008. This compares with the national average wage of about £24,000. Bear in mind, too, that being an MP is a part-time office, and many MPs earn substantial additional salaries for other jobs in farming, law, journalism, etc. Since 1996, they receive automatic pay rises tied to those of senior civil servants (to prevent MPs from having to vote on the specifics of their own annual salary increases), and civil service pay has risen sharply to try to attract high-fliers from the private sector.

In 2008, MPs bowed to public opinion and approved new methods of calculating their pay, by the Senior Salaries Review Body, which did not require the approval of Parliament.

MPs' expenses

MPs' claims for expenses are costly, controversial and sometimes difficult to verify. They include paying research and secretarial staff, office costs, housing (for MPs living away from home when in London), travel, telephone, stationery and postage.

In 2004, broad details of MPs' expense claims were made public for the first time – disclosures which were forced by the Freedom of Information Act. A London School of Economics study measured MPs' expenses against their voting records in the House between 2001 and 2004 – a crude kind of performance indicator – and (discounting frontbenchers, who have extra duties) found that Respect MP George Galloway was Parliament's most expensive backbencher, costing £1,491 for every vote he cast.[4]

In 2004, former Conservative leader, Iain Duncan Smith, was rebuked by Parliamentary Commissioner, Sir Philip Mawer, for paying his wife and two other employees from his parliamentary staffing allowance when part of their duties involved partisan party politics and not pure constituency work. Mr Duncan Smith was correct in responding that the rules were unclear. Some legislatures – as in America and Germany – have banned parliamentarians from employing their spouses and relatives, while the House of Commons gave no guidance at all. About one in four MPs 'employ' family members as staff on expenses. Each MP can hire three full-time and one part-time member of staff, at a cost of up to £102,650 per year.

This controversy escalated when, in 2008, it was revealed that Conservative MP, Derek Conway, allegedly paid his two adult sons £40,000 and £33,000 as parliamentary researchers, but no record could be found that any parliamentary work had been done by them. (Tabloid newspaper ire was fuelled by the fact that elder son, Henry, invited his friends to a 'Fuck Off I'm Rich' party before the scandal broke. He was subsequently reported as sending an email to 800 of his friends saying that the partying would go on.) Derek Conway had the Conservative whip withdrawn, was suspended from Parliament for ten days and was ordered to repay £13,161. He will not stand again at the next election. However, the police declined to investigate the case due to 'a lack of systems to account for MPs' expenses'. All the main parliamentary parties then ordered their MPs to declare any family members who worked for them.

In 2007, MPs' salaries were £60,277 a year plus pension, and each MP claimed an average of £135,000 in expenses to cover travel, staffing, stationery, office and staying away from home costs – a total of £87.6 million.

On the plus side, this information was obtained under the Freedom of Information Act 2000 – a good example of a significant trend towards more open government. In 2007, MPs were finally also forced under the Freedom of Information Act to reveal specific details of their £4.5 million travel expenses. Some MPs' expenses seemed unfeasibly high, while others had spent thousands of pounds on flights and car mileage rather than more environmentally sound train travel. Similar recent revelations by the Scottish Parliament resulted in a huge fall in the amount of travel expenses claimed by MSPs, and exposed abuse by two MSPs which led one to resign from the Scottish Parliament and another to resign as Conservative leader in Scotland.

However, in a move condemned by Liberal Democrat MP, Norman Baker, as 'deeply hypocritical', Westminster MPs voted by a majority of seventy-one in 2007 to pass a Conservative MP's Private Member's Bill exempting themselves, and the Lords, from the freedom of information laws. The MPs said that they wanted to protect the privacy of their constituents' correspondence, but this is, in fact, already safeguarded under the Data Protection Act. Critics claimed that MPs were simply trying to keep their expenses secret. Embarrassingly for supporters of the Bill, it failed to receive the support of a single peer when it went to the Lords. It was then sent back to the Commons where it was effectively scuppered by a handful of MPs who prolonged the debate until the Bill ran out of time.

In 2008 it emerged that MPs could claim substantial second home allowances – the so-called 'John Lewis list': for example, £10,000 for a new kitchen; £6,335 for a new bathroom; £2,000 for furniture; £1,000 for a bed; £750 for a TV or stereo; £600 for a dining table; £550 for a fridge-freezer; and £300 for a rug; all in addition to mortgages, utility bills and cleaning arrangements. A Conservative MP couple, Sir Nicholas and Ann Winterton, sought to defend their use of £165,000 of taxpayers' money to rent a flat that they already owned outright. MPs could also claim up to £400 a month for 'food' without receipts (although any supermarket item could legitimately come under that heading which, it transpired, included fish tanks and iPods); and a further £250 per item for other expenses without receipts, although this was recently been scaled down to £25 per item.

In 2008, the Commons lost a long court battle to block a freedom of information request for the detailed expenses of senior politicians such as Tony Blair, John Prescott, Gordon Brown, Michael Howard and Charles Kennedy (this time on the grounds that it could compromise MPs' security). All the MPs claimed mortgage interest payments on their second homes and five had their council tax paid. Conservative leader, Michael Howard (2003–4) spent the most on 'additional costs', including mortgages, utility bills, council tax, phone bills, cleaning, food and provisions and household repairs, claiming £20,347. Blair spent £15,490 and Brown £14,304. John Prescott claimed the most on food and groceries: £4,000. Blair's claim of £116 for a TV licence particularly angered groups such as the National Pensioners' Convention who pointed out that most people had to wait until they reached seventy-five before becoming entitled to a free licence.[5]

In the face of a steady stream of critical stories about MPs' expenses and obvious public dissatisfaction, Speaker Michael Martin launched an internal review of MPs' allowances by the Members Estimates Committee of the Commons, chaired by himself. However, he has also (2008 salary £137,000) come under criticism over his claims for £25,000 housing costs despite having state apartments at Westminster, £50,00 air travel expenses and £4,000 taxi fares claimed by his wife – into which the Parliamentary Commissioner for Standards launched an inquiry – as well as his past payments to his wife and daughter for working in his constituency office. He also spent over £20,000 of taxpayers' money instructing lawyers on a potential libel case if his impartiality was impugned.

There is no formal mechanism for recalling or sacking the Speaker – to protect his independence. By 2008, Speaker Michael Martin was being urged privately by colleagues to resign because of his embroilment in the row over MPs' expenses. However, most MPs refused to criticise him publicly because of his power to decide their right to speak in the chamber. His supporters, however, said that he was being targeted on class lines by Westminster snobs because he was a working-class, Catholic, teetotal Glaswegian with a broad accent. David Cameron blocked a plan by Conservative MPs to table a vote of no confidence in Martin for fear that it would backfire and rally Labour support around him.

Many commentators queried why the issue of MPs' expenses should be examined by MPs themselves rather than by independent outsiders. The MPs whom the Speaker appointed to the review were also were widely ridiculed as Establishment figures who had, themselves, been mired in controversy – including former Conservative chief whip, David Maclean, who used Commons allowances to buy a quad bike for £3,300 to get around his Cumbrian constituency, and whose Private Member's Bill had sought to prevent the Freedom of Information Act being applied to MPs. The review's main recommendation, for external auditing of MPs' expenses, was rejected in a Commons vote.

The major difference between the row over donations and the row over MPs' expenses is that the latter involves public money. Several MPs and media sources have called for the opaque and ill-regulated system of expenses to be scrapped altogether and, instead, for MPs' basic salaries to be raised by £40,000 to £100,000 so that MPs can fund all wider costs directly out of their own pay packets.

MPs and external interests

Many MPs have special personal interests (for example, former Labour MP, Jack Ashley, who is deaf, campaigned on behalf of the handicapped). They are often sponsored by pressure groups to act on their behalf. About one-third of Labour MPs are sponsored by trade unions (for example, Dennis Skinner, a former miner, is sponsored by the National Union of Mineworkers); here, the trade union pays some of the candidate's campaign costs in return for a voice in Parliament where possible. Such financial links are quite legitimate and no money goes into the MPs' own pockets.

Sleaze

Many other MPs are paid personal fees (ranging from £1,000 to £20,000 per year) as consultants or directors by pressure groups, private individuals and companies seeking to promote their own interests. This generated the 'cash for questions' scandal of the 1990s, where Conservative ministers such as Neil Hamilton and Jonathan Aitken tabled parliamentary questions in return for money from outside interests, notably from Harrods' owner Mohamed Al Fayed. Then Prime Minister, John Major, set up a Commission on Standards in Public Life chaired by a senior judge. In 1996 the following rules were agreed:

- MPs must register all outside interests with a Parliamentary Commissioner for Standards (currently Sir Philip Mawer);
- MPs must disclose sources and amounts of outside earnings;
- MPs are forbidden from tabling questions on behalf of outside paying interests and must declare such interests when speaking in debates;
- a Commons Committee on Standards and Privileges has been established to enforce the new rules.

Despite these new constraints, there is still concern about the activities of lobbyists, such as public relations and consultancy firms, and businesses who give financial, research and secretarial support to supposedly independent (informal) all-party, parliamentary groups of MPs (APGs) – nearly 300 of them at Westminster – who investigate controversial policies in which these businesses have a commercial interest. To give just one of many examples, the all-party MPs' group on Identity Fraud, which argued in 2006 that Christmas cards were a target for fraud and should be shredded, was funded by Fellowes, a company that makes shredding machines. Some lobbyists and industries even write policy reports in the name of such APGs – which sometimes like to act as though they have institutional status but which are, in fact, merely intra-parliamentary pressure groups. Lobbyists, as well as charities, are meant to reveal the names of their business clients to the Parliamentary Commissioner for Standards, but this is purely voluntary.

The conduct of some individual MPs has also raised eyebrows. In 2005, Conservative MP, Jonathan Sayeed, was suspended from the House of Commons for two weeks over claims that he was paid for arranging tours around the Palace of Westminster. Although he survived a deselection bid, he was expelled from the Conservative Party and stood down as MP at the general election on grounds of ill-health.

At the end of 2006, many senior Conservatives – including leader David Cameron, his predecessor Michael Howard, Shadow Chancellor George Osborne, policy chief Oliver Letwin, Shadow Trade and Industry Secretary Alan Duncan and a long list of back-benchers – faced an official inquiry by the Parliamentary Standards Commissioner, Sir Philip Mawer, into misuse of parliamentary premises to raise cash to fight marginal seats at the next election. The allegations concerned party patrons' clubs which charged a membership fee in return for access to dinners and private tours in the Commons and Lords. Among the many examples of patrons' clubs are platinum membership of Chester Conservatives – a constituency where Labour has a majority of 915 – which for £500 a year promises 'chances to meet leading party figures in a select environment, plus dinner at the House of Commons with a senior Conservative MP'. Parliamentary rules, however, state that 'The private dining rooms are not to be used for direct financial or material gain by a sponsor, political party, or any other person or outside organisation' and that 'The private dining rooms may not be used as an inducement to recruit new members of outside organisations or non-parliamentary associations'. Conservative peers were also accused of breaching these rules, including Lord Heseltine, the former deputy PM, and Lord Hunt of Wirral, a former cabinet minister. In 2007, Sir Philip Mawer upheld the complaints against Cameron and ten other Conservative MPs. Cameron wrote a letter of apology and no further action was taken.

The use and abuse of parliamentary privilege

Parliamentary privilege (see Chapter 2) is the exemption of MPs from some ordinary laws under the special laws and customs of Parliament. It is, therefore, a special category of constitutional law which breaches 'the rule of law' and principle of legal equality. It was originally a defence against the power of the Crown, and is now justified on the grounds that MPs can better represent the people if, for example, they have complete freedom of speech in the House. Thus, they are immune from slander or libel actions for words spoken in Parliament. This may be used to expose wrongdoing; for example Labour MP, Stuart Bell, used parliamentary privilege to expose the scandal of 'cash for questions' in the 1990s. However, this freedom may be abused by MPs; for example, in 1999, Unionist MP Ian Paisley – who became First Minister of Northern Ireland – named and accused a man of being an IRA killer although the police said that the man was an innocent farmer.

Other privileges, for example, freedom from arrest, may now seem anachronistic or excessive. The right of Parliament to control its own proceedings is, perhaps, quite reasonable, but its right to try and to punish outsiders for 'contempt of Parliament' is controversial.

Another little known privilege, introduced by former PM Harold Wilson in 1966, bans the tapping of MPs' telephones by the secret services: the so-called Wilson Doctrine. It was subsequently widened to cover all forms of communication, including electronic eaves-dropping, and to protect peers as well as MPs. No other legislature in the world – including the devolved assemblies and the European Parliament – has similar arrangements, and the security services have been calling for an end to the ban but then PM Tony Blair upheld it. However, when it was revealed in 2008 that conversations between

Labour MP, Sadiq Khan, and a constituent he was visiting in jail had been secretly recorded, no action was taken because the bugging – apparently routine in prisons – was approved by the police rather than by the secret services or ministers.

. . . .

What you should have learnt from reading this chapter

- This chapter has defined the key concepts of 'democracy' and 'representation' and has sought to assess how far they apply to Westminster's system.

- It has outlined the strengths and weaknesses of first-past-the-post and alternative electoral systems.

- It has assessed the merits and demerits of a party system and analysed five different ways of categorising the UK party system.

- It has highlighted the recent scandals surrounding party funding, the spiralling costs of election campaigning and the conflicting disadvantages of private versus state funding.

- It has then sought to assess how far MPs are representative of – and open with – their voters, whether in terms of social background, party loyalty, pay, expenses or paid interests. There are deficiencies, and current voter opinion is disillusioned, but that may well be because Parliament is now more open, not more corrupt, than before.

- Finally, the chapter has given some examples of the use and abuse of parliamentary privilege, a doctrine which breaches the 'rule of law' and the principle of legal equality.

Glossary of key terms

Adversary politics A period when the two main parties have polarised philosophies and policies.
By-election An election held in a single constituency, for example, when an MP dies.
Consensus politics A period when the two main parties share similar policies, for example, the 1960's economic boom.
Democracy Power of the people, by the people, for the people.
General election Election of the whole House of Commons.
Oligarchy Rule by the few.
Party system Political representation and power on the basis of formal, organised groups of people who put up candidates for election on a common policy programme.

Political equality One person, one vote, one value, and equal access to political office.
Representative democracy A form of indirect democracy reflecting the views, interests and/or typical social background of the electorate.
Safe seat A constituency which one particular party is virtually certain to win regardless of the candidate.
Short money The public grant provided to help opposition parties in the Commons with their parliamentary running costs.

Likely examination questions

Short questions:

- State a case against electoral reform at Westminster.

- Distinguish between a one-party system and a dominant-party system.

- Outline the diverse roles of an MP.

- What factors might explain the low turnouts in recent general elections?

Essay questions:

- Assess the nature of the UK party system.

- To what extent does the principle of political equality apply in Westminster's electoral system?

- How representative is the UK Parliament?

- Would proportional representation produce a more representative and effective Parliament than the first-past-the-post electoral system?

Helpful websites

http://news.bbc.co.uk

http://www.parliament.uk

http://politics.guardian.co.uk/foi

http://politics.guardian.co.uk/commons/comment/0,,1920277,00.html

http://www.hansardsociety.org.uk

Suggestions for further reading

Burall, S. et al., *Not in Our Name: Democracy and Foreign Policy in the UK*, Petersfield: Politico's Media, 2006.

Dale, I. and Fawkes, G., *The Big Red Book of New Labour Sleaze*, Petersfield: Politico's Media, 2007.

Johnston, R. et al., *From Votes to Seats: The Operation of the UK Electoral System Since 1945*, Manchester: Manchester University Press, 2001.

Morton, R., *The Bumper Book of British Sleaze*, London: Foxcote, 2007.

CHAPTER 6

The House of Commons: Scrutinising the Executive

Overview

This chapter outlines the constitutional purposes and procedures of 'parliamentary government', and assesses the reality of Commons control of government through, for example, financial scrutiny, Question Time, select committees and the **Ombudsman**. It evaluates the thesis of 'elective dictatorship' and highlights the limits to effective scrutiny by the Commons.

Key issues to be covered in this chapter

- Parliamentary government
- Scrutiny and control of the executive
- Evaluation of parliamentary control of the executive

Parliamentary government

In 'parliamentary government', the executive (government) is chosen from within the legislature (Parliament) and is, in theory, subordinate and accountable, that is, responsible, to the legislature. Parliament is, therefore, supposed to examine, debate, criticise and check the activities of the government, to publicise executive actions, to convey public opinion to the government and to authorise the raising and spending of money by government through, for example, debates, votes on government Bills, Question Time and committees. The ultimate form of control is a vote of no confidence against the government by the House of Commons, which would oblige the government to resign.

In a parliamentary system ministers should, by convention, be selected from either the Commons or the Lords. (In the American presidential system, by contrast, the executive may be drawn from the ranks of big business, the army, lawyers, academics, state governors, etc. as well as Congress.) However, MPs who see themselves as 'trainee ministers' may do little to control or criticise their own governing party, and ambitious MPs may hesitate to offend their party leaders. The parliamentary system – where MPs are meant to scrutinise and control the government but also provide the pool of future government ministers – thus creates 'role conflict' for many backbenchers. As Labour politician, Aneurin Bevan, once said, 'There are only two ways of getting into the Cabinet. One is to crawl up the staircase of preferment on your belly; the other way is to kick them in the teeth.' The number of iconoclasts – teeth-kickers – who make it to the rank of Cabinet is meagre, and, unless they conform, they rarely last long on the front benches.

Conservative MP, Charles Walker, has recently been quoted as saying: 'Being a minister looks like a rather crappy job, to be honest. We are moving towards a more presidential style of government and being a junior minister for paperclips looks extremely uninteresting.'[1] But there, of course, speaks an Opposition MP.

Scrutiny and control of the executive

Certain parliamentary institutions and procedures have been formalised in the UK constitution to facilitate executive scrutiny.

Her Majesty's Opposition

Her Majesty's Opposition (HMO) is the second largest party in the Commons and is a formal part of the constitution: the leader and whips are paid a special salary; and the Leader of the Opposition is given a chauffeur-driven car. HMO is traditionally consulted on bipartisan matters (for example, the invasion of Iraq) and is given special time and opportunities in Commons procedures which are unavailable to other, smaller parliamentary parties. Twenty Opposition Days are set aside in the Commons' yearly timetable for debate and criticism of government, with the topics chosen by the Opposition on seventeen of those days and by the Liberal Democrats on the other three. In 2008, for example, the Conservatives used an Opposition Day to call for an immediate inquiry into the Iraq war. They lost the vote, though by just twenty-eight, with twelve Labour MPs rebelling.

The role of the Opposition is to oppose, criticise and scrutinise the government. However, the Opposition is clearly weak against a majority government. The Opposition can never defeat a majority government alone and, in Westminster's two-party system, its main role is, therefore, to be the government in waiting, always ready with an alternative set of policies for the electorate to choose. Its formal recognition in the UK constitution epitomises pluralist choice in a liberal democracy.

However, voter choice, and parliamentary scrutiny of the government, are lessened when the Opposition chooses to support government legislation. In 2005, just prior to the general election, the Labour Government struck a deal with the Conservatives to save the Gambling Bill by agreeing to scale down plans from forty super casinos to eight, and then to just one. After the general election, Conservative votes ensured the passing of the government's Education Bill and renewal of the UK's nuclear weapons system despite large Labour backbench rebellions.

Control of finance

Scrutiny and control of the government's raising and spending of public money should be the Commons' most significant check, but 'estimates' of how much money is required by each government department are given only three days per year of parliamentary time, and no Budget item has been defeated since 1910.

The Commons Public Accounts Committee (PAC) and National Audit Office (NAO) – the latter with a staff of around 900 – check £200 billion per year of public money to ensure that it has been lawfully spent. However, the PAC has itself said that Commons control of government finance – 'Parliament's key constitutional function' – is 'largely a formality', because the estimates and accounts provided by Whitehall are both too vague about key financial categories and objectives, and too complex on minor details. The PAC was formed in 1861 and is now the oldest and most authoritative of the parliamentary committees, traditionally chaired by a senior Opposition MP. However, it can only criticise after the event, to little effect; for example, its criticism in 1998 of the underpriced privatisation of the Atomic Energy Authority as 'a staggering waste of public money', and of 'inexcusable mistakes' made in the government's handling of the 2001 £8 billion foot-and-mouth crisis. In 2007 the government simply brushed aside criticism from the NAO that they had undersold the privatisation of defence research firm Qinetiq by 'tens of millions', including an incentive scheme which netted the civil service bosses £100 million in shares. The budgets of the security and intelligence services – an estimated £1,000 million per year – are not subject to parliamentary scrutiny at all. The PAC also often accuses apathetic MPs of simply ignoring their many critical reports about government waste and mismanagement.

Question time and Prime Minister's Question Time

Question time is the noisiest and most publicised part of the Commons' day, and originated in the late nineteenth century. For some it epitomises the government's accountability to Parliament and turns a searchlight upon every corner of the executive; but others query the usefulness of the whole exercise, and it has been described as 'ritualised combat' and 'a Punch and Judy show'.

Prime Minister's Question Time (PMQT) was started by PM Harold Macmillan in 1961. Before then, Prime Ministers sat through questions to other ministers and awaited their own turn on the order paper. Thus, they spent far more time in the Commons and hence, as well as being more in touch with MPs' views and delivering many more Commons speeches, the likes of Gladstone, Balfour and Asquith answered far more parliamentary questions than do recent Prime

Ministers. For example, Gladstone was accustomed to answering questions on about seventy days per session, whereas Wilson, Heath and Thatcher averaged about fifty. In 1997 Blair changed PMQT to once instead of twice a week, without consulting Parliament at all. That said, he changed it from two fifteen-minute slots to one half-hour slot, and there is a case for saying that a longer period of sustained questioning is more challenging than two short slots when questions can be quickly brushed aside.

PMQT is a testing time for all Prime Ministers – Macmillan confessed that he used to feel physically sick before each occasion – but it is increasingly also a very public test of the oratory, confidence and backbench support of the Leader of the Opposition, who, by convention, is allowed to ask many more questions than other MPs. Former Conservative leader Iain Duncan-Smith – the self-professed 'quiet man' – was not a strong performer at PMQT, which partly explained his short duration as party leader.

Other ministers answer questions in the House only about once a month under a rota system. Confident ministers, well briefed by their officials and advisers, can usually deal easily with oral questions by giving combative or evasive answers. Sycophantic questions planted by the whips and asked by docile backbenchers make the process even easier for ministers. As Tony Benn said in 2001, 'Question Time now has so many planted questions, it might as well be called gardeners' question time'.

In 2004, the government was accused of dramatically reducing parliamentary accountability for the NHS when it announced that it would no longer answer questions about foundation hospitals. Foundation status confers a degree of autonomy from Whitehall because foundation hospitals are accountable to a local trust board. Then Health Secretary, John Reid, stated: 'Ministers are no longer in a position to comment on, or provide information about, the detail of operational management within such trusts. Any such questions will be referred to the relevant trust chairman.' Paul Burstow, the Liberal Democrat health spokesman, responded:

> We are talking about the growth of a **quangocracy** where people are placed, not elected, and are not answerable to their local community at the ballot box. It appears from John Reid's statement that they are not even answerable to him. This is all part of ministers

making it harder over time for Parliament to scrutinise the role of government.

Nevertheless, a genuine rottweiler – especially from the minister's own party – can highlight Question Time as a pure form of ministerial accountability, under the media spotlight, which can occasionally make or break ministerial careers.

Other, less public ways in which MPs can ask questions or express grievances include written questions – of which there are about 35,000 per year, at an average administrative cost to the taxpayer of £138 each. Written questions may not guarantee backbenchers their five minutes of fame, but they are often more searching and detailed than oral questions and they often elicit more genuinely useful and informative answers.

Select committees

Departmental select committees, established in 1979 and comprising backbench MPs from all the parliamentary parties, scrutinise each government department's policies, activities and spending. There are currently nineteen, each shadowing the work of a major government department. They generally conduct inquiries on specific departmental issues and publish reports, to which the government must respond. Often colloquially called 'watchdog' committees, they have been called the single most important weapon of increased parliamentary influence in the twentieth century.

The committees are attracting growing media attention: for example, the Treasury Committee's grilling of Northern Rock executives following the bank's near collapse in 2007. Committee members are rarely absent and they are quite independently minded: for example, in 2007 the Public Accounts Committee described the government's failure to get EU subsidies to thousands of farmers as 'a master-class in bad decision making'. They have also been able to extract valuable information from the government: for example, in 1999, the Commons Agriculture Committee strongly rebuked the Agriculture Secretary for hyping £1 million worth of new aid up to '£500 million'. The government has sometimes acted on their recommendations: for example, in 2004 the they took up the Home Affairs Committee's suggestion of more use of electronic tagging and other community sentences to reduce prison overcrowding. In 2001, the

Box 6.1 Departmental Select Committees, 2008

Business, Enterprise and Regulatory Reform
Children, Schools and Families
Communities and Local Government
Culture, Media and Sport
Defence
Environment, Food and Rural Affairs
Environmental Audit
Foreign Affairs
Health
Home Affairs
Innovation, Universities and Skills
International Development
Justice
Northern Ireland Affairs
Scottish Affairs
Transport
Treasury
Welsh Affairs
Work and Pensions

attempted removal by the whips of two feisty Labour select committee chairpeople (Gwyneth Dunwoody on Transport and Donald Anderson on Foreign Affairs) was defeated by the Commons – a rare example of the chamber exerting its will against a high-handed executive. In 2002, then PM Tony Blair agreed that he would henceforth appear twice-yearly before a special Liaison Committee made up of all the chair-people of the select committees. To his credit, he was the first Prime Minister ever to agree to appear before a parliamentary committee.

A mark of the committees' interrogative rigour is that the Financial Services Authority (FSA) has spent tens of thousands of pounds on training its senior officials to field MPs' questions in committee hearings. The Commons Treasury Committee, nevertheless, issued a scathing report in 2008 on the FSA's handling of the Northern Rock crisis, which Conservative spokesman Philip Hammond described as 'probably one of the most damning reports that any select committee has put out in recent times'.

However, the select committees lack the time, resources, staff, expertise, power and, perhaps above all, the will, to be more than an irritant to the government. Often the government simply ignores the criticisms and recommendations of the committees: for example, in 2000 a joint report of four major committees criticised arms sales to Zimbabwe, but it was simply ignored by the government.

When committee MPs grilled Work Secretary, Alan Johnson, in November 2004 about the much criticised Child Support Agency, the minister announced that its chief executive, Doug Smith, had resigned and was being replaced. In fact, he remained in the post until May 2005. A government spokesman said that no date was ever given for Smith's departure. Many observers were left with the impression that the select committee and the Commons had been misled in order to take the pressure off the Work Secretary and shift attention and blame elsewhere.

In 2007, the Public Administration Committee called for the civil service to be monitored by a new watchdog body – a National Performance Office similar to the National Audit Office – to remedy 'a lack of leadership and serious deficiencies on service delivery'. There was no immediate response from the government at all.

Departmental select committees cannot order the attendance of a member of either House – an interesting example of the paradoxes of parliamentary sovereignty. A committee cannot, therefore, insist on ministers attending its hearings. In 2000, Blair refused to attend – and refused to allow his chief of staff/spin doctor, Jonathan Powell, to attend – the Public Administration Committee to justify the increase in special political advisers in Downing Street. The government explicitly rejected suggestions from the Liaison Committee in 2002 for strengthening the committees' powers. Proposals to grant extra pay for committee chairs were passed (currently £13,000 per year), but attempts to wrest control of membership away from the whips were defeated.

Moreover, the balance of party power on the committees reflects that of the Commons as a whole, so backbenchers of the governing party are usually in a majority on the committees, and most government backbenchers, of course, want to be frontbenchers and may, therefore, be unwilling to be too critical:

> I was once, briefly, an adviser to a House of Commons select committee. It was a well-mannered, genteel body that would not hurt a fly. Each session was preceded by half an hour 'in camera' discussing

the next overseas trip, preferably somewhere warm. Whips sat at the back to see that no MP rocked any boat. The deal was simple.[2]

Parliament's Intelligence and Security Committee, in particular, has been criticised as a toothless watchdog. Its members are 'hand-picked by the Prime Minister' and its reports are comprehensively censored. For example, a 2008 report said that MI6 is:

> engaged in a range of counter-terrorism work; direct pursuit of terrorists, ***, capacity-building with key countries and – this is an absolutely vital point – ***. ***. ***. So put like that and defined like that, this takes up about 56% of our effort . . . and it is rising.[3]

Some staunch parliamentarians fear that the committees may detract from the work of the House as a whole, that MPs serving on them may become too specialised and narrow in outlook and interests, and that – since the committees are established for a whole parliamentary term – they might become too cosy with the department which they are scrutinising.

In sum, most commentators agree that the select committees have done little to shift the real balance of power between executive and legislature, though they do have influence and provide information, detailed scrutiny and public criticism of the government. Reformers say that they need bigger budgets, stronger powers and more capacity to conduct research, initiate debates and interrogate ministers and civil servants more rigorously. Such solutions lie largely in the committees' own hands.

The Ombudsman

This is a parliamentary bureaucrat, that is, a non-elected, non-political official, whose job is to investigate public complaints about government maladministration, but who, again, lacks power and resources.

In 2004, for example, the Liberal Democrats pressed the Foreign Office (FCO) to reveal the date on which it first sought legal advice on the invasion of Iraq. The FCO refused the request on the grounds that releasing the information would 'harm the frankness' of private talks. The Liberal Democrats complained to the Ombudsman, who rejected the FCO's reasoning and recommended that the information be released. The FCO simply refused.

The current Ombudsman, Ann Abraham, has recently threatened to resign because the government is still too secretive and it has also banned her investigations of ministerial conflicts of interest: for example, former PM Blair's private gifts from foreign leaders.

In 2006, she called upon the government to compensate 85,000 people who had lost some or all of their company pensions due, in part, to 'inaccurate, incomplete, unclear and inconsistent' government advice. Again, the government rejected her recommendations. However, in 2007, the High Court upheld the Ombudsman's finding. The courts are usually more robust constraints against government impropriety (see Chapter 9) than is Parliament, regardless of the theoretical doctrine of parliamentary sovereignty.

Impeachment
In 2004 a small group of MPs used age-old parliamentary powers in an attempt to impeach PM Tony Blair for misleading the public over the invasion of Iraq. This power can be used for 'high crimes and misdemeanours beyond the reach of the law or which no other authority of the state will prosecute'. Last used in 1806, it could, in unlikely theory, see Blair charged with improper conduct in office.

Blair is potentially charged with:

* misleading Parliament and the country over Iraq;
* negligence and incompetence over weapons of mass destruction;
* undermining the constitution;
* entering into a secret agreement with the US President.

Blair has acknowledged that there were 'intelligence errors' in the run-up to the invasion of Iraq, but denies misleading people.

Most of the MPs backing the impeachment campaign (see website reference at the end of this chapter) are Welsh and Scottish nationalists, but supporters include Conservate Mayor of London and former MP, Boris Johnson. In practice, it has little chance of success. As a parliamentary committee said in 1999: 'The circumstances in which impeachment has taken place are now so remote from the present that the procedure may be considered obsolete'. Lord Norton of Louth, Professor of Government at Hull University (a constitutional expert and self-confessed Conservative), said, 'It is still on the books so it's open technically for the Commons to vote for impeachment'.

He concluded, however, that it is more a way of highlighting an issue than of seriously pursuing a legal case.

Evaluation of parliamentary control of the executive

Some commentators argue that the task of Parliament is simply to scrutinise and sustain the government rather than to 'control' it. However, most say that, in the UK system of parliamentary government, Parliament should control the government but usually cannot, for the following reasons:

- majority governments;
- party discipline;
- government control of parliamentary time;
- government secrecy and obfuscation, especially on finance;
- government control of civil service personnel and information;
- the growth of delegated legislation;
- the lack of power of parliamentary committees and the Ombudsman;
- lack of resources and facilities for MPs;
- the weakness of the non-elected House of Lords;
- the growing influence on government of extra-parliamentary bodies such as the EU, business, pressure groups and the media.

For all of these reasons, but, above all, because of the power of a majority government in control of a sovereign Parliament with a flexible constitution, Lord Hailsham's phrase 'elective dictatorship' is often used to describe the UK system of government where the executive can almost always win its way in Parliament.

Frustration is often demonstrated by low parliamentary attendance of MPs. Another outlet for MPs' frustration is rowdiness in the chamber. Lively debate may be seen as a legitimate tradition of the House, but for some commentators, MPs' 'bad' behaviour is a symptom of the crisis of legitimacy developing in an unrepresentative, adversarial, executive-dominated House of Commons where the parliamentary process is slowly breaking down.

The reasons for executive dominance of the Commons are summarised below.

Majority

The nature of party government varies according to the balance of representation in the House of Commons, the attitude of MPs, the personalities and character of the Prime Minister and his ministerial colleagues, the actual and perceived roles of the party organisations, the attitudes of party supporters and their relationship with the leadership, and, by no means least, the prevailing political, economic and social situation at home and abroad.[4]

The decade after 1997 was characterised by exceptionally large government majorities in the Commons, an unusually dominant Prime Minister, an increasingly constrained Labour Party organisation and a stable economy which gave voters little cause for profound discontent. Hence, for example, the comment of the Power Inquiry (2006) into the state of UK democracy that 'The executive is now more powerful than since the time of Walpole'; and Labour Lord Hattersley's comment that current Labour backbenchers are 'the most supine MPs in UK history'.

Party

The key factor underpinning the increasing dominance of the executive since the nineteenth century has been the growth of party discipline, and MPs' increasing willingness to accept it. This is not to say that MPs are always, or even usually, spineless 'lobby fodder' or impotent victims of bullying whips. They have a strong and often long-standing ideological commitment to their party, and they owe it everything for their campaigning and electoral successes. There is a powerful bond of natural loyalty between MPs and their parties, and a profound belief that their party is the best for the country and that the Opposition would be ruinous. Rebellion hurts – it is unnatural, disloyal and painful. For MPs to revolt in sufficient numbers to bring down the governing party is virtually unthinkable. No majority government has been brought down by a backbench revolt since the 1880s.

Hence, whenever ministers want to distance themselves from a difficult or unpopular decision, they can simply say, 'It is for Parliament to decide'. It is, therefore, often argued that parliamentary sovereignty is usually, in reality, executive sovereignty; or that 'the contradiction at the heart of the UK constitution is the principle of parliamentary sovereignty being used by executives to minimise their accountability',[5] that is, being used as a legitimising cloak for executive power. One example of this occurred in 1992 when the then Conservative Government refused a public referendum on the Maastricht Treaty on the grounds that: 'The UK system is a parliamentary democracy: the government are accountable to Parliament and Parliament is accountable to the electorate . . . The government believes that is the right way to proceed in a parliamentary democracy.'[6]

Only three times in the twentieth century was a government Bill defeated in the House of Commons, and on only one of those occasions did the government have a majority: the Shops Bill 1986, which was intended to allow shops and other businesses to open on a Sunday. The Bill was defeated by an 'unholy alliance' of Labour trade unionists and a then record backbench revolt by Conservative traditionalists who, for very different reasons, wanted to prevent widespread Sunday trading. (Sunday shopping was eventually legalised in 1994 under pressure from the free trade EU.)

That said, Lord Hattersley's comment above was simply wrong. The scale of rebellions in the 2001–5 Parliament was the highest since 1945. The government remained undefeated until 2006 only because of its huge majorities. Early in 2005, on the draconian Prevention of Terrorism Bill, the government saw its 161-strong majority cut to just fourteen on a cross-party amendment to force the Home Secretary to apply to a court before being able to impose control orders. While the whips could clearly see that the government would not get the Bill through without big concessions, and while the Home Secretary was prepared to compromise, Blair's advisers were saying that he would not countenance compromise. However, he had to eventually. As one unnamed friend and senior minister said of this episode, 'He does not quite get Parliament'. In 2007, when the House of Commons held its first debate on Iraq for four years, Blair simply left the chamber – demonstrating his 'contempt of Parliament' according to critics. Later that year, he strained the loyalty of his MPs almost to the limit with the introduction of top-up tuition fees – explicitly renounced in the previous party manifesto – when his majority fell from over 160 to just five. Blair voted in only 5 per cent of Commons' divisions from 1997 to 2007 – a record low. His rare attendance in the House reduced his personal contact with MPs and his ability to sense the

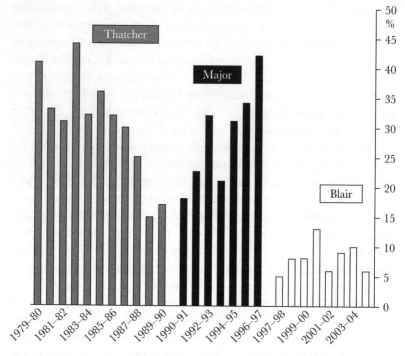

Source: *The Times*, 2 February 2006.

Figure 6.1 Graph of PMs' Commons voting records since 1979

mood of his own backbenchers: 'I've never pretended to be a House of Commons man' he admitted to nobody's surprise during his farewell performance at PMQT.

Since the 2005 General Election, the government has been defeated outright four times in the Commons despite a majority of over sixty: a historic first.

Government defeats in the Commons since 2005

First, in the Terrorism Bill 2005 the government sought to allow ninety days' detention of terror suspects without charge. Anticipating his defeat, Blair was defiant. He told the Commons that it was better to be right and lose, than to be wrong and win: he lost. MPs reduced the ninety days to twenty-eight days.

The second and third defeats came in the Racial and Religious

Hatred Bill 2006: MPs accepted the Lords amendments to the effect that a new criminal offence of incitement to religious hatred would require both 'intent and threat'; mere 'abuse, ridicule or insults' were excluded. On the second vote the government was defeated by just one vote: Blair had left the chamber. His Chief Whip, Hilary Armstrong, was deemed to have badly miscalculated the likely votes, and she lost her job in the next reshuffle. National Secular Society director, Keith Porteous Wood, said that these government defeats were 'the best news on freedom of speech for decades. Given we had to have this bill because it was a Labour manifesto commitment, having the Lords amendments agreed in full was more than freedom of speech campaigners dared hope for.'

In the fourth defeat, also in 2006, a rarely-used parliamentary mechanism forced Home Office ministers to go to the Commons to defend the government's extradition treaty with the United States, which many critics perceived as unbalanced and unfair. Speaker Michael Martin allowed an emergency debate on the case of the 'NatWest Three', where three former NatWest bankers were extradited to America to answer fraud charges relating to the collapse of the energy company Enron. MPs engineered a symbolic vote – technically on the adjournment of the House – to register their opposition to the treaty. The motion passed and the House adjourned. In other words, MPs effectively went on strike for the rest of the day, as the only method available to them to vote against this controversial government policy.

The government has also had to retreat at least partially on some measures, such as ID cards and the smoking ban, to avoid defeat, and won certain other measures, such as the Education Bill and the decision to renew the UK's nuclear weapons capability, only thanks to the backing of the Conservative Party.

Moreover, there were over sixty defeats of the government by the Lords in the 2005–6 Parliament, ten times more than in 1995–6. Since 1997, there have been around 400 amendments or defeats of government Bills in the Lords, of which 40 per cent have been accepted by the Commons and government.

Convention
The behaviour of some Conservative ministers in the governments of the 1990s, and their refusal to take responsibility for error and

wrongdoing, was one of the reasons why the voters rejected them so decisively and for so long. One notable example was Home Secretary, Michael Howard, who made a novel distinction between 'policy' and 'operational' responsibilities and sacked top civil servant Derek Lewis, rather than resigning himself over a series of prison crises. The 'new' Labour Government, therefore, came to power in 1997 apparently determined to be seen as open and accountable. Both Houses passed an identical resolution in that year, stating that ministers have a duty to account, and to be held to account, for the policies, decisions and actions of their governments. It was of paramount importance that they gave truthful and accurate information to Parliament. Inadvertent errors should be corrected as soon as possible and, should ministers knowingly mislead Parliament, they would be expected to resign.

However, there is always a fine line between being 'economical with the actualité' (as former minister Alan Clark famously admitted) and deliberately misleading Parliament. Moreover, the phrase 'ministers must not *knowingly* mislead Parliament' is a recent modification of the convention of individual ministerial responsibility (introduced by PM John Major) and is a crucial get-out clause, allowing ministers to blame civil servants for not telling them all of the facts. Under Blair's Government, Lord Falconer passed the blame for the Dome fiasco to civil servant Jennie Page, Defence Secretary Geoff Hoon blamed his officials for not telling him about reports of prisoner abuse in Iraq and Commons Leader, Peter Hain, blamed police operations rather than policy decisions for the breach of Big Ben's security by Greenpeace protesters in 2004. They all, therefore, successfully resisted pressures to resign. This is, arguably, unconstitutional.

The defects of procedures were demonstrated by the Budd Inquiry into the Blunkett/Quinn nanny's visa affair (when, in 2004, Home Secretary, David Blunkett, misused his office to grant a visa to his lover's nanny) and misuse of parliamentary allowances. The arrangements were hasty and haphazard and the inquiry was set up by Blunkett's Permanent Secretary himself, with narrow terms of reference and limited powers to compel full and honest answers from officials. Blunkett did, very reluctantly, resign, but remained in his £3 million official residence in Belgravia and was promptly, if briefly, reappointed to the Cabinet after the 2005 election.

In 2006, Blair partially heeded the recommendations of the Committee on Standards in Public Life and appointed Sir John Bourn (head of the National Audit Office) to advise him and ministers on potential conflicts of interest and clashes between ministers' public duties and private affairs and to investigate any claims that the rules may have been broken. Before Sir John's appointment, top civil servants in each government department had advised ministers about conflicts of interest and the Cabinet Secretary investigated possible breaches of the ministerial code. However, Sir Alistair Graham, chairman of the Committee on Standards in Public Life, said that this new appointment was inadequate, stating that:

> He [Sir John] has hardly any discretion to intervene on his own initiative – he has to wait until he is be asked to intervene by the Prime Minister – and there is no guarantee that any report he produces will be published. The government has not given an assurance that when Sir John is replaced there will be consultation with the opposition.[7]

When, later that year, there were scandals involving Deputy Prime Minister, John Prescott – first over his affair with one of his secretaries, then over him playing croquet with his officials at his grace and favour mansion Dorneywood, then over his visit to the American ranch of a billionaire businessman who had bought the Millennium Dome – Sir John Bourn was not asked to investigate whether Prescott had broken the ministerial code of conduct. This was because, said Number 10, 'he is the Prime Minister's independent adviser on ministers' *financial* interests' – a much narrower remit than had previously been implied. In any event, the ultimate decision on whether a minister should resign still rests – as it always did – with the Prime Minister. John Prescott did not resign.

Ironically, Bourn was himself informally criticised in 2007 for making forty-three foreign visits over the previous three years (twenty-two of them accompanied by his wife), to locations such as Mauritius, Ghana, India, Brazil and the Bahamas, at a cost to the taxpayer of £336,000. The details were only released after a freedom of information request by *Private Eye* magazine. He announced his retirement in that same year.

Secrecy

Secrecy remains a potent government weapon, despite the new Freedom of Information Act, which came into force on 1 January 2005. Whitehall promptly blocked an academic freedom of information request about the workings of the Freedom of Information Act itself. The civil service response (which took five months) was: 'Releasing information which would allow analysis of policy decisions affecting the operation of the Act would of itself be detrimental to the Act's operation because it may reveal sensitivities.'[8]

Thirty-three junior civil servants were given the task of handling appeals against refusals to disclose documents. By late 2005, they already faced a backlog of 1,200 cases which, at their current work rate, will take eight years to clear.

Summary

At the end of 2004 Lord Butler – former head of the civil service under Thatcher, Major and Blair – gave an interview to *The Spectator* magazine in which he was sharply critical of the way Blair's Government had operated:

> I think we are a country where we suffer very badly from Parliament not having sufficient control over the executive, and that is a very grave flaw. We should be breaking away from the party whip. The executive is much too free to bring in a huge number of extremely bad bills, a huge amount of regulation and to do whatever it likes – and whatever it likes is what will get the best headlines tomorrow. All that is a part of what is bad government in this country.[9]

Given Butler's status as the former top UK civil servant, the BBC's Andrew Marr called this 'a red card from God'.

Example of 'bad Bills'?

The Civil Contingencies Act 2004 (CCA) gives the government the power to suspend or repeal any Act of Parliament after a state of emergency has been declared – including core rights such as the Habeas Corpus Act 1816 and the Parliament Act 1911, which limits the duration of a Parliament to five years. In other words, this innocuous sounding law allows the government of the day to nullify most of the rights and freedoms of UK citizens in the event of a past, present or possible future 'emergency' – which may include not only terrorist threats and natural disasters such as storms, floods and droughts but also the fuel protests in 2000, foot-and-mouth in 2001 and 2007, bird flu and other potential epidemics, internet hacking, oil-spills, chemical leaks and domestic or international conflict, including strikes.

By executive decree, the CCA allows the requisition, confiscation or destruction of property, the shutting down of businesses, the suspension of Parliament, the prohibition or required movement of people, the prevention of assemblies, the prevention of travel, the deployment of the Army, longer periods of pre-charge detention and the creation of special courts. These powers are not purely hypothetical. The United Kingdom has, in fact, been in a 'designated state of public emergency in regard to international terrorism' (Home Office, 2003) since 9 September 2001.

There are some limitations on the scope of these powers: they can last no longer than thirty days, although they can be renewed at any time; and they can be challenged in the courts through the normal process. As the powers were made by secondary legislation they can, in theory, be struck down by the courts.

PM Gordon Brown in 2007 announced his intention to legislate to extend the twenty-eight-day period of detention for terror suspects. This was surprising for two reasons: first, it was the subject of an ignominious Commons defeat in 2005; and secondly, as Shadow Home Secretary, David Davis, pointed out, emergency powers in the CCA already allowed for an extension of pre-charge detention periods and, therefore, no new legislation was necessary.

The Inquiries Act 2005, which regulates the terms of judicial inquiries including those into the conduct and actions of government, slipped through Parliament on the last day before its dissolution in 2005. The Act gives the government the power to authorise any such inquiry and its terms of reference without parliamentary scrutiny, to decide whether it will be held in private, to bar disclosure of any evidence to the public and to dictate the content and publication of any final report. Amnesty International has urged judges to boycott any such inquiries, describing them as a sham. The Commons Public Administration Committee had urged, instead, the creation of a new

Parliamentary Commission of Inquiry, and also that ministerial decisions on setting up inquiries should be on the basis of published cri-
teria. The government rejected these recommendations out of
hand.

On the eve of the 2007 summer recess (under Gordon Brown's
new premiership) the government issued more than one hundred
parliamentary statements on subjects such as the use of Menwith Hill
RAF base for a US ballistic missile system, failings of the Child
Support Agency, the cost of ministerial cars, the role of the Attorney
General and the guest list at Chequers. The opposition said that the
timing gave MPs no opportunity to assimilate the information and to
question ministers. Shadow Commons leader, Theresa May, said that
this demonstrated the government's continuing 'disdain' for
Parliament. The Campaign for Nuclear Disarmament said that the
announcement about Menwith Hill was 'outrageous' and showed
'total contempt for democracy and consultation'.

· ·

✔ What you should have learnt from reading this chapter

- This chapter has outlined the constitutional theory of parliamentary
  scrutiny of government and has analysed the many institutions and
  procedures available to the Commons for executive scrutiny,
  including Her Majesty's Opposition, the Public Accounts
  Committee and National Audit Office, Question Time, Departmental
  select committees, the Ombudsman and the process of
  impeachment.

- It has found them all wanting because MPs lack the resources,
  time, power and, perhaps above all, the will to do the job very
  effectively.

- The main structural reasons for executive dominance of the Commons
  are the sheer voting arithmetic in the House combined with genuine
  party loyalty and enforced party discipline, the weaknesses of the
  doctrines of ministerial responsibility and the ongoing ethos of official
  secrecy (notwithstanding the impact of the Freedom of Information
  Act).

Glossary of key terms

Departmental select committees All-party committees of backbench MPs whose task is to scrutinise the activities of government departments and issues of public interest.

Impeachment A formal process for removing from office a politician for wrongdoing.

Quangocracy 'Rule by' quasi-autonomous non-governmental organisations, that is, bodies appointed by government but not a formal part of government, and meant to be impartial, to perform some administrative or regulatory function.

Ombudsman An official of Parliament who investigates public complaints of government maladministration.

Likely examination questions

Short questions:

- Define the concept of 'parliamentary government'.

- Outline three ways in which Parliament performs its function of scrutiny.

- Describe the role of Commons select committees.

- Suggest reasons for Parliament's limited control of the executive.

Essay questions:

- Is Parliament anything more than a 'rubber stamp' for executive policies?

- Assess the relationship between the office of Prime Minister and Parliament.

- Has the two-party system ceased to function effectively?

- How could government be made more accountable to Parliament?

Helpful websites

http://news.bbc.co.uk

http://www.parliament.uk

http://www.inthenews.co.uk/news/politics

http://www.number-10.gov.uk/output/Page1.asp

http://www.impeachblair.org

Suggestions for further reading

Budge, I. et al., *The New British Politics*, London: Longman, 2007.

Lord Hailsham, 'Elective Dictatorship', *The Listener*, 21 October 1976.

Jones, B. et al., *Politics UK*, London: Longman, 2006.

Judge, D., *Political Institutions in the United Kingdom*, Oxford: Oxford University Press, 2005.

CHAPTER 7

Parliament and the European Union

Overview

This chapter explains the developing relationship between the United Kingdom and the European Union since the 1960s, analyses the growing impact of EU membership upon the legal sovereignty and wider roles of Parliament, and considers possible future developments.

Key issues to be covered in this chapter

- The United Kingdom and the European Union
- The changing relationship of the United Kingdom and the European Union
- The issue of sovereignty
- The European Parliament
- The European Court of Justice (ECJ)
- Parliament and the European Union
- A European Union constitution?
- The impact of the European Union on UK political parties
- The European Union and Westminster: future challenges

The United Kingdom and the European Union

The then European Economic Community (EEC) was first formed in 1957, by just six countries: France, Germany, Italy, Luxembourg, the Netherlands and Belgium. The United Kingdom, Denmark and Ireland joined in 1973; Greece joined in 1981; Spain and Portugal joined in 1986; then Finland, Sweden and Austria in 1995. Norway had also planned to join in 1995 but its voters rejected membership in a referendum. Ten more (mostly former communist) states joined in 2004: Cyprus, the Czech Republic, Estonia, Hungary, Latvia, Lithuania, Malta, Poland, Slovakia and Slovenia. Bulgaria and Romania joined in 2007. There are now twenty-seven member states in total (490 million people).

The original creation of the EEC was intended to establish a common free market, economic and monetary union and 'an ever closer union among the peoples of Europe'. Thus, the visions of a single market and a federal Europe date from the 1950s (not from the 1980s or 1990s, as is sometimes suggested today). These goals were inspired by a desire for lasting peace and security after two world wars in Europe; awareness of growing economic and social interdependence and a desire for greater international co-operation between European countries; the advantages of large-scale markets; greater world influence; and the wish to challenge the blocs of the United States and the then USSR.

The main economic principle enshrined in the 1957 Treaty of Rome was free trade, that is, the removal of barriers and the establishment of common tariffs and policies (especially in agriculture, fishing, coal and steel) across Europe.

In 1967, the EEC became the European Community (EC). When the Maastricht Treaty came into effect in 1993, this institution became the European Union (EU). The changing labels are clearly illustrative of the broadening and increasingly integrated embrace of the EU.

The EU is a supranational institution, that is, not just an intergovernmental fraternity, but a sovereign power over member states with a body of law that takes precedence over national law.

The changing relationship of the United Kingdom and the European Union

The UK initially refused to join the EEC in the 1950s for a number of reasons: a sense of superiority and national pride after victory in war; a hankering after lost imperial status; the United Kingdom's international status and links with the United States and the Commonwealth; a sense of political and geographical difference – an island mentality, xenophobia (and mistrust especially of Germany and France); for the right wing of the Conservative Party especially, fear of loss of sovereignty and 'national' identity; and for the left wing of the Labour Party, dislike of the free market capitalist nature of the EEC. By the 1960s, however, it was clear that the EEC was an established success. The United Kingdom applied to join the EEC in 1961 but French President Charles de Gaulle vetoed UK membership, saying that the UK government lacked a clear commitment to European integration.

The United Kingdom eventually joined in 1973, under Ted Heath's Conservative Government. When the Labour Party came to power in 1974 they were very divided on the issue, so Prime Minister Harold Wilson held the first (and, so far, only) national referendum in 1975 on the question of staying in the EC. He lifted 'collective responsibility' and allowed his dissident left-wing Cabinet ministers (such as Tony Benn) publicly to divide on the issue. Two-thirds of the UK electorate voted to stay in Europe, thus legitimising Wilson's own support for the EC. At that time all the main UK parties and press were pro-European, so the solidly favourable referendum vote was to be expected.

UK elections to the European Parliament were first held in 1979. Until then all members of the European Parliament were also members of their national legislatures, but since the introduction of direct elections this is much less common.

The issue of sovereignty

'Sovereignty' means the legitimate location of power of last resort over any community. It may be defined purely in legal terms as the power to make binding laws which no other body can set aside or overrule. It may also be viewed as the autonomous power of a community to govern itself – a territorial concept relating to the powers of independent nation-states. The question of sovereignty is multi-dimensional.

The main issue since 1973 has been Parliament's 'legal sovereignty', which has been effectively negated (overruled) by the primacy of EU laws and treaties. Even on entry in 1973, the UK Parliament had to accept forty-three volumes of existing EU legislation. This loss of sovereignty to Europe has since increased, with the growing scope of European intervention and with reforms of European voting procedures. The most important reform was the change from unanimous voting in the EU Council of Ministers – that is, any one country could effectively veto any policy – to **Qualified Majority Voting** (QMV), under the Single European Act 1986 (introduced, ironically, by the eurosceptic Conservative PM Margaret Thatcher) – where several countries must now band together to veto a policy on a growing range of issues. For example, in 2008, contrary to the UK Labour government's wishes, an EU directive gave temporary workers the same employment rights as permanent workers.

Over 50 per cent of UK legislation now originates from the EU. No other continental country has (or had) parliamentary sovereignty, because they all have written constitutions and supreme courts; therefore, this issue matters more to the United Kingdom. However, observers might be forgiven for being sceptical about UK governments' expressed concerns about the loss of sovereignty to Europe, since the 'elective dictatorships' of some recent UK governments have done more than Europe ever has to undermine Westminster's real power, from within.

UK governments are generally more concerned about their own loss of 'national sovereignty', that is, their ability to pursue their own policies without external interference. From another perspective, however, the primacy of EU law has curbed the dangers of 'elective dictatorship' of a single-party majority UK government within a 'sovereign' Parliament with no codified constitution. The European Court of Justice (ECJ) has protected many civil liberties of UK citizens against UK law, for example, in relation to retirement ages, workers' hours and holiday entitlements, food and water standards and pension rights of part-time workers.

'Economic sovereignty' has become an important issue especially with the creation of the single European currency (euro). However, this has actually long been undermined in the United Kingdom by foreign ownership of businesses and industries, and especially by the United Kingdom's dependence on the health of the American economy – apparently with little hostility from the traditional right-wing eurosceptics. Moreover, the Labour Government's granting to the Bank of England of independent control of interest rates (immediately after the 1997 General Election) was a willing surrender of a key economic power which brought the United Kingdom into line with one of the conditions for joining the euro.

The euro was introduced in 2002, abolishing some traditional European currencies such as the French franc, although several EU member states – including the United Kingdom – have opted out of it. The post-1997 Labour Government was initially supportive but then Chancellor Gordon Brown set five economic tests (on issues such as the impact on jobs, financial services and foreign investment) as preconditions of joining the euro, subject to a referendum. Political interest in joining the euro has since waned in the United Kingdom – not least because a rather eurosceptic British public would most likely vote 'no'.

The 'political sovereignty' of the electorate has, arguably, been undermined by the 'democratic deficit' created by the EU: namely, that the only directly elected EU institution – the EU Parliament – is also the weakest. However, the EU Parliament is rapidly gaining political strength; it has given UK voters an added tier of democratic representation (via pure PR); and the issue of Europe did set the precedent, in the United Kingdom, for the holding of referenda on major constitutional issues.

A more positive view of EU membership argues that national governments benefit from pooling sovereignty to achieve policy goals which would be unattainable alone; and that EU decision making even helps to strengthen national governments by reducing the impact of domestic constraints.

The European Parliament

Elections to the EU Parliament are held every five years and member states have seats in proportion to their population sizes, ranging from

Germany with ninety-nine down to Malta with five. In 2008 the United Kingdom had seventy-eight of the 785 MEPs across twelve electoral regions, although it needs to cut this number to seventy-two by the 2009 EU elections to accommodate new EU member states. The Electoral Commission's recommendations would involve Scotland losing one of its seven MEPs, but the new SNP executive in Scotland has made vigorous protest against this.

The European Parliament is the only directly elected international assembly in the world. Though initially weak, its powers have been steadily increased over the last three decades. Although it is not a legislating body in the same way that the UK Parliament is, it examines draft legislation in committees and consults with the EU Commission and Council of Ministers. Most EU legislation now needs the approval of both the EU Parliament and the Council of Ministers before it becomes law. The Parliament also has the power to sack the Commission, it holds hearings on new commissioners and it has the last word on about half of the spending in the EU annual budget (which was €129 billion in 2008).

However, it has been widely criticised as a 'travelling circus' which is obliged by treaty to move between Brussels and Strasbourg on a monthly basis at an annual cost of £200 million. Many UK voters apparently regard the monthly parliamentary visit to Strasbourg as a money-wasting junket hugely enjoyed by MEPs, journalists and researchers. In fact, says BBC correspondent Mark Mardell, it is a money-wasting junket loathed by MEPs, journalists and researchers who complain about miserable journeys, lost luggage and pointless debates:

> This is not only a colossal waste of time and money, but also undermines the EU's hard work to tackle climate change, as the monthly move is producing 20,000 tons of carbon dioxide, the equivalent of 13,000 transatlantic round-trip flights.[1]

These criticisms were intensified by revelations in 2006 that the rent for the Strasbourg building had been overcharged by over £100 million since 1979. This scandal was particularly embarrassing for an institution which prides itself on being the watchdog against financial wrongdoing in the EU. However, Strasbourg is a powerful symbol of Franco-German reconciliation, and the parliamentary visits are a

Table 7.1 EU Parliament costs, 2008	
Annual budget of EU Parliament	€1.3 billion
Paid to Italian MEPs (the top earners)	€134,291
Paid to UK MEPs (the fifth-highest earners)	€87,358
Paid to Bulgarian MEPs (the lowest earners)	€9,276
MEPs' annual staff allowance	€185,952
MEPs' annual office allowance	€47,352

lucrative source of income for the city, so it is unlikely that the travelling road show will cease in the foreseeable future.

Just like the Westminster Parliament, the EU Parliament was, in 2008, mired in controversy about widespread misuse of expenses. One MEP paid a Christmas bonus to an assistant which was worth nineteen times his salary, several others set up arm's-length companies to pay bogus staff, about a third employ family members and many were filmed signing in to collect their daily allowance and then promptly leaving. MEPs voted to keep the auditor's report secret, but it was leaked by Liberal Democrat MEP Chris Davies. Austrian MEP Hans-Peter Martin said, 'This Parliament is a paradise of unjustified privileges and possibilities for real cheats. It is a central problem for democracy and credibility in Europe.[2]

The European Court of Justice

The European Court of Justice (ECJ) comprises judges appointed by member states for six-year renewable terms, and is based in Luxembourg. It interprets and enforces EU law, which takes precedence over national law. Its decisions are binding on EU institutions and member states. Courts in the United Kingdom are obliged to refuse to enforce Acts of Parliament which contravene European law.

This principle was established by the 1991 *Factortame* case about fishing rights in UK waters. Following the Icelandic cod war in the

1970s, Spanish fishing companies started buying UK-registered ships. In 1988, Westminster passed the Merchant Shipping Act, preventing the Spanish-owned ships from fishing under UK quotas. However, three years later the ECJ overturned the UK legislation, and also ruled that member states must pay compensation where a breach of European law was deemed sufficiently serious. In 1999, the Law Lords ruled that Britain would have to pay compensation estimated at £100 million to almost 100 Spanish fishing companies – including one called Factortame – whose ships were laid up from 1988 to 1991. The British judges said that, although the government's intention was to protect British fishing communities, the effect was to discriminate against Spanish nationals, thereby flouting one of the most basic principles of European law; and that the UK government had deliberately decided to run the risk of introducing the legislation, knowing that it could be unlawful.

Big fines can also be imposed for non-compliance with the ECJ's rulings. For example, when the EU's worldwide ban on the export of UK beef (over BSE) was lifted in 1999, France continued to ban imports of UK beef until 2002 when it was threatened with a daily fine of £100,000 by the ECJ.

EU decision making: a summary

At its simplest, EU decision making can be summarised as follows: the Commission makes a proposal; the Parliament offers its opinion and agreement; the Council of Ministers makes a decision; the ECJ interprets and enforces the decision; the member countries administer the decision.

Parliament and the European Union

Both Houses of the UK Parliament have established committees to scrutinise European legislation. The Lords EU Committee was established in 1974 and has wide terms of reference to scrutinise draft EU legislation, Commission proposals and EU policies. It can recommend a debate in the House on issues of sufficient importance. Its remit is wider than that of its Commons counterpart, and its prestige is probably higher.

One example is a report from the Lords EU Committee which said that the European Union should scrap the mechanism which sees it raise 15 per cent of its total funding from the VAT collected by member states, because the system is bureaucratic, confusing and costly. The system should, instead, be merged into the current main method of funding the EU, which sees national contributions based on a state's gross national income. The committee said that this would be both fairer and more easily understood by citizens. Peers also ruled out any move to introduce direct EU taxation of citizens.

In the Commons there is a dual system of standing and select committees for the scrutiny of EU legislation. The European Scrutiny Committee (ESC) is the most important body. It is an all-party select committee which can require submission of written evidence, examine witnesses, obtain specialist advice and ask other select committees for their opinions on a document. There are sixteen committee members with a quorum of five. The committee has a staff of fourteen. The Commons and Lords committees complement one another and there is close co-ordination between them. They have powers to confer and to meet concurrently in certain circumstances, but these powers are rarely exercised formally.

The ESC scrutinises about 900 EU documents every year, with those which are deemed sufficiently important (between fifty and seventy per year) being referred to a European Standing Committee, established since 1990. Ministers attend these meetings, whose resolutions and motions are reported to the Commons and occasionally debated there. The aim of this scrutiny process is to influence the relevant minister before he or she attends the European Council of Ministers. However, as usual, the parliamentary committees lack the power to control ministerial decisions. Also, as Peter Riddell points out: 'These scrutiny committees remain outside the political mainstream; their public meetings and frequent reports are largely ignored by fellow MPs and the press.'[3]

Ministers can also be held accountable for EU matters through debates and questions in both the Commons and the Lords, through ministerial statements after important meetings of the Council of Ministers and through the relevant departmental select committees.

However, the real issue remains the imbalance of power between the UK Parliament and government. The executive can sign up to EU legislation without first having sought agreement from Parliament by using an 'override' mechanism to avoid parliamentary scrutiny. The government has been using this override with increasing frequency: around 350 times since figures were first collected in 2001. Some controversial pieces of recent legislation have been exempted from parliamentary scrutiny in this way, including the creation of the EU Arrest Warrant and the setting up of the European Defence Agency. The Labour Government almost set an annual record in 2005 when it used the override seventy-seven times, including twenty-two during the UK's presidency of the EU Council, when in theory, use of the override should have been unnecessary given that the UK executive had control over the timing and agenda of Council meetings.

This contrasts markedly with the powers of scrutiny and control of EU legislation exercised by, for example, the Danish Parliament. Denmark joined the EEC at the same time as the United Kingdom but, from the beginning, Danish MPs ensured that they kept better command of what the Danish executive could agree to in Brussels. The Danish Government is required to get a 'mandate' from the Europe Committee of the Danish Parliament before it can sign up to any EU proposal. Most of the countries which have joined the EU more recently, such as Sweden, Finland, and several of the newer member states, have also set up Danish-style systems, with greater power for their Parliaments relative to their executives.

Also, the UK Parliament is in recess for around sixteen weeks a year on average, whereas the European Commission is only out of office during August. That leaves around three months each year when the EU is continuing to produce proposals for legislation which cannot be scrutinised in Parliament. According to a parliamentary written answer, in 2005 there were sixty-eight occasions where the Council of Ministers adopted proposals which had not been cleared by the ESC while the Commons was in recess. The Danish committee, by contrast, meets all year round, even if the Folketing (Parliament) is not in session. The only time it does not meet is during August when the European Commission is, itself, on holiday.

During a review in 2004, the then Leader of the House, Peter Hain, admitted:

The European Standing Committees have not worked out as it was hoped. It is hard to persuade members to serve on them. Few other members think them worth attending. Their proceedings have a ritualistic quality, and are largely devoid of much political interest; yet they consume a lot of time and effort. There is a very strong case for reform.

For this reason he proposed to abolish the European Standing Committee and instead refer significant documents identified by the ESC to departmental select committees. However, Hain's plans to reform the system fell by the wayside – as do most proposals to strengthen Parliament's scrutiny powers – and the UK government has yet to make any new proposals.

Assuming that the UK government would not countenance giving more substantive powers to the parliamentary scrutiny committees, other improvements are possible. MPs could hold a weekly Question Time with the UK's Permanent Representative in Brussels to keep themselves better informed about forthcoming EU proposals. ESC members could have substitutes to ensure full attendance (rather than the current average 40 per cent non-attendance). Whereas the ESC has just one page on the UK Parliament website, the Danish Parliament runs a full EU Information Centre, which answers questions from the public and interested parties, and it hosts a large website with much information on EU affairs.

However, some critics argue that many MPs are too fixated upon the general issue of loss of sovereignty to the EU to concern themselves with improving the processes of scrutiny. Such eurosceptic MPs – and, indeed, large sections of the media – generally ignore the reports of the various European committees, although they are quick to complain about the lack of information on EU matters, the 'democratic deficit' inherent in EU arrangements and the 'Brussels bureaucracy'. Such MPs also tend to be suspicious of MEPs – even those of their own party – for fear that they have 'gone native' and become overly supportive of the EU to the detriment of UK national interests. Riddell describes European scrutiny as 'a ghetto activity for enthusiasts (on both the pro and sceptic side) and the selflessly assiduous'.[4]

Overall, the influence of the UK Parliament upon the policy decisions of the EU – like that of many other national legislatures – is sporadic and marginal. There is also very little evidence that it has any impact upon the policy decisions of UK ministers in their dealings with the European Union.

A European Union constitution?

A constitution for the European Union was drafted in 2004. It brought together, for the first time, the many treaties and agreements on which the EU is based, defining the powers of the EU relative to member states and the diverse powers of the EU institutions. It enshrined the principle of **subsidiarity**: the principle enshrined in the EU Maastricht Treaty that power should be exercised at the lowest possible level compatible with efficiency and democracy; but, at the same time, the constitution extended EU legislative powers into new areas such as justice, immigration and asylum policies. Member states would retain their powers of veto over foreign policy, defence and taxation. It allowed for a longer term EU presidency with more influence and status than the current six-monthly rotation. The EU Commission would be slimmed down and the EU Parliament would have powers of 'co-decision' with the Council of Ministers. The constitution also contained a Charter of EU citizens' rights and freedoms.

Some commentators regarded the EU constitution as simply a tidying-up exercise to facilitate and streamline the workings of an ever larger Union. Others, especially eurosceptics, regarded it as the effective creation of a 'United States of Europe'.

The UK's Labour Government had promised to incorporate the provisions of the new EU constitutional treaty into UK law, subject to a referendum – the latter a concession which it was forced to make by the Conservative Opposition. Eighteen member states – representing 60 per cent of the EU's half a billion population – ratified the constitution. However, it required unanimous approval by all member states and France and Holland voted 'no' in their referenda on the EU constitution in 2005, which apparently killed it off. This let the UK government off the hook and no referendum was held in the United Kingdom.

However, several member states – notably Germany – were determined to resurrect the EU constitution in some form. An exhaustive 2007 EU summit agreed the key elements of a new treaty to replace the constitution. The language of the reform treaty was more legalistic and less penetrable than that of the draft constitution, but most European leaders agreed that 90 per cent of the constitution was carried over into the reform treaty. It omitted references to the EU anthem and flag and any reference to a constitution as such, but its provisions included:

- a President of the European Council chosen for thirty months, replacing the current system where countries take turns at being president for six months;
- a new post of High Representative combining the jobs of the existing foreign affairs supremo and the external affairs commissioner, to give the EU more influence on the world stage;
- a smaller European Commission, with fewer commissioners than there are member states, from 2014;
- a redistribution of voting weights between the member states, phased in between 2014 and 2017;
- new powers for the European Commission, European Parliament and ECJ, for example, in the field of justice and home affairs;
- further removal of national vetoes in a number of areas.

The reform treaty was passed by the Commons in March 2008. Liberal Democrat MP, Edward Davey, said that there were many 'firsts' in the treaty, including member states having the right to leave the EU and national parliaments being given a mechanism for calling a halt to EU legislation. He continued:

> This is a treaty which genuine Eurosceptics should be coming to praise – not to bury. . . . The fact that they don't now back these reforms that they used to call for reflects the reality that the vast majority of Eurosceptics aren't genuinely sceptical but actually are closed minded and predetermined in their opposition to everything European.[5]

Most member states were determined to avoid the political inconvenience of any further referenda (except Ireland, for whom it is a constitutional obligation). This dearth of democratic legitimacy may return to haunt them in the future. There were growing calls for a referendum in the United Kingdom not only from the Conservative Party and other right-wing eurosceptics, but also from some trade unions such as the GMB and RMT – historically left-wing eurosceptics who disliked the free market aspects of the EU. The GMB also criticised the UK opt-out from the EU Charter of Fundamental Rights: 'We want a social Europe. What sort of message is this preaching to developing countries that we are telling to raise working standards, when a government in Europe won't even accept them for its own people?'[6]

The right wing, europhobic, UK Independence Party (UKIP), which campaigns for Britain to leave the EU, gleefully picked up on left-wing calls for a referendum on the reform treaty. Its leader, Nigel Farage, said it was 'seriously good news' that unions were demanding a vote, adding:

> Gordon Brown must be the only man in the country who doesn't realise that we have to have a referendum on this treaty. Every other political leader in the EU has said that this is the constitution in all but name, and the Labour Party was elected with a manifesto to hold a referendum on that document. He is doing a rather splendid impression of an ostrich, surrounding himself with yes men who are trying to drown out the overwhelming calls for the British people to have their say.[7]

The UK government resisted such calls, arguing that the many opt-outs which it had secured meant that it was signing up to a more limited form of treaty than were many other EU states. The government's critics argued that these same safeguards were in the original constitution, on which it had promised a referendum. The opt-outs, in turn, raised a further problem.

For the United Kingdom, its many opt-outs on its so-called 'red lines' – from citizens' rights and criminal justice to asylum, immigration and home affairs – threatened to consign it once again to the margins of European power and influence. UK Liberal Democrat MP, Andrew Duff, has said: 'If it has not yet sunk in, in the UK, that it has effectively designed for itself a second-class membership of the EU, it is fast sinking in in Brussels'. A European diplomat based in London agreed, saying: 'Presumably, we now leave the Brits behind.' Others agree that the EU may now finally see the emergence of a core Europe, instead of struggling to agree at twenty-seven. As one French political observer put it:

We shouldn't totally exclude . . . a new discussion on a 'core Europe' making further progress on issues like economic governance, tax harmonisation, social protection, foreign and military co-operation, as several EU member states are not ready to make progress at the same pace.[8]

The impact of the European Union on UK political parties

Membership of the European Union has profoundly divided the two main UK political parties: Labour especially in the 1970s and the Conservatives especially in the 1980s and 1990s. Left wing Labour MPs have always been hostile to the EU, which they perceive as a free market 'capitalist club'. The 'new' Labour Government is now much more europhile (pro-European), although it has quietly kicked membership of the single currency into the long grass.

The Conservative Party, under Margaret Thatcher, became increasingly suspicious of the EC in the 1980s as they saw it extending beyond a free trade community to a supranational political power (which, in fact, it always was). Since 1990, divisions within the Conservative Party over Europe have been primarily responsible for some key events: Thatcher's prime ministerial defeat in 1990; the temporary withdrawal of the whip from several Conservative eurorebels which eradicated John Major's small majority; John Redwood's leadership challenge against Major in 1995; the defection from the Conservative Party of pro-European MPs to the Liberal Democrats or Labour, such as Robert Jackson in 2005; and the defection of some anti-Europeans to increasingly influential europhobic parties such as UKIP.

The current Conservative leader, David Cameron, is a eurosceptic who wants to remain 'in Europe, but not run by Europe'. The party's current policy on joining the euro is 'never'. They favoured a referendum on the EU constitution and on the replacement reform treaty because they believed that the UK electorate would vote 'no'. This was a rather opportunist position, because, philosophically, Conservatives oppose referenda in principle (the UK Parliament should be sovereign) and have never held one in practice.

During his campaign for the Conservative leadership in 2005, David Cameron pledged to pull out of the European People's Party

– the largest centre-right group in the European Parliament – because it was perceived by Conservative eurosceptics to be too pro-European. He promised to set up a new eurosceptic, pro-American group instead. This was one of his few concrete policy pledges in the leadership campaign, but he has since reneged on it, prompting new divisions within his party over the issue of Europe. Of the three main parties, only the Liberal Democrats are fully committed to the development of a federal Europe.

Euroscepticism in the United Kingdom has also generated the creation of some minor parties: most notably, UKIP, which dented the main parties' vote especially in the 2004 EU elections. UKIP seeks complete withdrawal from the EU. UKIP more than doubled its 1999 vote to take 16 per cent of the votes and twelve seats (on pure PR) in the EU Parliament, in so doing pushing the Liberal Democrats into fourth place. Labour's vote fell by 6 per cent to 23 per cent, their worst share of the vote since 1918. The Conservatives got more votes – 27 per cent – but that was still their lowest share of any nationwide election since 1832. UKIP MEP Robert Kilroy-Silk said in 2004 that he wanted to 'wreck' the EU Parliament by exposing the waste, corruption and the way 'it's eroding our independence'; but he then quit UKIP in 2005 because it would not elect him as party leader.

The Greens (left-wing eurosceptics) in 2004 held their two UK MEPs with 6 per cent of the total vote. Small parties are aided in European elections by an electoral system of pure proportionality (closed party list) which was introduced in the United Kingdom in 1999 – an election which also produced the lowest ever turnout in a national UK election, at just 23 per cent.

Whether the impact of the European Union upon UK politics has been, on balance, positive or negative is a matter of highly subjective and sometimes very emotive assessment. It has certainly done more to divide the main parties than any other issue for the last half century; but it has, perhaps, also done more to enhance the rights and freedoms of UK citizens than have any of those parties.

The EU and Westminster: future challenges

The EU reform treaty, designed to replace the unloved EU constitution proposal of 2004, has yet to be finalised. Its many opt-outs may promote a 'multi-speed' Europe rather than the intended consistency and harmony of the whole European Union with, perhaps, some ten out of twenty-seven countries progressing in a unified core with the others – including the United Kingdom – on various peripheral circles.

Other big future challenges include: energy policy – unbundling energy supply and ensuring energy security; negotiations on climate change and renewables; the EU's troubled enlargement process with Turkey (about which France, in particular, has doubts) and with the Balkans (notably Macedonia and Kosovo); and the perennial issue of the EU's budget and its expensive Common Agricultural Policy.

. . . .

 ## What you should have learnt from reading this chapter

- This chapter has outlined the process of formation and development of the size and scope of the European Union from just six member states in 1957 to twenty-seven in 2008, with several more (such as Turkey) still queuing to join.

- It has explained the United Kingdom's initial reluctance to join and has described the membership process in 1972–3, culminating in a seminal referendum in 1975.

- It has outlined and sought to evaluate the Westminster Parliament's growing loss of *de facto* sovereignty to the EU, especially since the adoption of QMV which has meant the ongoing reduction of unanimous voting in the EU Council of Ministers.

- It has briefly outlined the roles of some of the main EU institutions, notably the Parliament and ECJ.

- It has assessed the scrutiny processes of Westminster and its committees over EU legislation and found them to be worthy but wanting.

- It has outlined the continuing controversy over an EU constitution or replacement reform treaty – an issue which will not die.

- It has described the profoundly divisive impact of the European Union upon the main UK parties.

- It has discussed some of the challenges facing the EU and Westminster in the near future.

🔍 Glossary of key terms

Qualified Majority Voting (QMV) A formula for voting within the EU where several member states must band together to veto a policy.
Subsidiarity The principle enshrined in the EU Maastricht Treaty that power should be exercised at the lowest possible level compatible with efficiency and democracy.
Supranationalism The establishment of a sovereign international power over member states.

❓ Likely examination questions

Short questions:

- How did the United Kingdom formally accept the authority of EU institutions?

- Outline the effect of membership of the European Union on the sovereignty of Parliament.

- What areas of sovereignty has the United Kingdom retained in relation to the European Union?

- Outline the position of the Conservative Party on the European Union.

Essay questions:

- Where does sovereignty reside in the UK political system?

- Assess the impact of European institutions upon the UK political system.

- What are the advantages of European integration?

- What are the disadvantages of European integration?

🖥 Helpful websites

http://news.bbc.co.uk

http://www.parliament.uk

http://www.europarl.org.uk

http://news.bbc.co.uk/1/hi/in_depth/europe/2003/inside_europe/default.stm

http://news.bbc.co.uk/1/hi/world/europe/6481969.stm

Suggestions for further reading

Hix, S., *The Political System of the European Union*, Basingstoke: Palgrave Macmillan, 2005.

Leonard, D., *Guide to the European Union*, London: Economist Books, 2005.

McCormick, J., *Understanding the European Union: A Concise Introduction*, Basingstoke: Palgrave Macmillan, 2005.

Watts, D. and Pilkington, C., *Britain in the European Union Today*, Manchester: Manchester University Press, 2005.

CHAPTER 8

Parliament and the Devolved Bodies

Overview

This chapter explains the nature of the United Kingdom's unitary constitution, before going on to outline and assess the causes and consequences of **devolution** since the 1990s, including tensions and conflicts such as the **'West Lothian question'**. It ends with an analysis of possible future developments and their impact upon the Westminster Parliament.

Key issues to be covered in this chapter

- The UK's unitary constitution
- The processes of devolution
- The consequences of devolution
- Criticisms of devolution
- The future of devolution

The United Kingdom's unitary constitution

In a unitary system, ultimate power and authority for the exercise of the functions of a state are concentrated in the hands of a central body. The state may be sub-divided into smaller areas for administrative purposes, but these are the creation of the central body and their boundaries and powers can be altered, or abolished, by the central body. Unitary constitutions generally occur in small, stable and/or relatively homogeneous states with few sharp racial, religious or linguistic divisions. The United Kingdom, France and New Zealand are examples of unitary states.

The UK political system has one sovereign legislature, namely, the UK Parliament at Westminster, which has ultimate law-making authority over all other bodies within the United Kingdom. Although there are local government councils and now also local Parliaments throughout the United Kingdom, these bodies are subordinate to the central, sovereign, Westminster Parliament; and their existence and powers are wholly determined by Westminster which can limit the powers of such local bodies or, indeed, abolish them altogether at any time.

The United Kingdom has remained, for centuries, one of the most centralised political systems in the Western world because of the perceived disadvantages of decentralisation: namely, the neglect or abandonment of the wider national interest; the risk of inconsistent, unco-ordinated and potentially unjust provision of standards and services across different parts of the state; possible restrictions upon geographical mobility within the state; the danger that regional bodies may exceed their (weaker) local mandate to involve themselves in national issues, or that they may jeopardise overall control of public spending with populist and expensive local projects; the cost and potential inefficiency of added layers of local bureaucracy; and the possibility that devolution may entrench a regional 'elective dictatorship'.

However, the arguments in favour of decentralisation have become increasingly persuasive: namely, that local people know local needs best; regional assemblies provide vital checks and balances against the potential 'elective dictatorship' of a minority-vote government in a sovereign, unitary, Westminster Parliament – particularly one which may be neglectful of local wishes in areas where it is unpopular; regional assemblies also provide an added tier of democratic representation, participation and accountability; they have a mandate from local electors; they provide a training and recruitment ground for central government and Parliament; and they may even be cost-effective.

The processes of devolution

Devolution is a form of decentralisation – albeit a limited one. It means the delegation, that is, the passing down, of some legislative and/or executive functions of central powers to local bodies, while the national power remains responsible for major national issues such as defence, foreign affairs and macroeconomics. The local bodies are subordinate to the central legislature or executive, which can readily retrieve its powers. The system remains unitary because the centre is still sovereign. **Federalism**, on the other hand, entails greater local autonomy. Here the regions allocate certain national powers, such as defence and foreign affairs to a central body, and the local powers are, in theory, equal to the central power. The local powers have autonomy within their own, defined areas of decision making. Thus, central government cannot increase its powers at the expense of the regions or federal states. The courts arbitrate in cases of conflict. The United States and Australia are examples of federal systems. **Separatism** means complete political independence.

The United Kingdom has long had elements of executive and administrative devolution in local government, and Scotland and Wales had their own Secretaries of State with Cabinet status. Scotland's legal and educational systems have also long been quite different from those of England and Wales. Until 1999 there was, however, no legislative devolution; Westminster was the sole UK legislature since the suspension, in 1972, of the Northern Ireland Parliament (Stormont) and the introduction there of 'direct rule' from Westminster because of the growing political conflict in Northern Ireland at that time.

Encouraged by the rise of nationalist feeling in Scotland and Wales, Labour and the Liberals/Liberal Democrats since the 1970s advocated legislative devolution for Scotland and Wales; and the

Liberal Democrats also proposed elected local legislatures for the regions of England. A Labour Government in 1977 introduced a Devolution Bill, and held referenda on the devolution issue in Scotland and Wales in 1979. Wales voted against; Scotland voted in favour, but the 'yes' vote amounted to only 32.5 per cent of the total electorate, and the Bill controversially required approval by at least 40 per cent of the eligible electorate (a backbench amendment) so the issue was dropped.

Over the next two decades, support for the Scottish and Welsh nationalist parties increased, but the Conservative Governments of that period were firmly opposed to devolution. In the 1997 general election, the Conservatives won no Westminster seats at all in Scotland or in Wales; and Labour came to power with a mandate to hold new referenda on the question of devolution.

The Labour Party's motives for pursuing devolution were mixed. On the one hand, there was a perception that Westminster was simply not representing Scotland or Wales adequately. On the other hand, voter support for the nationalist parties was rising and draining votes from Labour in some of its bedrock areas of electoral strength, and the Labour Party wanted to win back some of those votes. Thus, the devolution agenda was prompted by both political principle and party pragmatism.

Scotland

Support for devolution in Scotland increased in the 1980s and 1990s for three main reasons: an unpopular Conservative Government at Westminster which imposed the hated poll tax and closed down the Scottish shipyards, steel mills and factories; the discovery of North Sea oil which, nationalists claimed, could enhance Scotland's financial autonomy; and membership of the EU which, it was hoped, could provide economic support to turn Scotland into the 'tiger economy' which EU regional financial aid had already fuelled in Ireland.

Scotland held a two-question referendum in September 1997, and 74 per cent voted in favour of a Scottish Parliament with 60 per cent agreeing that it should have tax-varying powers of up to 3p in the pound (turnout was 60 per cent). The Scottish Parliament came into being in 1999 with 129 members elected by the Additional Member System (AMS): seventy-three elected by first-past-the-post, and fifty-six

> ## Box 8.1 Policy areas for which the Scottish Parliament is responsible
>
> - Health
> - Education and training
> - Local government, housing and social work
> - Economic development
> - Employment
> - Transport
> - Law and home affairs
> - Police
> - Environment
> - Energy
> - Agriculture, forestry and fishing
> - Culture, sport and the arts
> - Administration of certain EU laws in Scotland (for example, civil nuclear emergency planning)

'top-up' members elected from closed regional party lists using the European parliamentary constituencies.

Westminster remains responsible for foreign affairs including relations with the EU, defence and national security, macroeconomic and fiscal matters, immigration, railways, shipping, airlines, pensions, employment law, broadcasting and telecommunications and much else. Overall, the Scotland Act lists nineteen pages of powers that are reserved to Westminster. In other words, devolution is a fairly limited form of decentralisation.

Wales

Knowing that nationalist sentiment in Wales was weaker than in Scotland, the Labour Government held the Welsh devolution referendum one week after the Scottish vote in 1997, in the hope of giving the 'yes' side a boost. Despite this, the 'yes' vote in Wales just scraped a 0.6 per cent majority (under 7,000 votes) on only a 50 per cent turnout. Although there has long been a sense of national Welsh culture, centred especially on the Welsh language, there was far less support for political nationalism in Wales than in Scotland because of the perceived economic and political benefits of the union with

Box 8.2 Policy areas for which the Welsh Assembly is responsible

- Economic development
- Agriculture
- Industry and training
- Education
- Local government services
- Health and social services
- Housing
- Environment
- Planning and transport
- Sport and heritage

England. The sixty-member Welsh Assembly – opened in 1999 – was, therefore, much weaker than the Scottish Parliament, with control over the spending of the £14 billion Welsh budget but with no taxation or primary law-making powers.

The Welsh Assembly (like the Scottish Parliament) is elected by the AMS system, with forty first-past-the-post and twenty party list members. It operates on the style of a local government committee system, with executive rather than legislative or fiscal powers: in effect, merely taking over the role of the Welsh Office in deciding how Westminster legislation is implemented in Wales (or passing secondary legislation), in the policy areas outlined in Box 8.2

Using the powers available to it, the Welsh Assembly government has, however, recently made some policy decisions different to those of Westminster. For example, Cardiff Bay was first to announce plans to abolish Key Stage 1 and 2 tests for school children. Wales was also the first UK nation to appoint a Children's Commissioner. Other examples include the abolition of prescription charges and a ban on smoking in enclosed public spaces which come into force earlier than that in England.

Northern Ireland

At around the same time as the Scottish and Welsh referenda on devolution, but for different reasons – namely, the Northern Ireland peace process – an assembly for Northern Ireland was re-established at Stormont (for the first time since its abolition in 1972) following the peace deal on Good Friday, 10 April 1998. In May 1998 a rapid referendum on the peace deal was held throughout Ireland and won substantial support, with Northern Ireland returning a 71 per cent 'yes' vote on 81 per cent turnout, and Eire 94 per cent 'yes' on 56 per cent turnout.

The peace deal provided for a Northern Ireland Assembly of 108 seats elected by a form of proportional representation; a twelve-member executive chosen from within and by the assembly in proportion to the parties' strengths in the Assembly (thus, for example, Sinn Féin were guaranteed two seats on the executive). The Northern Ireland coalition executive was formed in November 1999, and Unionists especially had to adjust to the new realities when former IRA commander Martin McGuinness was appointed Education Secretary.

In 2002, Stormont was suspended for the fourth time since 1972 over pressure on the IRA to decommission weapons and allegations – which later proved false – of an IRA spy ring inside Stormont. By 2004, the suspended assembly had cost UK taxpayers £37 million in ongoing salaries and administrative costs. Voters' growing anger about this stalemate, combined with strong pressure from the UK and US governments and ongoing concessions by the Northern Irish parties, eventually prompted profound shifts in the political landscape.

In 2007, new elections were held for the Northern Ireland Assembly, with the most radical parties on each side of the political divide – the DUP and Sinn Féin – emerging as the strongest. With disputes over the decommissioning of weapons and Sinn Féin's lack of support for the Northern Irish policing system behind them, the leaders of these two parties, Ian Paisley and Gerry Adams, held historic, face-to-face talks and they formed a new, power-sharing executive in the same year.

England remains the conspicuous hole in the UK constitutional doughnut. England does not have its own Parliament. Many English voters do not seem to recognise this fact – they appear to regard Westminster as their Parliament. However, Westminster is, of course, the sovereign Parliament of the entire United Kingdom. The more legislative and policy advantages are gained by Scotland, Wales and

Table 8.1 Northern Ireland devolution results, 2007

Party	Seats	+/–
DUP	36	+ 6
SF	28	+ 4
UUP	18	– 9
SDLP	16	– 2
AP	7	+ 1
GP	1	+ 1
PUP	1	0
UKUP	0	– 1
OTH	1	0

Northern Ireland, the more English voters' dissatisfaction seems to be increasing.

The consequences of devolution

The central government's Scottish and Welsh Offices – with their shrinking roles – were variously incorporated into wider departments: in Brown's first 2007 Cabinet, the Defence Secretary, Des Browne, also took on the role of Scottish Secretary, and the Work and Pensions Secretary, Peter Hain, also took on the role of Welsh Secretary.

Because various forms of PR are used in the devolution elections, no party has, to date, won an absolute majority of the seats in any of the devolved assemblies.

The nationalist parties are usually grouped together with the 'others' in UK party analyses – understandably, since over 80 per cent of UK voters live in England, where the Scottish and Welsh national-ist parties do not have a presence. Indeed, as many people live in Greater London as in Scotland and Wales combined. However, the

Table 8.2 Summary of devolved powers

Type of devolution	Powers	Scottish Parliament	Welsh Assembly	Northern Irish Assembly
Legislative	The power to pass, amend or repeal laws	✔	✘	✔
Financial	The ability to raise or lower taxes independently	✔	✘	✘
Administrative	The power to run services	✔	✔	✔
Administrative	The power to allocate funds	✔	✔	✔
Administrative	The power to organise administration	✔	✔	✔

SNP and Plaid Cymru are currently (2008) in government in Scotland and Wales. The nationalist parties are, therefore, now a significant force in UK party politics.

Scotland
In Scotland, the primary consequence of devolution was an eight-year Labour/Liberal Democrat coalition from 1999 to 2007. During that time, the Scottish Parliament voted to abolish tuition fees for Scottish students (the price of Liberal Democrat coalition support); then to repeal section 28 (which banned the promotion of homosexuality in local government and state schools) just after the House of Lords had blocked its repeal at Westminster; then to support universal free personal care for the elderly; then to ban fox hunting, and the smacking of children; then to reject foundation hospitals for Scotland – all clear examples of a devolved body flexing its muscle in the face of central opposition.

The arrangements for Scotland generated the 'West Lothian question' (so-called because it was first raised by the MP for that area, Tam Dalyell): that Scottish MPs at Westminster continue to have law-making powers over areas of English policy such as health and education, while English MPs have no such power over Scotland because the Scottish Parliament now legislates on such matters. In 2003, for example, Scottish Labour MPs helped the government at Westminster to push through foundation hospitals for England, which had already been rejected for Scotland. In 2004, forty-six Scottish Labour MPs voted with the Labour Government at Westminster to push through top-up tuition fees for England on a total majority of just five votes, although the Scottish Parliament had already rejected tuition fees for Scotland. As one Conservative MP has said:

> We have MPs from Scotland essentially telling England what to do when they are doing the opposite in Scotland, have no control over what they are doing in their own constituencies in Scotland and are not in any way accountable for the effects their actions have in England.[1]

The Conservatives' solution to the 'West Lothian question' is to propose barring Scottish MPs from voting on English legislation at Westminster. The Labour Government rejects this on the grounds that it would create 'two classes of MPs at Westminster' and would undermine collective responsibility; but objective observers cannot help but note how the removal of Scottish MPs' voting rights at Westminster would dent Labour's majority on key items of English legislation. Such a reform would also impinge upon the leadership credentials of PM Gordon Brown, who represents a Scottish constituency. Conservative MPs such as Alan Duncan were saying, rather mischievously, in 2006, 'I'm beginning to think it is almost impossible now to have a Scottish Prime Minister because they would be at odds with the basic construction of the British constitution.'[2] (The Liberal Democrats are reserving judgement and calling for 'a Constitutional Convention to provide a constitution for a twenty-first century Britain'.)

Scotland has also long had a disproportionate number of Westminster MPs relative to its population size. The number of Scottish seats at Westminster was, therefore, reduced from seventy-two to fifty-nine for the 2005 General Election by redrawing constituency boundaries. Ten of the thirteen lost seats belonged to Labour MPs. Critics of the Labour Government argue that the government will not contemplate reducing voting rights for the remaining Scottish MPs at Westminster because so many of those MPs are still Labour. Such critics argue more broadly that devolution in Scotland and Wales was an example of the Labour Government's ambivalent attitude towards power: namely, decentralising only on Labour's own terms and to its own advantage, as far as possible.

However, if that motivation was ever true, it was dealt a blow in the 2007 Scottish parliamentary election which saw the SNP become the largest party with just one seat more than Labour. When the Liberal Democrats ruled out a new coalition with Labour, that left the way clear for a historic, albeit minority, SNP Government in Scotland, led by Alex Salmond. Churlishly and unconventionally, the then PM Tony Blair refused to call Salmond to congratulate him. Salmond made gentle mockery: 'He never phones, he never writes . . .' and pointedly travelled to Brussels to champion Scotland's cause in Europe.

The SNP Government is promising a freeze on council tax, free school meals for all pupils, abolition of prescription charges, Scottish control of Scottish broadcasting and votes at sixteen. At the end of 2007, the Scottish police got their backdated pay deal, while the English police did not.

Wales

In the Welsh Assembly there has usually been a minority Labour executive (which briefly formed a coalition with the Liberal Democrats in 2000–3). In February 1999, the Welsh Labour Party elected its leader for the Welsh Assembly: the Welsh First Secretary. Blair's favoured candidate, Alun Michael, beat the traditionalist, 'people's choice' Rhodri Morgan by 5 per cent, in what some critics saw as a 'stitch up' by the party machine. However, in 2000, Alun Michael had to resign over a funding crisis, and Rhodri Morgan, the man whom the Labour leadership had tried hard to block, took over.

It did not take long for the Welsh people and politicians to start questioning and criticising the limited powers of the Welsh Assembly, especially compared with those of the Scottish Parliament. Following a Commission of Inquiry chaired by Lord Ivor Richard in 2004, and a White Paper in 2005, the Labour Government in Westminster passed the Government of Wales Act 2006, strengthening the legislative powers of the Assembly, the changes taking effect after the 2007 devolution elections. The Assembly can now pass its own legislation – but only after the Welsh Secretary lays an order before Westminster, and then ninety-minute debates and votes in both Houses of Parliament grant it permission, and only in the specified policy areas for which the Assembly already had responsibility.

So, on the one hand, the parliamentary stage is much faster and simpler, and the end result will be to let the Assembly pass its own laws or repeal laws passed at Westminster. On the other hand, the central government's minister responsible for Wales has to trigger the process, and Westminster remains sovereign and can still stop the Assembly in its tracks or, of course, even abolish it.

The 2006 Act also allows the Assembly to hold a referendum on gaining full law-making powers like the Scottish Parliament, as long as two-thirds of Assembly Members (AMs) vote for one and a simple majority in favour is achieved in the House of Commons and the Lords. In practice, that means Labour currently has a veto on the referendum option. Should, for example, a Conservative Government at Westminster be hostile to a Labour-controlled Assembly, then this route to full law-making powers might be pursued in Cardiff Bay.

Plaid Cymru said that the provisions were a 'major disappointment to anybody wishing to see Wales gaining a proper Parliament', falling short of law-making powers recommended by the Richard Commission and Welsh public opinion. The Richard Commission had also recommended additional numbers of AMs and said that it was 'desirable, though not essential' for the Assembly to have the power to vary tax.

The 2006 Act also modified the electoral system. In the 2003 Assembly election in Clwyd West three of the four candidates defeated on the first-past-the-post ballots nevertheless made it into the Assembly. They got in through the regional list ballots. The government said that this was unfair and confusing, making winners out of losers. The 2006 Act, therefore, forces would-be AMs to choose one or other route in future. Opposition parties say that this rigs the system because, as things stand, it will not damage Labour as much as other parties. The Electoral Commission also criticised the change.

Further examples of decentralising only on Labour's own terms and to its own advantage, as far as possible?

That said, in 2007 Labour entered into a historic coalition with Plaid Cymru in Wales, making it more likely that the devolution agenda in Wales will progress rather than stagnate or regress.

By 2008, therefore, nationalist parties were in government in Scotland, Wales and Northern Ireland: a historic first. Devolution certainly seems to be, not just an event, but a process.

England
The Labour Government did try, in a limited way, to address the 'English question', that is, the conspicuous omission of England from the devolution project. In 1999, non-elected regional economic development agencies (RDAs) were set up for the eight English regions outside London; but there were already growing calls for elected English regional assemblies. Some ministers of the time, such as John Prescott, wanted these to be part of the framework for an element of regional representation from all parts of the United Kingdom in a reformed second chamber at Westminster.

In 2004, a test referendum was held in the north-east of England on the proposal for an elected regional assembly. (Originally, referenda were also planned in the north-west and Yorkshire and Humberside, but the government dropped them because, it said, of problems with postal voting in those areas. The decision was attacked by critics as a cynical move to avoid contests in the two regions least likely to deliver a 'yes' vote.) In the event, the north-east referendum was roundly defeated by 78 per cent to 22 per cent – on a quite respectable 48 per cent turnout – probably because the assembly's proposed powers were conspicuously weak. It would have had a budget of around £500 million – mostly inherited from transferred government functions – and influence over a further £500 million. It would have distributed investment for affordable housing and become the new fire and rescue authority, but it would not have had powers over the health service, police or transport. Local government expert, Tony Travers, compared the proposed assembly to a Christmas tree: 'That is, it's completely bare when you buy it, but with the hope you can buy interesting things – in this case new services – to hang on it.'[3]

In the wake of this heavy referendum defeat, English devolution now seems to be off the agenda for the foreseeable future.

Criticisms of devolution

Some parties have criticised devolution for going too far; for others, it has not gone far enough.

Summary of the main parties' views

The Conservative Party were always against devolution on principle: they favoured politically strong, centralised government and feared that devolution might be the first step down the slippery slope towards the complete break up of the United Kingdom. However, largely for political and pragmatic reasons, they will not now reverse the devolution processes. When David Cameron was elected leader of the Conservative Party in 2005, he gave an assurance that devolution would be allowed to function freely under a future Conservative Government and that the Scottish Parliament's tax-varying powers would remain – but he also said that the relationship between Westminster and Holyrood would have to be spelled out more formally ahead of the possibility that the Conservatives might win power at Westminster while other parties were dominant in the Scottish executive. He also urged the Scottish Conservatives to campaign for tax cuts.

The Labour Party have long favoured devolution to different degrees in different parts of the United Kingdom; which, critics say, has been a largely self-serving agenda. They have also tried, but not always successfully, to control the leaderships of the new institutions. However, they do not favour any greater degree of decentralisation, such as UK federalism.

The Liberal Democrats have always favoured federalism, that is, much greater local autonomy, in a consistent pattern across the whole United Kingdom. For them, Labour's programme of devolution has not gone far enough.

The nationalist parties (SNP, PC, SDLP and SF) ultimately favour separatism, that is, the complete independence of Scotland, Wales and Northern Ireland from the United Kingdom. However, they are largely content to accept degrees of devolution for the foreseeable future; although, to fulfil a manifesto promise, the SNP published a White Paper containing proposals for a referendum on independence, just three months after taking power in 2007. (Opinion polls suggest around 30 per cent support in Scotland for full independence.)

Devolution has, undeniably, created imbalances and inconsistencies of political power, representation, services and standards across the United Kingdom as a whole. The 'West Lothian question' and the imbalances in Scottish representation have already been addressed above.

One final controversy was the spiralling cost of the Scottish parliamentary building (Holyrood) from an original estimate of £40 million to over £400 million. The New Welsh Senedd at Cardiff Bay, by contrast, cost just £67 million.

The future of devolution

The current devolution arrangements are, unquestionably, unbalanced. The lack of any legislative devolution in England remains the biggest inconsistency.

Vernon Bogdanor, professor of government at Oxford University, has put it strongly:

> England has no constitutional status. 'Smile at us', G. K. Chesterton wrote in his poem, The Secret People, 'pay us, pass us, but do not quite forget; for we are the people of England that never have spoken yet'. England has never spoken because, constitutionally England does not exist . . . There has been no English Parliament since 1536. There is no English Office comparable to the Scottish, Welsh or Northern Ireland Offices, the 'English' ministers being so only because their non-English functions have been hived off to the territorial departments. The 'English' legal system comprises both England and Wales, the Treaty of Union which the Scots claim to have agreed with the 'English' in 1707, was agreed, certainly, with the English state but this at the time comprised both the English and Welsh people.[4]

Many voices have been calling for a single English Parliament to complete the devolution process. In 1998, the eurosceptic Conservative backbencher, Teresa Gorman, introduced a Private Member's Bill calling for a referendum on an English Parliament to resolve the constitutional dilemmas to which asymmetrical devolution gives rise. It failed.

Canon Kenyon Wright, an architect of Scottish devolution, said in 2006 that it was 'undemocratic' that Scottish MPs could vote on English legislation but not vice versa and that he wanted to see 'a strong English Parliament' and a strengthened Welsh legislature. Conservative critics fear the break up of the United Kingdom but Canon Wright has argued that a rebalancing of the devolution arrangements would strengthen the Union and 'may well save it'.[5] He said that the failure of the referendum in the north-east of England had persuaded him that England has a growing sense of collective national identity every bit as strong as that of Scotland.

An English Constitutional Convention (ECC) was set up in 2006 by the English Democrats and the Campaign for an English Parliament. Its chairman, Michael Knowles, said that devolution has led to a 'constitutionally and politically bizarre, inflammatory and divisive' situation with particular inconsistencies and injustices in health and education policies. 'We don't want to take anything away from Scotland and Wales, we just want the same thing for people in England', he told a meeting at Westminster in 2006.[6]

A Mori poll in 2006 found that 41 per cent of respondents wanted 'England as a whole to have its own national Parliament with similar law-making powers to the Scottish Parliament'.

Critics of this view include Campbell Christie, who sat on the Scottish Constitutional Convention, an unofficial cross-party body (chaired in the 1980s by Canon Wright) whose name is echoed by the ECC:

> The consequence of creating a Parliament of nine-tenths of the UK is that it would almost definitely lead to the break up of the UK. That parliament would not be content with just the powers that the Scottish Parliament has. It would want to handle foreign affairs, taxation and economic affairs.[7]

Bogdanor agrees:

> An English parliament would hardly avoid becoming a real rival to Westminster. A federation consisting of four units – England, Scotland, Wales and Northern Ireland – would, the Royal Commission on the Constitution declared in 1973, 'be so unbalanced as to be

unworkable'. It would be dominated by the overwhelming political importance and wealth of England. The English Parliament would rival the United Kingdom federal Parliament; and in the federal Parliament itself the representation of England could hardly be scaled down in such a way as to enable it to be outvoted by Scotland, Wales and Northern Ireland, together representing less than one-fifth of the population. A United Kingdom federation of four countries, with a federal Parliament and provincial Parliaments in the four national capitals is therefore not a realistic proposition.[8]

The more balanced solution does seem to be devolution to the English regions – but exactly which regions, and what powers should be devolved, remain unanswered questions: 'In much of England, the regions are little more than ghosts'.[9]

Conclusion

Frequent reference by the Labour Government to the current devolution arrangements as the 'settled will of the people' seems at best, misguided and, at worst, misleading. Devolution seems very likely to be, not an event, but an ongoing process, with increasing impact particularly upon English constitutional arrangements. English (as opposed to UK) nationalist sentiment has been growing perceptibly since the turn of this century, and the flag of Saint George has replaced the Union flag as the symbol of choice for English nationalists of all sorts, whether liberal, conservative or chauvinist.

From a weak base – more cultural than political – Welsh nationalist sentiment has also strengthened since the creation of the Cardiff Bay Assembly and its powers are now, accordingly, increasing.

The election of a nationalist executive in Scotland (albeit very much a minority government with just forty-seven out of 129 seats) suggests the same trend there. One 1998 poll indicated that 65 per cent of Scots believed that Scotland would be wholly independent by 2013. This was one reason why the Conservatives and others used to reject devolution entirely, fearing that it might be the first step towards the complete break up of the United Kingdom.

The Westminster Parliament, meanwhile, would certainly resist – and could, of course, legally obstruct – any genuine threat to its supremacy.

Devolution, which began as a largely well-meaning process of limited democratic decentralisation, could yet escalate beyond the imaginings of its founders.

. . . .

 What you should have learnt from reading this chapter

- This chapter has outlined the *de jure* unitary nature of the UK constitution but has considered the possibility that, *de facto*, it may be threatened by the processes of devolution and the rising tide of nationalism.

- It has outlined the causes, processes and key consequences of devolution since the 1970s and especially the 1990s.

- The forms and the outcomes of devolution have differed in the constituent parts of the United Kingdom because of the varied history and strength of nationalist sentiment in different parts of the country.

- This chapter has attempted to illustrate some of the merits and demerits of devolution.

- It has described the main parties' diverse views on decentralisation, and especially on the asymmetric nature of the devolution arrangements across the United Kingdom since the 1990s. This does not seem to be a sustainable situation. Devolution is a process in flux.

Glossary of key terms

Devolution The delegation, that is, the passing down, of some legislative and/or executive functions of central powers to local bodies, while the national power remains responsible for major national issues. The system remains unitary because the centre is still sovereign.

Federalism Division of power between central and local executive and legislative bodies, with both, in theory, supreme in their particular fields, that is, there is shared sovereignty and the centre cannot override the local bodies. Contrasts with a unitary system where there can be devolution but no genuine regional autonomy.

Separatism Complete political independence and sovereignty.

West Lothian question Scottish MPs at Westminster have law-making powers over areas of English policy where English MPs have no such powers over Scotland.

? Likely examination questions

Short questions:

- Distinguish between a federal and a unitary constitution.
- Why did the Labour Government introduce devolution in the 1990s?
- Describe the powers of the Scottish Parliament.
- Outline the main differences between the powers of the devolved bodies in the United Kingdom.

Essay questions:

- What have been the main effects of devolution in the United Kingdom?
- How has the party system changed since the 1970s?
- Has Scottish devolution been a success?
- Assess the case for devolution in the United Kingdom.

🖥 Helpful websites

http://news.bbc.co.uk

http://www.parliament.uk

http://www.cewc-cymru.org.uk

http://www.scottish.parliament.uk/home.htm

http://www.wales.gov.uk

http://www.niassembly.gov.uk

Suggestions for further reading

Deacon, R. and Sandry, A., *Devolution in the United Kingdom*, Politics Study Guides, Edinburgh: Edinburgh University Press, 2007.

Dickinson, H. and Lynch, M., *The Challenge to Westminster: Sovereignty, Devolution and Independence*, East Linton: Tuckwell Press, 2000.

Hazell, R., *Devolution, Law Making and the Constitution*, Exeter: Imprint Academic, 2007.

O'Neill, M., *Devolution and British Politics*, London: Longman, 2004.

Trench, A., *The Dynamics of Devolution: The State of the Nations*, Exeter: Imprint Academic, 2005.

CHAPTER 9

Parliament, the Courts and Civil Liberties

Overview

This chapter explains and assesses the relationships between Parliament and the courts – both British and European – and it evaluates the changing and often strained relationships between the politicians and the judges. It goes on to examine the impact of the Human Rights Act 1998 upon these relationships, especially in the light of the authoritarian approach to criminal justice policy taken by recent governments.

Key issues to be covered in this chapter

- Parliament and the UK courts
- The courts and the executive
- Parliament and the judges
- A Bill of Rights for the United Kingdom: the Human Rights Act 1998
- 'New' Labour authoritarianism on law and order
- Parliament and the European courts

Parliament and the UK courts

United Kingdom constitutional theory is simple: it asserts that the Westminster Parliament is legally sovereign. The UK courts, therefore, cannot challenge or veto the law of Parliament; they can only interpret and enforce statute law as it is written. Statute law, in turn, takes precedence over all other forms of domestic law, such as **case law** and common law. Ironically, this doctrine of parliamentary sovereignty is not, itself, statute law; it only exists as common law because the UK judges have, since the Civil War, accepted the primacy of Parliament and exercised a self-imposed veto to their own powers to strike down parliamentary legislation.

However, in practice, the relationship between Westminster and the UK courts is rather more complex. The primary complication is that EU law takes precedence over all UK law and, where they conflict, the UK courts are required to enforce EU law. This was established by the *Factortame* case of 1991 which upheld the rights of Spanish trawlers to fish in UK waters, contrary to the Merchant Shipping Act 1988. In this case, the House of Lords held that when Parliament accepted the Treaty of Rome by passing the European Communities Act 1972 which ensured that European law takes precedence over all domestic sources of law, it had – contrary to previous constitutional theory – bound its successors on EU law so long as the United Kingdom remained in the European Union. Parliament remains technically sovereign in that it could, in theory, pass a law expressly overriding European law or, indeed, it could withdraw from the EU altogether – but this is unlikely in practice.

Secondly, Parliament's law may be unclear or ambiguous; in a test case, the judges must interpret the law precisely, which can allow a very 'creative' judicial role amounting effectively to 'law-making' by the judges. This is called case law. Some examples include: in 2004, the UK courts gave some protection to the model Naomi Campbell's right to privacy, and gave the right of anonymity to Maxine Carr (former girlfriend of Soham murderer Ian Huntley) upon her release from prison. The courts also ruled against the indefinite detention in the United Kingdom of foreign terror suspects on the ground that it was contrary to human rights law. In 2006 a Muslim schoolgirl lost the right to wear the traditional gown (jilbab) in repeated hearings against her school. A mother was refused parental 'right to know' if daughters under sixteen were given an abortion. In 2007, a woman left infertile by cancer treatment lost her five-year court battle (which went all the way to Europe) to use her frozen embryos because her former partner withdrew his consent.

Conservative journalist William Rees-Mogg has objected strongly to the growth of such case law, saying: 'The rule of Parliament is challenged by the growth of judicial interpretation, which amounts to legislation by judges.'[1] He likens the process to the 'political decisions' of the US Supreme Court and his particular complaint is about the Naomi Campbell judgment of 2004 which ruled that the publication of photographs of the supermodel outside a clinic constituted a breach of privacy which overrode freedom of the press and hence freedom of speech. He asserts that the judges, not Parliament, have 'made a new law' protecting privacy and eroding the principle of free speech: 'Parliament could have passed an Act protecting privacy . . . Parliament has decided not to do so . . .' However, he neglects to point out that Parliament has also chosen not to pass an Act protecting the principle of free speech and that, if it had, the judges would be bound by it in a state where – unlike the United States – the principle of parliamentary sovereignty is still the central doctrine of the UK constitution.

Thirdly, the courts and Parliament may clash when the courts interpret a statute in a way in which Parliament did not intend. Parliament may then, of course, rewrite the law; it can thus 'legalise illegality' or set aside court decisions. It may even do this retrospectively.

There has always been debate about the actual merits of Parliament's sovereignty over the UK courts. For example, Lord Denning – formerly a Law Lord and Master of the Rolls – has argued that judges should be able to veto parliamentary statutes:

> Every judge on his appointment discards all politics and all prejudices. You need have no fear. The judges of England have always in the past – and I hope always will – be vigilant in guarding our freedoms. Someone must be trusted. Let it be the judges.[2]

He gave the hypothetical example of wishing to obstruct any attempt by a radical left-wing government in the Commons to abolish the

House of Lords, which seemed, to some critics, to demonstrate the very 'politics and prejudices' he sought to deny. Also, without a written constitution or Bill of Rights at the time of his lecture, there were no clear, consistent and overriding constitutional principles against which judges could challenge parliamentary statutes. This is, of course, the fundamental reason for the doctrine of parliamentary sovereignty itself.

The new UK Bill of Rights (Human Rights Act 1998) has undoubtedly extended the role of the UK judges; but it expressly maintains the principle of parliamentary sovereignty and says that the judges cannot set aside parliamentary statutes when they conflict with the Human Rights Act; the judges can only point out such conflicts and leave it for Parliament to resolve them (as in the Law Lords' 2004 ruling against the internment of foreign terror suspects at Belmarsh, where Parliament subsequently rescinded the internment law). In other words, the UK Human Rights Act has no superior legal status – it is not entrenched in the way that the American Bill of Rights is.

The courts and the executive

Administrative law is the term applied to the whole package of laws which apply to executive and other public bodies. The ordinary courts may hear civil or criminal actions against central or local government members or departments. The courts may declare the orders or actions of a minister or department to be *ultra vires*, that is, beyond their legal powers, either because of what was done or because of the way in which it was done. There is no distinct body of administrative law or courts in the United Kingdom (unlike, for example, France) – in other words, such cases are heard and enforced in the same way as all other types of law.

Such **judicial review** of executive action has increased markedly since three significant rulings against the government in 1976, concerning attempts to ban Laker Skytrain (the first ever low-cost UK airline), to stop people buying TV licences early to avoid a price increase and to hasten the introduction of comprehensive schools in Tameside. (This last case, incidentally, involved Lord Denning again displaying his own 'politics and prejudices' when he said to parents trying to prevent the closure of a grammar school: 'Search as I may, and it is not for want of trying, I cannot find any abuse or misuse of power by the education authority . . . It is sad to have to say so, after so much effort has been expended by so many in so good a cause.')

Those were all rulings against a Labour Government, but later Conservative Governments were overruled by the UK courts more often than any previously: notably Michael Howard's Home Office being ruled illegal fifteen times in the 1990s, for example, over cuts in compensation for crime victims and illegal deportation of asylum seekers. Since 1997, the Labour Government has been ruled illegal many times. Some examples include: the domestic ban on beef on the bone during the BSE scare; the secret extension of genetically-modified crop research; NHS restrictions on the prescription of Viagra; the indefinite detention and deportation of some asylum seekers; the fining of lorry drivers who (often unwittingly) carry stowaways (under article 6 of the European Convention on Human Rights protecting the right to a fair trial); the detention of child asylum seekers in adult prisons which was ruled illegal in 2007; and, also in 2007, the government's consultation process on nuclear power was also ruled 'seriously flawed, procedurally unfair and misleading'.

In a single week in 2008, there were five headline-grabbing examples of judicial review. First, the High Court ruled that the government acted unlawfully in retrospectively tightening up immigration rules for highly skilled workers who wanted to stay in the United Kingdom. Then it ruled that the government and Serious Fraud Office had acted unlawfully in dropping a corruption probe into a £43 billion Saudi/BAE arms deal on grounds of 'national security' (although it was apparent that the government's concerns were primarily commercial, also contrary to law). The government has since threatened to increase the power of the Attorney General to give him or her the right to stop the courts from intervening at all whenever the government pleads 'national security'. The courts also ruled, contrary to government insistence, that human rights laws can be applied to soldiers in combat zones (in the case of a UK soldier who died of heatstroke in Iraq due to inadequate kit); and, in the same case, that coroners could not be banned from using critical phrases such as 'serious failure'; and, in another case, that illegal asylum seekers cannot be denied NHS care. However, in the same week the Law

Lords rejected an attempt by the parents of two dead UK soldiers to force the government to hold a public inquiry into the invasion of Iraq.

However, any central government usually has a majority in a sovereign Parliament and, therefore, if it is ruled illegal by the courts it may use Parliament to rewrite the law and so legalise itself. It may even backdate the rewritten law so that the government was never technically illegal – so-called 'retrospective law'. This tactic was employed frequently during the 1980s under Margaret Thatcher's Conservative Governments. Some examples include: Environment Secretary, Nicholas Ridley, taking £50 million too much from the Greater London Council (then led by Ken Livingstone and just prior to its abolition by Thatcher) to finance the new London Regional Transport body (1985); increasing toll charges for the Severn Bridge (1986); authorising the building of the Okehampton by-pass through Dartmoor National Park (1986); DHSS Secretary, Norman Fowler, imposing cuts in board and lodging allowances (1986); cuts in opticians' fees (1986); and the Local Government Act 1987 which retrospectively legalised central government's grant allocations to local authorities, which, it was discovered, had been technically illegal since 1981. Subsequent Labour Governments have also employed this tactic, though much less often. Labour Chancellor Gordon Brown's 1998 budget, for example, contained a retrospective law closing an offshore tax loophole.

The courts' control of central government is, therefore, limited, and is inextricably bound up with the issue of parliamentary sovereignty. It is also, of course, debatable how far non-elected and arguably unrepresentative judges *should* control 'democratic' public bodies. Some commentators such as Griffith[3] do not, in Lord Denning's words, 'trust the judges' to interpret and enforce the law in a liberal and progressive way, because they see UK judges as unrepresentative, unaccountable and largely conservative.

Others used to argue that, in cases of dispute between the state and the citizen, UK judges may 'show themselves more executive-minded than the executive' (Lord Atkin), especially on issues of national security and official secrecy in the mid-1980s such as the banning of trades unions at the government's 'spy centre' at GCHQ, and the *Tisdall* and *Ponting* government secrecy cases; and also in key industrial disputes such as the 1984–5 miners' strike.

Nevertheless, such cases of judicial review continue to rise (to around 5,000 per year currently): perhaps because the judges are less 'executive-minded' nowadays; or because citizens are increasingly aware of their legal rights against government; and/or because governments are increasingly careless about adhering to the letter of the law.

Parliament and the judges

There has been friction between politicians and judges for at least three decades – superficially over sentencing limits but, more fundamentally, over perennial conflict between the doctrines of parliamentary sovereignty and the rule of law. The Human Rights Act 1998 sought to balance these rival doctrines by preserving the legislative sovereignty of Parliament, while allowing judges to make 'declarations of incompatibility' between ordinary legislation and the Human Rights Act. Although Parliament can, in theory, simply ignore such declarations, the legal and political pressures to acknowledge and respond to them are weighty. Recent judgments over, for example, the rights of prisoners, asylum seekers and suspected terrorists goaded Tony Blair, Gordon Brown and David Cameron into musing publicly about reviewing, that is, limiting, the provisions of the Human Rights Act or even abolishing it altogether (see also below).

The question is who should decide the balance between the rights of the individual and the security of society: the judges or the politicians? Most politicians argue that it is, ultimately, for elected representatives to decide. Some senior judges, however, argue that politicians may often have their own short-term electoral interests at heart rather than the genuine longer-term interests and freedoms of society.

Freedom or security?

Lord Denning (again) presided over the well-known 'ABC trial' in 1978 when two journalists, Crispin Aubrey and Duncan Campbell, and ex-soldier John Berry were charged under the Official Secrets Act for compiling information – from already published sources – about British intelligence to produce a kind of 'do it yourself' official secret. Lord Denning summed up: 'When the state is in danger, our own cherished freedoms and even the rules of natural justice have to take second place' – a view contrary to that of liberal democratic theory.

A current example of this apparent, ongoing dilemma between freedom and security arose from the Terrorism Act 2001 which allowed some foreign nationals to be detained indefinitely in Belmarsh high security prison without any charge or trial – and, by 2005, some had been interned for three years. The United Kingdom was the only country to have opted out of part of the European Convention on Human Rights in order to introduce these measures. Even the Conservatives, who are generally strong law and order advocates, described this law as 'needless totalitarianism'. In a landmark ruling, the Law Lords ruled in 2004 that such internment was contrary to both UK and European human rights laws. The foreign nationals were all released because there was insufficient admissible evidence to press any charges, although they were then often subject to 'control orders' amounting to stringent house arrest.

After the suicide bombings in London in 2005, PM Tony Blair publicly announced (apparently without consultation even with the Home Office) proposals for yet more restrictive anti-terror laws. Before any parliamentary process had begun, Opposition Leader, Michael Howard, entered the fray in support of the Prime Minister and warned judges 'not to thwart the wishes of Parliament'. Writing in the *Daily Telegraph*, he said: 'Parliament must be supreme. Aggressive judicial activism will not only undermine the public's confidence in the impartiality of our judiciary. It could also put our security at risk.'[4] He cited the Law Lords' 2004 ruling over the Belmarsh detainees as an example of judicial interference. He was especially critical of Lord Hoffmann's comment that: 'The real threat to the life of the nation . . . comes not from terrorism but from laws such as these.' Blair also warned the judges that 'the rules of the game are changing' – both politicians apparently impinging on judicial independence. However, Howard primarily blamed, not the judges, but the Labour Government for drawing the judges into the 'political sphere' by passing the Human Rights Act. Liberal Democrat peer, Lord Lester QC, on the other hand, said that judges were charged under the Human Rights Act to interpret and enforce the laws of Parliament and not to thwart them. 'It is completely astonishing', he said, 'that a modern day Conservative Party should wish to whittle away the safeguards for you and me by creating weaker, less effective judicial remedies than we have at present.'[5]

The Labour Government sought to replace the internment law with a ninety-day detention period for foreign terror suspects but, in 2005, it suffered its first Commons defeat since 1997 (and the largest post-war defeat on such a significant issue), thanks to Conservative and Liberal Democrat opposition combined with forty-nine Labour rebels. Parliament did, however, agree to extend the potential detention period from fourteen to twenty-eight days.

Within a month of taking office in 2007, new PM Gordon Brown said that he wanted to double to fifty-six days the period that terrorist suspects could be detained without charge. However, the joint Lords and Commons Committee on Human Rights said that there was insufficient evidence to justify this. The committee's Labour chairman, Andrew Dismore, pointed out that there was only one serious alleged plot where six people had been held for up to twenty-eight days – three of whom were then released. Even the police were not asking for an extension yet. The cross-party committee's report concluded that the law should be changed only if it was 'justified by clear evidence that the need for such a power already exists'. It also backed a full adversarial hearing before a judge when deciding if a suspect needed to be detained for longer without charge. Currently, this period of detention can be extended in the detainee's absence and can be based on information not available to them. This is 'very far removed from anything we would consider to be a fair procedure', the report said. The parliamentary committee also recommended the production of an annual report on any police use of the power to detain without charge beyond fourteen days.

It became increasingly clear that the government would not get fifty-six-day detention through the Commons. By 2008, the government was seeking to extend from twenty-eight to forty-two days the period that terrorist suspects could be detained without charge, but this was ultimately defeated by the House of Lords.

This legislative conflict between Parliament, government and the judges has been one of the most seminal constitutional disputes for some decades in the United Kingdom. It poses fundamental questions about the freedom and security of UK citizens, and about the roles of politicians and judges in defending public rights and safety.

From some liberal perspectives, of course, there is no real dilemma here: as the quotation (probably wrongly) attributed to Benjamin Franklin famously goes: 'Any society that would give up a little liberty to gain a little security will deserve neither and lose both.'

A UK 'supreme court'

The UK's most senior judges – the Law Lords – have long breached the liberal democratic principle of the separation of powers, since they are members of both the judiciary and the legislature. The Labour Government, therefore, decided to remove these judges from the House of Lords and establish them as a separate court altogether independent of Parliament.

The judges initially resisted these changes. Aside from their natural conservatism, they feared that it might actually weaken their judicial role. They also valued their legislative voice in the Lords, not to mention their membership of 'the best gentlemen's club in London'. They questioned the cost of the reform – an estimated £50 million. They, therefore, dug their heels in, largely by the tactic of rejecting the buildings offered for the new and separate court as insufficiently prestigious: 'The building in which the court is housed must reflect the importance of the rule of law in a modern democracy.'[6] The government's response to this was to grant a £30 million contract to a team, headed by top architect Lord Foster, to redesign and renovate Middlesex Guildhall in Parliament Square as the new supreme court building by 2009. The Law Lords eventually accepted this new arrangement.

Importantly, the label 'supreme court' is rather a misnomer. The new court, like the Law Lords before it, will have 'constitutional' responsibilities in overseeing the relationship between the devolved administrations and the centre, as well as its adjudication of the Human Rights Act. However, the new court will have no new powers; crucially, unlike the American Supreme Court, it will not be able to veto parliamentary legislation.

A new Judicial Appointments Commission has also been created which is now responsible for drawing up shortlists of judicial candidates – taking over this role from the Lord Chancellor. However, the final decision on appointments will still rest with a politician. With the formation of PM Gordon Brown's first Cabinet, the Lord Chancellor was no longer even a lord. Instead, Labour MP Jack Straw combined the offices of Secretary of State for Justice and Lord Chancellor (briefly the Secretary of State for Constitutional Affairs). He still has the ultimate power of veto on senior judicial appointments, so the process has only partially been separated from the political sphere.

A Bill of Rights for the United Kingdom: the Human Rights Act 1998

In the United Kingdom, until the enforcement of a domestic Bill of Rights in 2000, few rights were guaranteed in law; such rights as citizens possessed tended to be negative: that is, they were allowed to do something if there was no law against it. The Human Rights Act 1998 (HRA) incorporated the European Convention on Human Rights into UK law, and it came into force in 2000 after UK judges had undergone relevant training. However, in cases of conflict between the HRA and ordinary parliamentary statute, UK judges are required to enforce statute (to maintain the principle of parliamentary sovereignty); they can only point out any such conflicts to Parliament for possible action (or not). The HRA also has sweeping exemptions 'in accordance with the law and the necessity for public safety, prevention of disorder or crime, protection of public health or morals or rights and the freedoms of others'. It is, therefore, much weaker than, for example, the US Bill of Rights, but it has prompted more 'rights awareness' in the drafting of laws, in judicial interpretation of those laws and, increasingly, among the general public – and even the politicians.

The Human Rights Act has generated significant conflict between Parliament, government and the courts. In the view of Scottish judge, Lord McCluskey, the Act has established 'a field day for crackpots, a pain in the neck for judges and legislators and a gold mine for lawyers'.[7] Some senior politicians have breached convention by publicly criticising judges' human rights rulings, including Jack Straw and David Blunkett calling the judges 'bonkers' over the anti-internment ruling, and Blair and Cameron calling the judges' ruling in favour of the Afghan hijackers 'an abuse of common sense'. Opposition

Leader, Michael Howard, in 2005, blamed it for bringing courts and judges into the political sphere. This is disingenuous: the courts have always been charged with interpreting statute law and ruling on the legality of executive actions – unavoidably political spheres. The Human Rights Act has provided more codification, clarity and consistency for these rulings and has put them in a previously rather neglected context of citizens' rights.

However, both Gordon Brown and David Cameron have recently criticised the Act and/or its application. The Human Rights Act enshrined the European Convention on Human Rights into British law. The Conservatives say that they want a Bill of Rights specifically designed to fit British needs and traditions. David Cameron says that the Human Rights Act has resulted in some 'perverse' judgments stopping suspected terrorists from being deported and that it has not protected key rights either, with ministers threatening the right to trial by jury in some cases:

> Let's look at getting rid of the Human Rights Act and saying instead of that, instead of having an Act that imports, if you like, a foreign convention of rights into British law, why not try and write our own British Bill of Rights and Responsibilities, clearly and precisely into law, so we can have human rights with common sense.[8]

However, Cameron said that he was not proposing withdrawal from the European Convention on Human Rights, nor did he want to prevent people pursuing cases at the European Court of Human Rights in Strasbourg. To both pro- and anti-European critics, this seemed illogical.

Gordon Brown, meanwhile, has suggested the idea of a new Bill of Rights and Duties to run alongside the UK Human Rights Act. This seemed, to many, equally illogical.

As has often been pointed out, the European Convention was written by British lawyers – led by Conservative Lord Chancellor Kilmuir – after the Second World War. Essentially, British concepts of human rights were imported into Europe rather than vice versa. As former Lord Chancellor, Lord Falconer, said in 2006: 'Human rights are as British as the Beatles. As British as the BBC. As British as bitter beer.' Recent legislative trends under Labour Governments have, however, called Falconer's statement into question.

'New' Labour authoritarianism on law and order

'New' Labour has passed sixteen Criminal Justice Acts and created over a thousand new crimes in the decade since it came to power in 1997.

The introduction of these and many other illiberal laws, on the one hand, has employed Parliament in the most sweeping curtailments of the liberties of UK citizens for over three centuries and, on the other hand, seems certain to pave the way for an increase in the number and scope of future judicial rulings on human rights.

The people's voice

The 'new' Labour government pushed through one particularly controversial and illiberal law during its term in office. The Serious Organised Crime and Police Act 2005 (SOCA) included a clause requiring all protests within a half-mile exclusion zone around Westminster to have prior police permission, otherwise the Home Secretary has the power to ban them. The Opposition described the new law as 'a contempt of democracy and a contempt of people's right to protest'. The new law was actually targeted at lone anti-Iraq war protester Brian Haw – who has been in Parliament Square since 2001 – because many ministers and MPs regarded him as an embarrassing eyesore and a disruptive nuisance. Ministers particularly disliked his habit of shouting abuse at politicians through a megaphone. However, the law was not backdated; and an amendment which attempted to backdate it was rejected by the judges because it was done through secondary legislation. Lady Justice Smith expressed surprise in court that the government had attempted to use such an order 'to criminalise conduct which would not otherwise be criminal. If Parliament wishes to criminalise any particular activity, it must do so in clear terms. If it wishes to do so, Parliament can amend this Act,' she said. Ironically, therefore, Haw is now the only person in the country allowed to protest outside Parliament without authorisation as his six-year vigil predated the new law. In the predawn hours of a morning in 2006, seventy-eight police raided his protest site and removed most of his placards – an exercise which cost the taxpayers £27,000. Later that year, he and his supporters marked 2,000 days of his continuous anti-war vigil, and he remains there to this day, despite

Box 9.1 Examples of illiberal legislation introduced by 'new' Labour since 1997

- Reducing the age of criminal liability and extending abolition of the right to silence to 10 year olds.
- Curfews for children under ten and electronic tagging of 10 year olds.
- Retrospective restriction of the **double jeopardy** rule.
- The United Kingdom now has more CCTV cameras per head of the population than any other country in the world.
- The prison population in 2008 was a record 81,000, and female prisoner numbers have increased by 180 per cent since the 1990s.
- The Anti-Social Behaviour Act 2003 redefined a 'public assembly' subject to police restrictions from a gathering of twenty people or more to just two.
- New and draconian anti-terrorism laws were passed in 1998, 2000, 2001, 2005 and 2006.
- The UK government is pressing ahead with compulsory national identity cards despite substantial parliamentary and public opposition.
- Criminal Justice and Human Tissue Acts 2001–4 allow for the taking of DNA by the police – and its commercial, academic or security analysis – which can then be stored indefinitely, from a person who is never charged, let alone convicted, and without their permission. There are already around three million people on the national DNA database in the United Kingdom – by far the highest proportion in the world.
- The Civil Contingencies Act 2004 gives the government sweeping powers to amend or repeal any Act of Parliament after a state of emergency has been declared, including the Habeas Corpus Act 1816 and the Parliament Act 1911 which limits the duration of a Parliament to five years. An 'emergency' can be declared orally, without a written order, by any senior minister. According to this law all ministers are 'deemed to always act reasonably and cannot be criminally liable for misuse of these emergency powers' – in other words, this law itself explicitly places the government above the rule of law. This law was passed while the United Kingdom was already declared to be in a 'state of public emergency' in 2001–5 (see below).
- Restrictions on protests around Parliament under the Serious Organised Crime and Police Act 2005 (see previous page).

the continuing court challenges launched by the government, mayor and police – most recently in 2007 when the police tried to argue that terrorists could hide bombs under his banners and placards without him knowing.

Others, however, have been excluded from peaceful protest outside Parliament. There were thirty-three arrests at protests in Parliament Square in the year after the new SOCA law came into force. For example, at the end of 2005, a young woman – Maya Evans – was arrested, charged and convicted under the new law for standing by the Cenotaph memorial in Whitehall – which falls within the exclusion zone – and reading aloud the names of UK soldiers killed in Iraq. She was given a conditional discharge and ordered to pay £100 costs. In 2007, new PM Gordon Brown suggested the need to review this law.

Parliament and the European courts

Besides the UK courts, the United Kingdom is a member of two separate European courts. The first is the European Court of Justice (ECJ) at Luxembourg which enforces European Union law, for example, on the world-wide beef ban, the forty-eight-hour maximum working week, against the UK's discriminatory retirement ages for men and women, pollution of UK beaches, etc. As an EU institution, this court has *de jure* sovereignty over all member states and can enforce heavy fines against those which breach its rulings (see Chapter 7).

The second is the European Court of Human Rights (ECHR) at Strasbourg. This is nothing to do with the European Union and it pre-dates its creation. It enforces the 1950 European Convention for the Protection of Human Rights, ratified by forty countries including the United Kingdom. However, its rulings are not formally binding in the way that EU law is: for example, in 1990 the ECHR ruled illegal the detention without charge of three men for over four days under the UK Prevention of Terrorism Act; but the UK government said that it would simply ignore the ruling. Also, as aforementioned, the Labour Government opted out of article 5 of the European Convention on Human Rights and of its own Human Rights Act, which guarantees the right to liberty and grants protection against detention without charge or trial, to introduce internment in 2001. In order to do this, the Home Secretary had to declare that the United Kingdom was in a 'state of public emergency', which was not lifted until 2005.

The ECHR has ruled against UK governments on many issues, including: phone tapping by government agencies; corporal punishment in state schools; torture of prisoners in Northern Ireland; press censorship; and discrimination against women, gays and ethnic minorities. In 2004, the ECHR ruled that the UK's blanket ban on votes for prisoners was a breach of free elections, free expression and anti-discrimination laws. Until 2000, UK governments had lost more cases at the ECHR in Strasbourg than had any other governments, largely because the United Kingdom had no domestic Bill of Rights and did not enforce the European Convention in its own courts; and also because much UK government action is still based simply on convention rather than on law.

The ECHR also, of course, rules on human rights cases which do not directly involve the UK government. In 2002, for example, the ECHR refused to allow terminally ill Diane Pretty's husband the legal right to help her to die. Such cases often raise conflicting rights issues. In 2007, for example, Natallie Evans lost her long fight for the right to use the frozen embryos that she had created with her former partner because he withdrew his consent for her to try to conceive with the embryos. The seventeen judges in the Grand Chamber in Strasbourg ruled against her – with some expressing personal regret – by 13:4.

• •

☑ What you should have learnt from reading this chapter

- This chapter has returned once again to the central doctrine of the UK constitution – that of parliamentary sovereignty – and has explained its practical applications and limitations with reference to the courts.

- It has also cited both a defence and a critique of the principle of parliamentary sovereignty itself.

- It has gone on to describe the courts' facility for judicial review of executive actions and its rapidly increasing application since the 1970s; but also governments' ability to circumvent it, employing the doctrine of parliamentary sovereignty.

- It has also highlighted friction between Parliament and the courts, using the case study of the Terrorism Act 2001 and the controversial issue of detention without charge.

- This chapter has also outlined and assessed the creation of a UK 'supreme court' – a misleading label for a process of separation between Parliament and the senior judges.

- It has gone on to highlight the contradiction between 'new' Labour's introduction of the Human Rights Act 1998 and its conspicuously authoritarian legislative agenda on criminal justice, anti-terrorism, citizens' rights of protest and ministers' emergency powers.

- Finally, it has outlined the nature of the UK's membership of two European courts, the ECJ and the ECHR – of which only one, the ECJ, has formal sovereignty over Westminster.

Glossary of key terms

Administrative law The body of laws which apply to executive and other public bodies.
Case law Judge-made law as interpreted by the courts in significant test cases.
Double jeopardy Legal principle which prevented anyone from being tried twice for the same crime.
Judicial review Court hearings against actions of central or local government or other public authorities.

Likely examination questions

Short questions:

- What are civil liberties?

- Explain the difference between judicial neutrality and judicial independence.

- In what ways is the independence of the judiciary upheld?

- What is meant by 'judicial review'?

Essay questions:

- Is it important that judges should be representative?

- How independent are UK judges from Parliament and the executive?

- Do the benefits of the Human Rights Act outweigh its problems?

- How effective are judges in protecting civil liberties in the United Kingdom?

 ## Helpful websites

http://news.bbc.co.uk

http://www.parliament.uk

http://www.amnesty.org.uk/education

http://www.liberty-human-rights.org.uk

 ## Suggestions for further reading

Atkins, C. et al., *Taking Liberties*, San Diego, CA: Revolver Books, 2007.

Fenwick, H. (ed.) et al., *Judicial Reasoning Under the UK Human Rights Act*, Cambridge: Cambridge University Press, 2007.

Hoffman, D. and Rowe J., *Human Rights in the UK: An Introduction to the Human Rights Act 1998*, London: Longman, 2006.

Le Sueur, A., *Building the UK's New Supreme Court: National and Comparative Perspectives*, Oxford: Oxford University Press, 2004.

Wadham, J., *Blackstone's Guide to the Human Rights Act 1998*, Oxford: Oxford University Press, 2007.

CHAPTER 10

Conclusion: The Future of Parliament in an Age of Reform

Overview

This concluding chapter presents an outline and analysis of the current state of Parliament and of likely, possible and desirable future reforms. First, it outlines the government's 2008 White Paper proposals for future reform of the Lords and highlights several possible problems arising from them. It then outlines the limited reforms to date of the Commons, and a range of ideas for future reform from diverse sources. Readers, ultimately, must evaluate the extent to which Parliament is going to be an influential and authoritative fulcrum of democracy, or a marginalised and supine talking shop.

Key issues to be covered in this chapter

- The story so far
- The Lords
- The Commons
- Westminster and the European Union

The story so far

The Labour governments since 1997 have been the boldest constitutional reformers for a century. Their motives have been mixed: partly a natural instinct for modernisation; partly to reduce or remove the 'forces of conservatism' perceived in, for example, the House of Lords; partly, after eighteen years in opposition, a desire to curb the power of any future Conservative Government; partly – through devolution – an attempt to forestall growing nationalist sentiment in the regions of the United Kingdom and to steal votes from the nationalist parties; and partly to shore up their own political strength in Scotland, Wales and the regions.

The overriding impression given by Labour's reform programme, therefore, is that it has been piecemeal, selective and self-serving. It has also been combined with a growing centralisation of executive power in the hands of the prime minister and his unelected advisers; and it has, paradoxically, been accompanied by an increasingly illiberal programme of legislative changes in the spheres of criminal justice, law and order, anti-terrorism, state security, asylum and immigration.

'Parliament isn't working': this trenchant statement formed the first sentence of a weighty pamphlet from Parliament First, a cross-party group of MPs committed to reform of the Commons.[1] It points out that recent changes 'fail to distinguish between the modernisation of customs, conventions and ceremonies and the political reform of Parliament'. Their recommendations fall under four headings. First, improving scrutiny, notably by making the committees more independent. Secondly, strengthening the legislative process, for example, by strengthening scrutiny of Bills at an early stage. Thirdly, changing the balance in the relationship between Parliament and government by reducing the number of ministers and putting most prerogative powers, such as public appointments, on a statutory basis and subject to the approval of MPs. Finally, putting the Commons more in charge of its own business such as the timetable, and making it more professional in the process.

Almost all such reforms involve the surrender of powers by the government and hence might well be resisted by the government. The answer, as always, lies in MPs' own hands.

Before looking in more detail at possible future reforms of the Commons, this chapter will examine the current position and possible future of the House of Lords.

The House of Lords

Labour's 2005 election manifesto pledged that: 'In our next term we will complete the reform of the Lords so that it is a modern and effective revising chamber'. They proposed, specifically, to remove the remaining ninety-two hereditary peers and consider an elected element, but also to reduce the Lords' one-year power of legislative delay to just sixty sitting days. The Conservatives said that the government was trying to 'disable' the House of Lords and accused the prime minister of showing contempt for Parliament. The Liberal Democrats described it as 'improper and unconstitutional' to put a time limit on how long Bills can spend in the Upper House when there is no evidence that the Lords has abused its powers.

By 2008, the Labour Government was adjusting its proposals to head off growing opposition to reform from peers who feared for their jobs if and when an elected system was introduced. After deadlock between the two chambers for much of the 2005 Parliament over the future of the Lords, in mid-2008 the government produced a White Paper outlining their latest proposed reforms, to take place after the next general election in 2010. Justice Secretary Jack Straw said that it had never been the government's intention to legislate in the 2005 Parliament, explicitly contradicting Labour's 2005 manifesto. The government's procrastination did not surprise some seasoned observers: 'The solution to the long-term future of the Lords is always after the next election, and has been for a century . . . Do not expect early action from a Cameron government . . . So current peers need not fear early execution.'[2]

Now the government made no mention of curtailing the powers of the Lords; instead, the White Paper focused on composition. It suggested that most, if not all peers would be elected and would serve single, non-renewable terms of three electoral cycles, between twelve and fifteen years. (Both government and Opposition continue to favour some appointees to ensure an independent element.) Elections would be at the same time for those as MPs.

Four possible electoral systems were suggested: first-past-the-post (favoured by the Conservatives and many Labour MPs); AV; STV; and open or semi-open party list. Only the last two are forms of proportional representation. The method of election would, of course, be crucial to whether the government of the day would have a majority.

The Lords would be reduced in number from more than 700 to a maximum of 450. The ninety-two hereditary peers would be abolished but the bishops would stay. (The Law Lords will already have been separated out by 2010.) Members would be paid a salary between that of members of devolved legislatures and Westminster MPs (rather than claiming allowances, as now). It is estimated that this would raise costs from £13 million to £41 million per year.

The government emphasised that: 'The White Paper represents a significant step on the road to reform and is intended to generate further debate and consideration rather than being a final blueprint for reform.'[3] Justice Secretary Jack Straw insisted, however, that the Commons would retain primacy in policy and decision making.

Certain flaws – or, at least, question marks – about these proposals are immediately apparent. The question of how to reduce the number of peers has not been addressed; transitional arrangements could be long and complicated; for example, how long would existing peers serve, or would they just be allowed to die off? The government's earlier thinking was that, instead of the mass expulsion of all hereditary and many life peers, voluntary retirement and natural wastage through death would cut the number of peers over a couple of decades from around 740 to 450. In the short term, this would mean a substantial increase in the number of peers as elected members came in without existing peers being forced out. A 'redundancy package' may be offered including severance pay and pensions arrangements (this despite the fact that peers are not, currently, salaried).

The percentage of elected peers is not addressed, nor how and by whom the remainder would be chosen. The Labour Government leans to having 50 per cent elected members. The Conservatives have expressed support for a 300-member 'Senate', 80 per cent elected – presumably out of a desire to embarrass the Labour Government rather than for any reasons of principle since they are not, by nature, reformists. David Cameron sought to reassure a meeting of peers in 2006 that a Conservative Government under his leadership would not address the issue of Lords' reform until its third term. The Liberal Democrats have long argued for a fully elected second chamber but, by 2006, had modified their stance to advocate an 80 per cent elected chamber. Of course, peers will very likely continue to oppose the idea of elections entirely.

Following the 'cash for honours' scandal of 2007, a report from the Commons Public Administration Committee recommended a new Corruption Act which would enable MPs and peers to be prosecuted for bribery, and would grant new powers to public funding watchdogs, notably the Electoral Commission. It also said that the Prime Minister should give up the right to create peerages and to appoint the people who vet the nominations. Currently, too, the House of Lords Appointments Commission only has an advisory role and its decisions are, in theory, subject to a veto by the Prime Minister. The report also suggested that a peerage granted as a political honour should not allow the person to sit in the House of Lords. All recommended names should be published and all peers should pay British taxes. The report said pointedly:

> The current Prime Minister could make changes without needing parliamentary approval. For example, he could implement tomorrow all the changes we suggest to the House of Lords appointment procedures. He could call on all parties in future to submit long lists of nominees to the Appointments Commission without legislation, and give the commission the formal power of selection. He could undertake never to veto or change any decision on either honours or peerages, effectively withdrawing himself from the process. The point is that it could be done now if the government wanted to. We believe it should, as an immediate and proper response to the lessons to be learned from recent events.[4]

The MPs also called for a system enabling corrupt or criminal peers to resign, or be compelled to leave, which is not currently available.

Further potential problems arise from the government's White Paper proposals such as: if members of the second chamber were elected at the same time as MPs, this could produce a close reflection of the first chamber, undermining the Lords' usefulness as a check upon the Commons and exacerbating the possibilities of an 'elective dictatorship' in the UK political system. This is why most other bicameral systems around the world ensure that members of the Upper House are elected in the mid-term of the Lower House.

The idea of members of the second chamber serving 'non-renewable terms' is likely to be even more contentious, since it renders them unaccountable and largely negates the purpose of election.

The retention of the 'lords spiritual' – Anglican bishops – in the legislature of a twenty-first century, multi-cultural and largely secular society may also be questioned by some.

Overall, the government's proposals err on the conservative side, and seem designed to do little to increase the checks and balances on the government of the day, or even to make Westminster conspicuously more democratic. Above all, there is simply no consensus on the whole question of reform of the Lords – except, perhaps, for the name 'Senate', to which the government will not commit, to avoid preoccupation with name over composition and role.

Meanwhile, the House of Lords is to spend £100 million on new offices opposite Parliament, complete with a wine cellar, an art store and chandeliers costing £130,000. There may be a tunnel connecting the new offices to the Palace of Westminster, which would more than double the cost. Since there will be room for only 117 of the 733 current peers in the new offices, this will amount to at least £1 million per peer, even without the tunnel.

For at least one commentator, Johann Hari, the solution is to get rid of the House of Lords altogether:

> What is the function of the second chamber? It is to provide checks and balances, to ensure the Commons does not rush into bad or foolish legislation, and to prevent democracy from descending into a tyranny of the majority. Can these functions be carried out better elsewhere? I think they can – within a remade House of Commons itself.[5]

His solutions are: PR – hence coalitions; and real, substantial powers to select committees, such as far greater resources, the legal power to subpoena witnesses, and the right to scrutinise and veto government appointments.

Supporters of the House of Lords, however, point out that the upper chamber is now more representative and active than ever before: the House has a higher number of female legislators than the Commons, sits for about 170 days per session (longer than the Commons), attendance averages 400 peers per day, and it now inflicts twice as many defeats upon the government since the 1999 reforms, two-fifths of which are broadly accepted by the Commons. Yet peers are still not salaried but, instead, receive a daily attendance allowance and expenses. Perhaps unsurprisingly, most peers routinely claim the maximum amount whenever they attend – up to £48,000 a year, for which they do not have to submit receipts or pay tax. As noted by Peter Riddell:

> There is a populist paradox in our attitudes to Parliament. The political class, its perks and privileges, are deplored in the same breath as we seek more assertive legislators. We cherish the myth of the amateur, independent MP or peer, but expect him or her to be largely full-time in upholding our rights and interests.[6]

If we expect our legislators to perform their roles in a professional way, perhaps we should treat and pay them accordingly.

The House of Commons

Since 1997, the Labour Government has made some quite small and piecemeal reforms of the Commons (apart from devolution, which was a major constitutional change):

- Changes to the Commons timetable, so that its proceedings start and finish earlier in the day. This was done to reduce the number of late-night and all-night sittings and to make the place more 'family friendly', especially for its women members.
- A new building – Portcullis House, next door to Westminster – has given MPs added office space.
- PM Tony Blair cut PMQT from twice to once per week.
- The Prime Minister has taken questions from the Commons' Liaison Committee (of Select Committee chairpeople) twice a year since 2002.
- The Electoral Administration Act 2006 lowered the age limit for MPs from twenty-one to eighteen, bringing it into line with the voting age. This has prompted renewed calls for a lowering of the voting age to sixteen from the Liberal Democrats and others, and

the government is considering this, due mainly to concerns over low voting turn outs. The new law also tightened the rules on postal voting, making it an offence to apply fraudulently for a postal vote and banning political parties from collecting postal vote applications from voters. The opposition parties said that this did not go far enough, because it did not require voters to register individually rather than by household. Individual registration in Northern Ireland led to a large drop in the numbers registering to vote and, therefore, the government rejected it for the rest of the United Kingdom. The new law also allowed foreign election observers access to all stages of the electoral process.

In the 2007 local elections, several new voting and vote counting methods were trialled including internet and telephone voting, early voting and electronic scanning technology to count ballot papers. The Electoral Commission had opposed almost all of them on grounds such as possible technological flaws, fraud and breaches of ballot secrecy; but the government brushed aside their concerns, prompting one newspaper editorial headline, 'What's the point of the Electoral Commission?'.[7]

Similarly, in 2008 the government decided to push through measures to reduce Conservative spending in marginal seats outside of election periods (during which party spending is limited by law to about £11,000 per constituency), despite objections from the Electoral Commission. Conservative deputy chairman, Lord Ashcroft, had angered the government by directing millions of pounds into target constituencies, which was credited with securing many of the thirty-three gains made by the Conservatives at the 2005 General Election. Conservative spokesman, Francis Maude, said:

> For a governing party to rig election rules just months before an election in order to cling on to power has all the hallmarks of a banana republic. It is quite proper for the Electoral Commission to raise concerns over such partisan moves by the government, and there is also a real prospect of a legal challenge in the courts against such flawed new laws.[8]

Following the furore over Conservative MP, Derek Conway, who paid his full-time student son over £40,000 as a parliamentary researcher, the government in 2008 also proposed banning MPs from employing their children using taxpayers' money. At the time of the government's proposal, at least twenty-two MPs employed their children (the exact number was unclear because it became compulsory to register them only in August 2008). Some employed more than one: for example, spouses Peter and Iris Robinson, both DUP MPs, employed two sons, a daughter and a daughter-in-law between them.

In 2008, the Commons finally lost its hard-fought court battle against the forced disclosure of MPs' expenses (which totalled £93 million per year) under the Freedom of Information Act; including a detailed breakdown of second home allowances of up to £24,000 per year per MP – the so-called 'John Lewis list'. A subsequent review of MPs allowances recommended abolishing the John Lewis list. MPs – including thirty-three government ministers – initially rejected the recommendations but, two weeks later, under pressure from party leaders, backed plans to change the John Lewis list, restricting claims to £2,400.

Whither the Commons?

In 2004, the post-Iraq Butler Report strongly criticised Blair's style of government for bypassing Cabinet, over-dependence on political appointees and spin doctors, over-emphasis on spin and centralised control and too much whipping and insufficient parliamentary control of the executive. Butler stated:

> I think we are a country where we suffer very badly from Parliament not having sufficient control over the executive, and that is a very grave flaw. We should be breaking away from the party whip. The executive is much too free to bring in a huge number of extremely bad bills, a huge amount of regulation and to do whatever it likes – and whatever it likes is what will get the best headlines tomorrow. All that is part of what is bad government in this country.[9]

Given Butler's status as the former top UK civil servant, the BBC's Andrew Marr called this Report 'a red card from God'. It helped to stimulate serious consideration of significant political reforms from all quarters, aided by a change of Prime Minister.

Gordon Brown took over as Prime Minister in 2007 with a substantial agenda of constitutional reform proposals designed, in part, to signify a change from the days of Blair's premiership, and also to reconnect the voters with the political process. He highlighted twelve areas where power held by the government should be surrendered to MPs or limited 'to make for a more open twenty-first century British democracy which better serves the British people'. These are:

- the power of the executive to declare war;
- the power to request the dissolution of Parliament;
- the power over recall of Parliament;
- the power of the executive to ratify international treaties without decision by Parliament;
- the power to make key public appointments without effective scrutiny;
- the power to restrict parliamentary oversight of the intelligence services;
- the power to choose bishops;
- power in the appointment of judges;
- the power to direct prosecutors in individual criminal cases;
- power over the civil service itself;
- powers to determine the rules governing entitlement to passports;
- powers to determine the rules governing the granting of pardons.

Brown also proposed limiting the 2005 law which restricted the right to demonstrate in Parliament Square, and he suggested introducing Commons committees for each English region, perhaps lowering the voting age from eighteen to sixteen and allowing election day to be moved to weekends. He said that a paper on the electoral system would be produced later. He has long expressed his opposition to PR but is prepared to debate reform. His proposals for reform of the Lords have already been outlined above. There are even tentative proposals for a whole new written constitution and a Bill of Rights and Duties to run alongside the Human Rights Act. Potentially, these could be the biggest changes to the UK political system in living memory.

However, Brown rejected the idea of resolving devolution's 'West Lothian question' by allowing only English MPs to vote on English laws at Westminster, saying that it would create two classes of MPs. Former Conservative leader, Michael Howard, said that devolution had already created two classes of MPs. Then Liberal Democrat leader Sir Menzies Campbell called for a full 'constitutional convention' to discuss changes.

Westminster's Joint Committee on Brown's Draft Constitutional Renewal Bill responded in July 2008, saying that the proposals were 'a step in the right direction' but that 'further work' was needed before a full Bill could be drawn up. They agreed with cutting restrictions on protests in Parliament Square but said that such freedom 'must be balanced against the need for the police and other authorities to have adequate powers to safeguard the proper functioning of Parliament and protect the amenity value of Parliament Square'. They also argued that the proposed reforms of the judicial system came 'too soon' after the 2005 changes to the process of judicial appointments. However, six members of the committee, led by a Liberal Democrat, broke ranks and said that the reforms did not go far enough. They called for the separation of the Attorney General's legal and political roles and for the removal of the office from Parliament.

A month later, the Joint Committee on Human Rights called for an extended Bill of Rights for the United Kingdom, to include social rights to housing, education and a healthy environment as well as greater protection for children, the elderly and those with learning difficulties, plus the right to trial by jury, the right to administrative justice and international human rights which do not yet feature in UK law.

Boundary changes to Westminster constituencies take place every decade or so, to take account of population shifts. The next set of boundary changes in England will be put in place before the next general election – largely in response to a population drift to the suburbs. They will, therefore, favour the Conservatives more than now (although there will still be a big electoral bias against the Conservatives). The overall number of seats will increase from 646 to 650, but the constituencies of some prominent MPs will be abolished altogether: for example, that of Labour Secretary of State for Children, Schools and Families, Ed Balls, and of Liberal Democrat Education spokeswoman, Sarah Teather.

Traditionally, the Conservative Party is not predisposed to radical constitutional change. However, David Cameron is a 'moderniser' who wants to change the image of the party and to outflank Labour on the issue of political reform. The Conservatives had already said in 2004 that, if and when elected, they would reduce the number of MPs by about one-fifth as part of their 'smaller government' plan. This, they said, would save £15 million per year in pay and allowances and £10 million in Commons' administration costs. They would also reduce the number of peers, ministers, government departments, special advisers and civil servants. They also said that they would hold a referendum in Wales to decide whether to abolish the Welsh Assembly. This last proposal seems much less likely to happen now as the Assembly's popularity grows and the current mood is actually to increase its powers: in 2008 the All Wales Convention met to consider full law-making powers for the Welsh Assembly. The Convention was a key commitment of the 2007 Labour–Plaid Cymru coalition deal, although many Labour MPs opposed the idea.

In 2005 Cameron called for a whole raft of reforms, including fixed-term Parliaments, a largely elected Lords, the election by backbenchers of select committees, weakening of government control of the Commons timetable, restrictions on the number of ministers and special advisers and more 'sunset clauses' for controversial legislation. He quoted Disraeli: 'I am conservative to preserve all that is good in our constitution; a radical to remove all that is bad.'[10]

He has expressed support for Gordon Brown's proposals to require parliamentary approval for executive decisions to deploy troops or sign international treaties, formal scrutiny by MPs of significant public appointments such as the head of the NHS or BBC, and of major changes to government structure and organisation. He has rejected changes to the personal prerogative powers of the monarch such as the appointment of PM and dissolution of Parliament, largely to appease traditionalists. He has also rejected plans for compulsory voting, as outlined in a recent pamphlet by the think tank IPPR, saying that not voting should never be a crime. He evoked his party's opposition to compulsory ID cards as he criticised moves to alter the relationship between the citizen and the state. However, like Brown, he rejected the use of proportional representation to replace the UK's first-past-the-post electoral system, arguing that the present link between MPs and their constituencies was 'human, transparent and unambiguous'. Whether Cameron will be able to carry his party with him on what is, for them, an exceptionally radical set of proposals for political change, remains to be seen.

The Liberal Democrats have always been the party most committed to constitutional reform. They would like a codified constitution, proportional representation for general elections, fixed-term Parliaments – probably every four years – removing the Prime Minister's power to decide the date of general elections, reform of the Commons to make it more effective in scrutinising and holding the government to account, the strengthening of the Human Rights Act so that it takes precedence over primary Westminster legislation, a stronger Freedom of Information Act, a stronger Welsh Assembly and elected regional assemblies for England. Such a catalogue of changes would have a profound impact upon the role and status of Parliament.

Other commentators have yet other ideas. For instance, business tycoon, Archie Norman, tried to modernise parliamentary and party procedures while he was a Conservative MP prior to 2005. He said of Parliament: 'When I stepped into Westminster [in 1997] it was like stepping backwards into the 1960s'. It was 'anarchically organised, or rather, disorganised', hidebound by tradition and self-regard, lacking computer and technological resources and skills, and out of step with the United Kingdom it was meant to represent. He continued: 'I hadn't realised the extent to which those cultural things, the obsession with protocol and status and mannerisms actually colours the working effectiveness of the debates.'[11] He believed that it is particularly dangerous when an MP with no management training or skills is put in charge of a vast government department and a multi-million pound budget. He left politics, a frustrated man, in 2005.

An Ofsted survey of fourteen to sixteen year olds in 2005 found that only a quarter knew that Labour was in power and only one in six could identify then Conservative leader, Michael Howard, in photographs. The House of Commons Modernisation Committee has called for Parliament to be a more voter friendly place and more interesting for young people by, for example, a new visitor centre to explain the work of Parliament, a big overhaul of Parliament's website with virtual tours and email newsletters, a guide to be sent to all new voters on their eighteenth birthday and parliamentary roadshows touring schools. When MPs are not at work the chamber should be available to students and members of the National Youth Parliament for debates.

There is also room for reform in MPs themselves. Some male MPs' attitudes are still, apparently, remarkably sexist. A survey of female MPs in 2004 contained accounts of male MPs juggling imaginary breasts and shouting 'melons' as women tried to speak in the Commons, and asking to 'roger' colleagues. Some young female MPs said that colleagues and officials often assumed, at first, that they were secretaries or researchers. Female MPs were expected to stick to traditional 'women's issues' such as education and family policy. When one of only two female MPs resigned from the Defence Select Committee, its chairman, Bruce George, stood up and said, 'Well, I have to make this announcement: one down, one to go.' When another female MP was promoted to the Cabinet, she was asked 'Who have you been sleeping with?'. For many of the women it was quite a culture shock. When Labour's Claire Curtis-Thomas first arrived at Westminster and saw red ribbons hanging from the coat-pegs, she assumed they were to commemorate AIDS day, only to be told that they were for members to hang their swords upon: 'And that's when I knew it really was in the dark ages'.[12] As Lovenduski says, 'All institutions are resistant to change and this is a really traditional institution'. However, with the arrival of more female MPs, Commons' hours have been made a bit more 'family friendly' and the culture is slowly changing.

That said, however, the reforms to the Commons' timetable, introduced by Robin Cook when he was Leader of the House, have been gradually and quietly reversed by traditionalists – with a little help from the government. In 2005, Leader of the House, Geoff Hoon, astonished MPs when he announced provisional recess dates for 2006 running from late July to 9 October, apparently trying to kill off September sittings. He claimed to be responding to 'strong feelings' among MPs who felt the midsummer sitting to be disruptive; but several MPs, from both sides of the House, protested that the new timetable would give the government a free ride over the summer when the public expected Parliament to be holding it to account.

In the 2005 general election, for the first time in history those voting for the winning party were outnumbered by those who didn't vote at all. This prompted one of the most far-reaching explorations of political reform in recent decades, that is, the eighteen-month

Power Inquiry, set up to consider how political participation and voter engagement in the United Kingdom could be increased and deepened. It was established by the Joseph Rowntree Trust, headed by reforming Labour peer, Baroness Kennedy, and cost £800,000. The Inquiry concluded in 2006 that UK politics must become cleaner, fairer and more democratic. Its recommendations included:

- PR;
- age limit for both voting and standing for Parliament should be reduced to sixteen;
- the power of the whips in the Commons should be curbed;
- More power to cross-party parliamentary select committees;
- a £10,000 cap on donations to political parties;
- large organisations, such as trades unions, should be able to donate only £100 per member;
- more state funding of political parties;
- abolishing the £500 election deposit;
- enabling voters to give £3 each from public funds to the political party of their choice as they vote on polling day;
- members of the public should be able to propose legislation;
- voters could compel the government to hold a referendum if they can get two million signatures on a petition (a system of citizens' initiatives that operates in some other countries around the world, most famously Switzerland);
- seventy per cent elected members in the second chamber;
- every member of the House of Lords must be over forty;
- monthly, published logs of ministerial meetings with lobbyists, pressure groups and companies for greater accountability;
- a Royal Commission on the high concentration of media ownership in the United Kingdom;
- a new, independent information service to provide key political facts and news free of political spin.

In 2007, the Commons Modernisation Committee issued proposals designed to strengthen the role of the backbencher and to make better use of non-legislative time in the House. They suggested that a weekly ninety-minute debate be held 'in prime time' on a 'big issue of the day', and that MPs should sometimes be allowed to ask topical questions of ministers without having to give the usual three days' notice. They also said that MPs might be more willing to sit for hours through debates if they were allowed to take mobile phones into the chamber and 'multi-task' by checking emails and texts.

In 2008, in response to a request from Gordon Brown, Commons Speaker, Michael Martin, announced his intention to hold a Speaker's conference to find ways of getting more women and people from ethnic minorities to become MPs. (Currently, about one in five MPs is female, compared with half the UK population.) The Speaker will also hold a conference to consider the state of UK elections, including ideas such as weekend voting and lowering the voting age to sixteen. Speakers' conferences, held only five times since they began in 1916, aim to achieve a cross-party consensus following confidential talks. Papers of the conference are not made available until thirty years after they occur. There is no obligation upon the government to accept their recommendations but most are usually adopted.

Westminster and the European Union

It is widely argued that there should be improvements in the connections and scrutiny processes between the national legislatures and the institutions of the European Union. Some pro-Europeans, such as Michael Heseltine, have suggested the creation of an upper chamber of the EU Parliament, containing members of national Parliaments, with a scrutinising role over EU legislation. However, the EU Parliament is very largely hostile to this idea, and it seems an unlikely option for the foreseeable future.

An alternative is to give MEPs access to meetings of UK parliamentary committees on European matters. The Westminster Parliament does not favour this idea. Aside from the geographical, logistical and practical difficulties of bringing members of the diverse legislatures together, there is a sheer lack of political will on both sides to improve links, relationships and scrutiny processes.

Less radically, more issues could be discussed in the Commons and Lords rather than being tucked away in committee meetings and buried away in unread committee reports. A wider range of European matters, including defence and foreign affairs, could be included in the scrutiny process. Official texts of proposals could be made available for scrutiny before decisions are made by ministers – who could be required to report back to the UK Parliament in detail what has been decided in EU Council meetings.

The UK media have a potentially important role in this area. As long as a largely europhobic press is fixated on mythical fears about bent bananas and straight cucumbers, political and public understanding of the impact of Europe will be limited and Westminster's interest and involvement in maximising the benefits of EU membership will be inadequate.

. . . .

✓ What you should have learnt from reading this chapter

- Reforms of the Westminster Parliament over the last decade have taken small steps towards making the United Kingdom a more open and accountable liberal democracy but, for most commentators, they have not gone far or fast enough.

- There is a veritable cornucopia of progressive and productive ideas for further reform among the diverse sources mentioned above. The outlook for change seems more positive than for decades, with the current leaders of all three main parties in modernising mood.

- However, an Electoral Commission survey in 2006 found that 17 per cent of the UK population do not want a say in how the country is run. Maybe we get the democracy we deserve.

? Likely examination questions

Short questions:

- What factors limit the accountability of ministers to Parliament?

- In what ways has Parliament become more open in recent years?

- Outline the advantages and disadvantages of televising the proceedings of Parliament.

- To whom are MPs responsible?

Essay questions:

- How has the role of Parliament changed over the last century?

- Assess the role which Parliament plays in UK democracy.

- 'Parliamentary sovereignty is the major problem of the UK political system.' Discuss.

- What are the main weaknesses of the UK Parliament?

Helpful websites

http://news.bbc.co.uk

http://www.parliament.uk

http://www.electoral-reform.org.uk/index.php

http://www.hansardsociety.org.uk

http://www.ukwatch.net

 Suggestions for further reading

Barnett, A. and Carty, P., *The Athenian Option: Radical Reform for the House of Lords*, Exeter: Imprint Academic, 2008.

Giddings, P. (ed.), *The Future of Parliament: Issues for a New Century*, Basingstoke: Palgrave Macmillan, 2005.

Great Britain, Parliament, House of Commons (2007) Constitutional Reform Bill, London: Stationery Office Books.

Kelso, A., *Parliamentary Reform at Westminster*, Manchester: Manchester University Press, 2006.

References

Chapter 1

1. Bagehot, W., *The English Constitution*, London: Chapman and Hall, 1867.
2. Silk, P., *How Parliament Works*, London: Longman, 1987, p. 7.
3. *The Times*, 4 March 2005.
4. Assinder, N., 'Appreciating Betty Boothroyd', at: http://news.bbc.co.uk, 12 July 2000.
5. Lord Howe in Lords' debate, 12 July 2004.
6. Lord Hewart, *The New Despotism*, London: E. Benn, 1945.

Chapter 2

1. Dicey, A. V., *Introduction to the Study of the Law of the Constitution*, London Macmillan, [1885] 1961, quoted by Adonis, A., *Parliament Today*, Manchester: Manchester University Press, 1993, p. 8.
2. Michael Howard, 'Judges must bow to the will of Parliament' at: http://news.bbc.co.uk, 10 August 2005.
3. Lord Hailsham: 'Elective dictatorship', *The Listener*, 21 October 1976, p. 497.

Chapter 3

1. Thomas, G. P., *Parliament in an Age of Reform*, Sheffield: Sheffield Hallam University Press, 2000, p. 124.
2. Andrew Pierce, 'Blair sets record for rewarding party donors with life peerages', *The Times*, 14 November 2005.
3. Anthony Howard, 'Why is corrupt practice now deemed acceptable?', *The Times*, 14 November 2005.
4. Adonis, A., *Parliament Today*, Manchester: Manchester University Press, 1993, p. 217.
5. Lord Howe of Aberavon, 'Why elected peers would be an expensive mistake', *The Times*, 5 January 2007.
6. Johann Hari, 'Don't reform the House of Lords – close it', *The Independent*, 24 April 2006.

7. Quoted in Sam Coates and Patrick Foster, 'Lords' expenses are compromise, not sign of corruption, peer says', *The Times*, 12 November 2007.
8. Conservative leader Michael Howard's speech in response to the 2003 Queen's Speech.
9. 'Making subjects custodians', *Guardian Unlimited*, 3 April 2007.
10. Alan Duncan MP, Conservative spokesman on constitutional affairs, quoted in: http://news.bbc.co.uk, 19 January 2005.

Chapter 4

1. Quoted in Patrick Barkham, 'Out to grass', *The Guardian*, 6 April 2007.
2. Lord Morrison of Lambeth, *Government and Parliament: A Survey From the Inside*, Oxford: Oxford University Press, 1964, p. 114.
3. Greg Hurst and David Charter, 'How comic's supporters kept their heads down and used their cunning', *The Times*, 2 February 2006.
4. Quoted in Philip Webster, 'MPs under fire after giving themselves 91 days' holiday', *The Times*, 19 October 2007.
5. Riddell, P., *Parliament Under Pressure*, London: Gollancz, 1998, p. 16.

Chapter 5

1. Johann Hari, 'Don't reform the House of Lords – close it', *The Independent*, 24 April 2006.
2. Report by the Sutton Trust Charity, 2005.
3. http://news.bbc.co.uk, 26 June 2007.
4. http://news.bbc.co.uk, 18 January 2006.
5. http://news.bbc.co.uk, 4 April 2008.

Chapter 6

1. Charles Walker, Conservative MP for Broxbourne, quoted in *The Times*, 4 December 2006.
2. Simon Jenkins, 'A Parliament that is unworthy of the name', *The Times*, 1 February 2002.
3. Richard Norton-Taylor, 'When you put it like that . . .', *The Guardian*, 30 January 2008.
4. Rush, M., *Parliament and the Public*, London: Longman, 1986, p. 23.
5. Judge, D., *Political Institutions in the United Kingdom*, Oxford: Oxford University Press, 2005.

6. *Britain in Europe*, pamphlet published by the Foreign Office, 1992.
7. Sir Alistair Graham, Chairman of the Committee on Standards in Public Life, quoted in http://news.bbc.co.uk, 21 May 2006.
8. *The Times*, 3 October 2005.
9. *The Spectator*, 11 December 2004.

Chapter 7

1. Gary Titley, Labour MEP, quoted in 'Giving up the Strasbourg junket', Mark Mardell at: http://news.bbc.co.uk, 4 December 2007.
2. David Charter, 'Whistle-blower criticised as MEPs vote to keep their scams secret', *The Times*, 27 February 2008.
3. Riddell, P., *Parliament Under Pressure*, London: Victor Gollancz, 1998, p. 38.
4. Riddell, *Parliament Under Pressure*, p. 52.
5. Quoted in 'EU treaty bill clears the Commons' at: http://news.bbc.co.uk, 11 March 2008.
6. Kathleen Walker-Shaw, European Officer of GMB, quoted in 'Brown rejects union EU vote call' at: http://news.bbc.co.uk, 23 August 2007.
7. Kathleen Walker-Shaw, http://news.bbc.co.uk, 23 August 2007.
8. Quoted in Kirsty Hughes, 'EU eyes its next big challenges', at: http://news.bbc.co.uk, 10 July 2007.

Chapter 8

1. Conservative MP Alan Duncan, quoted in http://news.bbc.co.uk, 2 July 2006.
2. Alan Duncan, 2 July 2006.
3. Quoted in http://news.bbc.co.uk, 18 October 2004.
4. Bogdanor, V., *The British-Irish Council and Devolution*, London: LSE, 1999.
5. Quoted in 'Fresh calls for English Parliament' at: http://news.bbc.co.uk, 24 October 2006.
6. Quoted in http://news.bbc.co.uk, 24 October 2006.
7. http://news.bbc.co.uk, 24 October 2006.
8. Bogdanor, The British-Irish Council.
9. Bogdanor, The British-Irish Council.

Chapter 9

1. William Rees-Mogg, 'We must not allow unelected judges to usurp the powers of Parliament', *The Times*, 10 May 2004.
2. Lord Denning, Dimbleby Lecture, 'Misuse of Power', 1980.
3. Griffith, J. A. G., *The Politics of the Judiciary*, London: Fontana Press, 1997.
4. Michael Howard, 'Judges must bow to the will of Parliament', *Daily Telegraph*, 10 August 2005.
5. Quoted in Michael Howard, 10 August 2005.
6. Law Lords' formal response to government proposals, 4 November 2003.
7. Quoted in Michael Howard, 10 August 2005.
8. David Cameron at: http://news.bbc.co.uk, 25 June 2006.

Chapter 10

1. Parliament First, *Parliament's Last Chance*, 2003.
2. Peter Riddell, 'Missed the Lords reform? There'll be another along soon', *The Times*, 15 July 2008.
3. Jack Straw, Justice Secretary, quoted in: http://news.bbc.co.uk, 14 July 2008.
4. Quoted in David Hencke, 'Honours system damned by Westminster inquiry', *The Guardian*, 18 December 2007.
5. Johann Hari, 'Don't reform the House of Lords – close it', *The Independent*, 24 April 2006.
6. Peter Riddell, 'Basis of the Lords has changed, but we still expect a bunch of amateurs', *The Times*, 4 June 2008.
7. 'Ballot paper tiger', *The Times*, 2 March 2007.
8. Quoted in http://news.bbc.co.uk, 1 August 2008.
9. Former Permanent Secretary Lord Robin Butler, interview with *The Spectator*, 11 December 2004.
10. David Cameron, speech to the Carlton Club, 26 July 2005.
11. Quoted in Helen Rumbelow, 'Asda boss returning to real life', *The Times*, 13 December 2004.
12. Lovenduski, J., *Whose Secretary Are You, Minister?*, Birkbeck College, 2004.

Index

Bold indicates that the term is defined